From the Author of Grey Matter Book Series…

A Daily Message of

Encouragement and Wisdom

For year _____

Written By:
Anthony S. Parker

Copyright © September 2023

By: Anthony S. Parker

All Rights Reserved. Published in the United States by

KDP Publishing / Independently Published

Printed in Milford, Delaware

No part of this publication may be reproduced, distributed, or transmitted in any from or by any means, including photocopying, recording, or other electronic or mechanical methods, without the prior written permission of the Author, except in the case of brief quotations embodied in critical reviews and certain other noncommercial uses permitted by copyright law. For permission requests for the text or artwork in this book please email the Author, addressed "Attention: Anthony Parker," at:

Regarding Copyrights

Email: authoraparker@gmail.com

ISBN-13: 9798687803014

1. The main category of the book —

a. Nonfiction > Self-Help > Motivational & Inspirational

2. Another subject category

a. Nonfiction > Self-Help > Personal Growth > General

First Edition. Volume. 1

Also, by Anthony S. Parker:

1. Grey Matter Series Volume 1: The Story of Mark Trogmyer in The World of the Unknown
ISBN 9781723022494
2. Grey Matter Series Volume 2: The Wrath of Nerogroben
ISBN 9781534993518
3. Grey Matter Series Within the World of the Unknown Volumes 1 & 2
ISBN 9781707117291
4. Grey Matter Series Volumes 3 & 4 Within the World of the Unknown
ISBN: 9798630793065
5. Grey Matter Series Volume 3: Secrets of The World of the Unknown (2nd Edition)
ISBN 9781729565520
6. Grey Matter Series Volume 3: Secrets of the World of the Unknown (3rd edition)
ISBN: 9798575161264
7. Grey Matter Series Volume 4: Mark Trogmyer and the IFRD
ISBN 9781729565216
8. Dreams: An Interactive Journal
ISBN 9781729745885
9. Dreams: The Official Notebook for Dreams: An Interactive Journal
ISBN 9781695288881
10. Grey Matter Series Volume 5: The Story of Thomas Joshua McPherson
ISBN 9781088990247
11. Grey Matter Series Book of Illustrations
ISBN 9781095428160
12. A Step into Self-Publishing Your Own Book
ISBN 9798623551559
13. A Daily Message of Encouragement and Wisdom
ISBN: 9798687803014
14. The City of Sandglass Volume 1 : The Story Untold - TBA
15. Mindset Mastery Volume 1: - TBA
16. Guardians Volume 1- TBA
17. The Flame that Flickered - TBA

Check out:

Author Website: www.authoraparker.com

Instagram: @authoraparker

Facebook Pages: @authorofgreymatterbookseries

@readersofgreymatterbookseries

For updates, Reviews, and upcoming books and events!

In Dedication

To those who are lost,
who may need a little push in their life,
encouragement, decompression, distraction, or daily guidance.

Extended Special Dedication:

I am reminded of a friend of mine, Julio Caesar Gonzalez Jr, who was only 26 years old when he passed away in September 2021 of COVID-19, in Harlingen, Texas. He was there during the start of my journey into Personal Development and my becoming an Author. He once said "YOLO" to me, "You only live once." He was all about taking advantage of the opportunities that were before him. He knew extremely well of what some of us know as "the struggle," and yet he never seemed to let it hold him back. He had even said once to me that, "When there is a will, you will find a way." He was an incredibly big hearted, loving, caring, and kind man who was a good husband and father. My heart goes out to his family and to my friends who knew him and through my shock as I write this today. I am reminded of the sobering fact that we don't know how much longer that we have on this Earth, and that "Death is the one thing that we all share on this path called life." – Steve Jobs.

Julio Caesar Gonzalez Jr in his lifetime had also stressed something that we all learned together in our own personal development journey, and this was "We need to be grateful for what we have in life and to live in a constant state of positivity and gratitude whenever and as much as we can."

Be sure to post a selfie with you and this book on social media!

Tag @authorofgreymatterbookseries and check out my Instagram page!

Don't Forget to post your review of this book on the

"Submit a Book Review Tab" on my website for a free discount on one of my other books – Exclusively at www.authoraparker.com

Autograph Page

_____

<u>My inner most feelings quote:</u>

Love is love. There is nothing about love that discriminates, or separates our souls, nor is there a difference between the color of our blood from each other. Humanity is love. It is my opinion, that if we were to understand that love is love, and that in its essence, it is the most important in any and in all circumstances around us when it comes to our lives, families, friends, and those we come to know, it shouldn't be taken for granted. Through it, we will find inner peace amongst ourselves by being understanding and accepting of these inner differences of each other. You will see that it can be a positive contagion in the world around us. You are not the victim of the circumstances that have happened to you and around you…
You are an overcomer! Being alive right now is a gift no matter who you are. Right now, looking back at your life, you need to realize that you personally have made it through so many trails and struggles in life, and you can make it through anything else that may be put before you in the future! What you do or don't do right now in the present affects your future. What you don't want to do out of fear may even affect you as soon as your own tomorrow by putting your own success backwards, it could put things off by I don't know how far. Put into action today the goals and the dreams that you wish to accomplish. Don't let anyone or anything dictate your own value or self-worth. Don't live by trying to please others and then you forget to live. Keep pushing forward. Be the light in the world for others around you, so that they too may have the hope, tenacity, and the strive to be the better person than they were yesterday and in the past. Let me repeat this in emphasis, your past does NOT and will NEVER have to dictate the person who you will become

tomorrow! I believe in second chances for others who make mistakes or who have traveled down the wrong path. Those people can still find a short cut path to go back in the right direction. People really do change, and learn from their mistakes, sometimes it's just too late to undo what has been done. Sometimes others don't accept that you can change and that is their loss to see the changes that you make on your own going forward. Life is too short to waste time on what was and what could have been. So be a support for others in life as well because if today was not your day, today is supposed to be you making someone else's day! Above all, remember to have gratitude and the gift of giving, either through money, time, or patience, or even helping someone else, through gratitude you can find within yourself a new sense of purpose and inner peace. Never give up hope, or faith in yourself. Remember that you may feel alone sometimes, but you aren't, and you are loved, and you are cared about, and you do and already have had a huge influence and impact on those around you! Everything is going to be okay.

Introduction

As I sit here and think about what I want to say, I thought that maybe you would like to know what this book is about – even more clearly - What is its purpose?

My goal is simple, every day when you wake up instead of looking at your phone, I challenge you to keep this book at your bedside and read the daily message that I have inscribed for each day, and I also added a segment after the daily quote to ponder about throughout the day. It is my intention to be a help to you as you go through this year. Maybe offer an opinion or thoughts about the quote or an anecdote to hear me out on. I know it is difficult for those of us with busy lives to read every day, much less read a whole novel. I would still like to make a difference in your life, by helping you reflect on something short, and sweet, at the beginning and end of each day. It is my hope that little by little it will also encourage you to read more. Perhaps pick up a healthy habit of reading for a few minutes or hours daily. Please keep a pen in this book and keep it handy as you go along. Then, before you go to sleep each night. Behind the morning page, write a few things that [you] are truly grateful for but the challenge is DO NOT repeat what you've written before. Even if you had a bad day. There is still good that happens every day all around us and there is so much to be grateful for, you must look for it, think about it, and see it around you. Then write down some things that you have learned that day. Every day is not a waste, especially if we can say we have learned from it or that there was something we can take from that day, or especially if there was someone that we helped and have learned from that experience of helping someone else. Maybe it was a lesson in an argument within a relationship or friendship, or in an interaction that we had. Finally, write down a few things that you wish to do or need to remember to do the next day before going to sleep. This will keep you off your phone before you go to sleep and help you to relax your mind as well before you go to sleep. It is my hope that every day for the next year, this book will find you well, or if not, hopefully you will be even better prepared for the next day.

JANUARY
Capricorn

A New Year's Resolution? What if this name was changed to a long-term goal or dream? What are you most passionate about? I challenge you to start this year with a goal of not only finding YOUR happiness but being in a state of total and complete bliss, in doing what you are most passionate about every day. You can do this! Things to focus on this month: Try to be more positive, Brave, admit when you make mistakes and try to be flexible in your decision making. It is okay to admit if you are wrong sometimes. Don't feel like you must have your guard up all the time. Some people are not out there to hurt you but want to help so don't be afraid to share information with people when you know it could help them out. Focus on being giving to others and sharing how you feel about situations to your family and friends. Being more open to others will help you get along better with others around you and have someone to talk to when you are feeling down or depressed this month. There is no such thing as a perfect person, we make mistakes in life and try to push ourselves to that limit and can end up being self-destructive in this way of thinking. I know that at a younger point in my life that I had always wanted to be a writer. Not just any writer but a NY TIMES BESTSELLING AUTHOR, an influential and thought-provoking writer. It was a big goal for me. A dream. But the point is, once you have one, put what you need to do into action to become and be who you want to be, there are no limitations in life except for the ones that you place on yourself. If you are passionate about something in life and you believe in yourself, follow through with it. If you work hard enough at it, things will eventually come to life and will happen around you. Sure, it will be difficult to accomplish your dream, but no one said life is easy. For every human in the world, they have dreams, they have goals and aspirations in which they want to accomplish but to every dream and goal, there is a process to get to that next level. Sometimes to get to that next level, there is some pushback or some roadblocks that need to be faced. It doesn't matter who you know or where you come from or how much money you have, if you can dream it and believe it, it's possible to do it and you will get better at it over time. We all make mistakes down this road, and you will get dirty, but you can do this, I dare you!

End of Day Reflection

Five Things I am grateful for:

1

2

3

4

5

What did I learn today?

1

2

3

TO DO TOMORROW

1

2

3

4

5

JANUARY 2
Capricorn

Have a sense of gratitude daily - Start with this gratitude journal. Many people are fault finders as if they get a reward for it, instead of trying to be a gratitude finder. Find things that are in your life that you can be grateful for and that make you happy and feel positive about your life. In these troubled times it is so easy to push yourself to the point where you are negatively putting yourself down in your mind. Making yourself feel smaller or less than others without you even realizing it. Let this journal bring out the best in you every day. When you find yourself striving towards better and better things around you, you will also find that inner peace that makes you feel successful and more positively inclined towards others. You will find that positivity also attracts more people to you. People who want to be around that energy. If you think about it, have you ever wanted to surround yourself with people who constantly put you down? Who doesn't support you? Who is constantly negative in your life?

Maybe at one point in our lives, some of us are guilty of this, of being that energy vampire and pushing people always from us who could have potentially been a great part of our lives and sometimes it has dramatic effects to the point where they avoid you forever and there is no going back from that. As the saying goes you can attract more bees with honey than vinegar and the same is true for people and their personalities. Take apart your day today gradually and find things that you are grateful for. Start simple and then get gradually more and more intense. DO NOT REPEAT What you are grateful for daily in this journal if you can help it. This will keep things challenging for you. Next attempt to find three things that you learned about yourself, others, or new things you learned in general, keep changing this too. DO NOT REPEAT! Then write down things that are keeping you from sleeping tonight, what is on your mind that you must remember to do for tomorrow?

End of Day Reflection

Five Things I am grateful for:

1

2

3

4

5

What did I learn today?

1

2

3

TO DO TOMORROW

1

2

3

4

5

January 3
Capricorn

"Find what makes you happy, find who makes you happy. OQP (Only Quality People) are the five people who you want to surround yourself with in your life. These are the top people in your life who support you, who are there for you, and who want more out of life, not just for themselves, but for you as well – For your benefit of betterment. "Birds of a feather flock together." - Les Brown

Wanting to be happy is the most basic human need in life. Somewhere along the way, we forget about this, and we feel that we NEED to have more materialistic things in life to find happiness. When even the wealthiest of people lack happiness. With more money comes more responsibility and there are things in life that money cannot buy. Money can buy you a house, but it cannot buy you a home. Money can buy you companionship, but it cannot buy you a good friend. Money can help those who are struggling with the basic needs of life but in the past that is only greed and suffering and the realization that money isn't everything in life.

Of Course, everyone says that they want to win the lottery or become a million or billionaire but after most of the necessities are covered you can get consumed by societal luxuries within the ability to have money, and you can begin to lose your way. Just as much as not having money can destroy people, having money can also be destructive because you must be more responsible. Things around you become transactional between you and people around you. Love cannot be bought, and people around you can easily become greedy if they know you have money and can take advantage of you.

Upon seeing the effects of money on people around me I have seen that if this ever became a situation for me, I would need to be logical and anonymous and learn to still get by with only what I need to survive. Money can blind you and ruin the relationships that you have with people around you if you let it consume you. Be careful out there is all I can add to this thought.

End of Day Reflection

Five Things I am grateful for:

1

2

3

4

5

What did I learn today?

1

2

3

TO DO TOMORROW

1

2

3

4

5

January 4
Capricorn

"If you let people's perception of you dictate your behavior, you will never grow as a person, but if you leave yourself open to experience, despite what others think, then you will learn and grow." – Mr. Feeny, Boy Meets World

Having an open mind is sometimes difficult if we only have a one-track mindset. By not being open to change or new ideas, we limit ourselves from experiencing new opportunities that may arise by following through with certain things that may be suggested to us. As humans, we have the unique ability to adapt over time. We also can learn and grow daily to be better and better each day as we go through various life experiences. As you go through life, having an open mind will allow you to open doors to new opportunities that come knocking. You are going to get exactly what it is that you want as soon as you let go of what is holding you back from receiving it.

End of Day Reflection

Five Things I am grateful for:

1

2

3

4

5

What did I learn today?

1

2

3

TO DO TOMORROW

1

2

3

4

5

January 5
Capricorn

"Difficult roads lead to beautiful destinations!"

Sometimes it is the journey that matters more than the destination in the end. There can be a lot of struggles on the road while going to where you want to be in life. What matters more, is how strong you remain while on this path and focusing on the destination. BE STRONG! It is easy to give up, but I challenge you when you get out of bed this morning to PUSH YOURSELF FORWARD! P.U.S.H – PRAY UNTIL SOMETHING HAPPENS and BE THE ANSWER to people's prayers!

No one has ever said that the road of life that you are traveling on is going to be easy. Sometimes it is difficult to reflect on the present moment in our lives and realize that there are others who are on an even more difficult path but that doesn't make you better or any less of a person for having to face these obstacles. It makes you human. To say you want to give up or that you need help or need to take a break is okay. Taking "the easy way out and give up" doesn't resolve the issue for those around you. Some have told me in the past, oh my uncle or my mom or my brother told me that showing emotions or asking for help is wrong. That it makes you vulnerable and shows weakness. Sometimes you must understand that to get by in life it is okay to reach out and to ask for help from those around you if you realize that you need to be there for them for when their cards are down or when they want to give up or when they are dealing with a difficult situation as well. As they say, it takes a village to raise a child, but it also takes a village to grow and support and be there for one another and through life's difficulties you will all grow stronger through the worst of times and be there for each other during the best of times. KEEP GOING! You can handle whatever you are struggling with and whatever difficulties that you may have come your way! Just don't forget you aren't alone, and you can ask for help occasionally!

End of Day Reflection

Five Things I am grateful for:

1

2

3

4

5

What did I learn today?

1

2

3

TO DO TOMORROW

1

2

3

4

5

January 6
Capricorn

"A struggle in life is merely a learning curve or a new challenge, so take those times moment by moment and come up with a plan of logical action to cope with it."

"The hard times you will realize will not come to stay, but they will come to pass!" – Les Brown

This is a lot easier to say than to do for most of us. Almost all the time we may catch ourselves wanting things to happen and occur exactly as we plan them. This goes to show that even the best laid plans can always fall short. Things happen. We missed the meeting we were supposed to be at by a few minutes. We were late to class because we were talking to someone else and lost track of time. We were a few meters too short running the race because we were too slow. The inches that we need are all around us. We can't be caught up in what we are short on in life. Realize that yes you can put all or nothing effort into things and sometimes the results are or aren't what you expect but the challenges are to learn and grow and live and learn and share the wisdom with others along the way.

End of Day Reflection

Five Things I am grateful for:

1

2

3

4

5

What did I learn today?

1

2

3

TO DO TOMORROW

1

2

3

4

5

January 7
Capricorn

"There are no mistakes in life, only lessons. There is no such thing as a negative experience, only opportunities to grow, learn and advance along the road of self-mastery. From struggle comes strength. Even pain can be a wonderful teacher." — Robin Sharma

"In life, the biggest regret of those who are dying is never becoming your ideal self. I do believe that we are thrust into a world that we don't fit in, and the journey is a lot of people sell you a lot of things along the way, that if you receive a lot of certain rewards, you mean something. If you go to a certain school, you get it. You are cute, classical beauty and you get the right man and the right zip code, and you swim through all that filthy swill, and you come to that conclusion that you want to become deep within the person you are supposed to be, that is transcends status and that at the end of the day we are only here to love." – Viola Davis

This is of course all a matter of perspective. One can look at your day today and assume everything could go unbelievably bad and you can visualize these occurrences today as negative and bad. Or you can see today as a chance to grow and learn and get better at what you made mistakes in today. It will be a good day, full of positive experiences and you are open-minded enough to see everything as a learning experience. Today allow yourself to be open to new opportunities that others might never have had. This doesn't mean that you need to suffer, in order to grow, or learn. You can learn from the mistakes of others around you as well as help them to have a better day. The choice is yours. Your destiny awaits!

End of Day Reflection

Five Things I am grateful for:

1

2

3

4

5

What did I learn today?

1

2

3

TO DO TOMORROW

1

2

3

4

5

"There is no need to rush, only to be consistent with a plan of action. We can all hope and wish for change, but hope isn't an action, it's only a feeling behind an idea without an exact timeline of which to accomplish it."

"No matter how small you start, start something that matters."
– Brendon Burchard

"Sure, the road to success will not be easy, but sometimes the things that are worth having in life are not easy to work for and the things that come easy to us in life are usually not worth having."

These are quotes that I have carried with me since I was younger. I am not sure exactly who said the last one-off hand only that this has made an impact on my life in one way or another. This is the price of hard work and determination to want to be successful or at least a better person than I was yesterday. I feel it goes hand in hand with what you have as your constant mindset as well.

End of Day Reflection

Five Things I am grateful for:

1

2

3

4

5

What did I learn today?

1

2

3

TO DO TOMORROW

1

2

3

4

5

January 9.
Capricorn

A week has passed since the new year. If you haven't already, start new positive habits daily, and everyone will change around you once you change.

Study personal development and watch daily motivational videos to get yourself in the right constant mindset. YouTube University is an excellent resource to use when trying to find these types of motivational videos daily.

"One day you are going to decide this isn't who you want to be anymore, and this isn't how you want to feel and only when you choose, that's when the power will come back to you, and you will begin to do better." - @cross.novia

This is a matter of whether you are ready to be open minded about change, or at least open to seeing things from a unique perspective and improving yourself in ways that you want to see in yourself. There are many benefits to studying personal development and getting yourself motivated at the beginning of the day.

End of Day Reflection

Five Things I am grateful for:

1

2

3

4

5

What did I learn today?

1

2

3

TO DO TOMORROW

1

2

3

4

5

January 10
Capricorn

"Sometimes you have to lead by being the change you want to see in those around you."

In many respects, people don't receive the idea of being bossed around too easily or even micromanaged for that matter. For comfort there are some who don't like to run into confrontation but want to be a leader. Sometimes the best way to lead is by leading by example. When others around you see what you are doing, they will catch on and try to do the same without you having to say anything. Or they may take the opposite approach and do less knowing that you may do it for them instead. So, this is a double-edged sword depending on the type of people you are surrounding yourself with.

Other times, perhaps in the working environment, you may wish for others to pull their share of weight and instead they do a lot of talking. Sometimes in that scenario, you must keep pushing on and keep quiet, and keep working. Others will take the hint that they are talking too much and will get back to work once they notice that they have fallen behind. Do not let these types of people get to you in life. Letting people have control over you and getting under the skin of the hardworking person within a working or home environment is not worth the energy.

End of Day Reflection

Five Things I am grateful for:

1

2

3

4

5

What did I learn today?

1

2

3

TO DO TOMORROW

1

2

3

4

5

"Read a new book daily/weekly/monthly however long it takes you to read. If you read, it will take you to places you've never been, and you will hear tales you had never heard before and learn and grow from the experiences of others while becoming wiser."

The more you read, the more you will learn and grow, and it will also improve your writing. Reading gives you the ability to grow in your own creativity and realize that you never thought were even possible for other characters and people to go through and grow through. Within our reading we can not only improve communication skills, our language comprehension and vocabulary but also you can learn so many skills and transform yourself from having that wealth of knowledge. Never be afraid to grow or be something bigger than yourself. Libraries are all around us, just take some time to visit one and check out some books and get lost for an hour of reading a day! I challenge you to grow and strengthen in wisdom and face the dragons and magic in your reading.

End of Day Reflection

Five Things I am grateful for:

1

2

3

4

5

What did I learn today?

1

2

3

TO DO TOMORROW

1

2

3

4

5

January 12
Capricorn

"Hope gives us the courage to see things in a brighter light. But do not depend on just hoping for your dreams to just magically come true, put them into action and set an exact time and deadline!"

Very few have the ability and the hope to see the positive in everything around them. Especially when things are not going well around them, which is why if you do have that ability, it's so much more important for you to show the hope that you have in others around you. Encourage those around you to be positive and try to improve other people's days around you. I challenge you to make this contagious thinking.

I challenge you to make a difference in someone's life that you don't know and get to know one random person for an hour or two!

End of Day Reflection

Five Things I am grateful for:

1

2

3

4

5

What did I learn today?

1

2

3

TO DO TOMORROW

1

2

3

4

5

January 13
Capricorn

"It is easy to criticize when someone screws up. People do this so they can try to make themselves look better, however in reality, when we criticize, we don't attract many, and people won't be as easily able to gravitate towards you."

Buy a coffee for someone today and talk to them in the coffee shop and learn two things from them about them that they enjoy!

As the old saying goes, "you can attract more bees with honey than with vinegar." Also, if you want to correct someone there are two things you might want to consider: pull them aside and talk to them away from others. Also, instead of focusing only on what they may have done wrong, tell them what they did right and "for next, this is how you can improve." Be more encouraging, it will also bolster their self-confidence and want to do better for you next time.

End of Day Reflection

Five Things I am grateful for:

1

2

3

4

5

What did I learn today?

1

2

3

TO DO TOMORROW

1

2

3

4

5

I challenge you to find a way to compliment 5 people on doing good things and be encouraging to them as well.

"Humans have the potential not only to create happy lives for themselves, but also to help other beings. We have a natural creative ability, and it is very important to realize this." – Dalai Lama, Little Book of Wisdom, Page 17. ISBN 9781571746283

To add to this thought for today, I couldn't help but think that ultimately our goal in life is to find that thing and the things around us that make us happy. It is usually not the material things in life that can bring us the simple pleasures in life that I have found in my experience. It's the things that material money cannot buy, that is what is more important in life, they are timeless, precious, and at times irreplaceable memories and times with those we love.

End of Day Reflection

Five Things I am grateful for:

1

2

3

4

5

What did I learn today?

1

2

3

TO DO TOMORROW

1

2

3

4

5

"Many people fear the unknown in life and are afraid to change and change their habits. They think, what if something goes wrong? What if something bad happens? Instead of thinking about what could go wrong, think about what can go right! Accept changes that happen around you, and even the new challenges that come with making those changes." – Anthony Parker

Challenge of the day: Do two things that you fear doing and reflect on it and decide what you learned from that experience.

Happiness is crucial in life. Without it, we can lose our sense of purpose and sometimes we can be overcome by grief and sadness and sometimes in frustration with ourselves we can become angry because we are not where we want to be in life. A negative outcome just means a new challenge in life to overcome and once it's overcome, you see things in a new perspective. If you are not happy with where you are, who you are, or the people you hang around with, do something about it. Incorporate the changes you think you need and don't be afraid of what could go wrong. BE EXCITED about the new opportunities coming your way!

End of Day Reflection

Five Things I am grateful for:

1

2

3

4

5

What did I learn today?

1

2

3

TO DO TOMORROW

1

2

3

4

5

In life, people make mistakes, they do and say things they don't mean. They live in regret for what they did or didn't do right - Sometimes they even do you wrong by accident - sometimes you may even end up holding a grudge against that person - the best advice I can give you is to forgive that person. Life is too short to hold these meaningless grudges and it hurts you more than it hurts them. People end up suffering because of lost time as well depending on the circumstances around the grudges."

"I am a firm believer in giving people second chances in life. Forgiving others not only empowers you, but it also releases you and them of regret and further hardship and <u>ill-resolve.</u>"

If you hold onto a grudge, it can destroy you. It doesn't hurt the other person. They may have wished things turned out differently but in the end, when you forgive someone, you are in some respect releasing the power that you and they hold over you/them.

Life is too short to hold grudges against others. Live your life to the fullest and never forget to live and to find your purpose in life. Once you have figured this out and live on track to accomplishing that purpose, along the way, don't forget to help others find what their purpose in life is and what their goals and dreams are.

End of Day Reflection

Five Things I am grateful for:

1

2

3

4

5

What did I learn today?

1

2

3

TO DO TOMORROW

1

2

3

4

5

Find your happiness…. Do that which brings you happiness and peace.

"The great existential miseries of life come when too many days stack up where we are conforming and posing while doing things that we have no passion for. Personal Freedom means we are being fully ourselves and striving for things that bring us joy and meaning. The opposite is life slave to conformity and boredom." Brendon Burchard, The Motivation Manifesto

People today are living mundane lives because they have grown comfortable with being comfortable and have gotten used to doing the same things repeatedly day in and day out. They are not growing, and they are just settling with that which they have in life and are just content with that. There is nothing wrong with contentment and the mundane if you are happy but I CHALLENGE YOU, IF you are unable to be happy when you wake up every morning, if you find yourself stuck in an endless cycle, do something that will break that cycle, change your routine and take some time out of your day to do that which makes you unconditionally and unconventionally happy. There are people that are out there living their lives based off what people are telling you to live by and do. This is not going to bring you happiness in the end if this is not where your heart desires to be. I think that if you have an unpleasant taste of the mundane in your life you need to do something about it and do what makes you most happy. Forget how much money that your dreams/goals may or may not make you, live your dream as if it's your last day on Earth as we don't know when our last day is. Living in happiness is ultimately key. Life is fragile and to go about life and not do what you most want to in life because someone is telling you no or that it's impossible or because you aren't going to make money or because it isn't what they want you to do is not living your life to the fullest.

End of Day Reflection

Five Things I am grateful for:

1

2

3

4

5

What did I learn today?

1

2

3

TO DO TOMORROW

1

2

3

4

5

Successful people talk about innovative ideas, unsuccessful people talk about people.

This is a huge difference in the type of people that you will come across in your day to day. Surround yourself with people who talk about new ideas and goals and who encourage you with your own dreams, goals, and aspirations. These will be people who want more for you and want you to be successful. These will also be the type of people who will go out of their way to make sure you are okay too and check up on you.

There are those out there in the world that just like to gossip and talk about others and put others down and thrive in this type of living. These are people who may or may not be secretly miserable or who may become miserable. The negativity is the gas that gets them nowhere but only attention. Sometimes there are people who just want to complain about the problems that they have in life and not do anything about them. These people may not even want you to provide them with an answer or a solution but only want the attention that comes of this conversation which will not lead them anywhere. Always look for people who are trying to grow and become better than they were yesterday!

There is a secret that you need to be aware of in life, there is no rule book so what is or isn't possible. If you want to travel and see the world sell your things and travel and explore and settle where you will be happiest. If you want to become a teacher, find out what it takes to do so and do it! If you want to become a lawyer, or an author, do research to find out what it takes and realize that as long as you continue to work towards your dream, it will become your next reality. Dreams are not limited to those who are the top 1% or only to those who are without kids or pets. You can live your dreams!

End of Day Reflection

Five Things I am grateful for:

1

2

3

4

5

What did I learn today?

1

2

3

TO DO TOMORROW

1

2

3

4

5

January 19
Capricorn

"I challenge you to continuously ensure you are learning. As you learn and grow you become more resourceful, and successful. Remember this, you don't know what you do not know." – Anthony Parker

In school, many may have found it challenging and "not fun," but teaching yourself can be fun, it is all merely a matter of perspective. I have found YouTube to be a great source of learning material from cooking to car help, to just basic general learning. It is so amazing to be able to teach yourself and learn and grow to be different and more cultured. Not many take the time to invest in themselves to learn and grow. Take advantage of the ability to teach yourself.

End of Day Reflection

Five Things I am grateful for:

1

2

3

4

5

What did I learn today?

1

2

3

TO DO TOMORROW

1

2

3

4

5

"Better to be yourself than try to be someone else."

I read this quote when I was a kid, "We live alone, we die alone, everything else is just an illusion, it used to keep me up at night, we all die alone. So why am I supposed to spend my life, working sweating, struggling for an illusion? Because no number of friends, no significant other, no assignment about trying to be determining the square root or a hypotenuse is going to help me avoid my fate, I have better things to do with my time." – The Art of Getting By

Living a lie or living the life someone else wants you to live just to make them happy is not worth it, because you will end up miserable. Be who you are and be proud of the person you are today. Stand up and look up at yourself in the mirror and say, "I HAVE MADE TO BE _____ YEARS OLD AND I AM PROUD OF THE PERSON YOU HAVE BECOME!!"

Raise your potential and destroy the walls around you which limit your beliefs in who you are and what you can do as a person!

End of Day Reflection

Five Things I am grateful for:

1

2

3

4

5

What did I learn today?

1

2

3

TO DO TOMORROW

1

2

3

4

5

January 21 Aquarius

"There is a reason why everyone is different, otherwise the world would be a pretty boring place."

There is nothing wrong with being yourself and it's our differences that make us all unique human beings and make us all special by giving us unique identities. Although we are different and come from different places, it's the different cultures that we can all learn and grow from. Not everyone has been raised the same so not everyone's life experiences are the same. We all have gained various wisdoms of life along the way that have helped us to grow and be the very people we are today. It's in sharing these individual experiences that we have had that could help others also learn and grow around us. Liking different things and not having things in common with others is okay. Let us be more open minded this week about the differences of others and show others a hand outreached to them to help them or help them grow or feel more accepted. Be open-minded and more accepting of others around you and you will find that making new friends along the way a lot easier.

You need to realize that "YOU ARE AMAZING! YOU ARE A SHINING BRIGHT STAR IN THE EVENING NIGHT SKY!!" BE THE STAR! Don't worry about what others think and say if they are or aren't burning as brightly as you or brighter than you, BE UNIQUE, BE YOURSELF! SMILE!

End of Day Reflection

Five Things I am grateful for:

1

2

3

4

5

What did I learn today?

1

2

3

TO DO TOMORROW

1

2

3

4

5

"It is okay to not own the next best thing, sometimes all we need is just the basics in life to find true happiness."

Sometimes we go through life looking for, "the next best thing" in life. Whether it is the need to have the new iPhone, or the new android phone or the newest piece of technology and we forget that sometimes even the material things in life don't always fill the emptiness that we feel inside of ourselves. It may not make you more courageous or confident or braver by having that next best thing. It might make you feel unsettled, or it may even bring a temporary mask of happiness that isn't intentionally fully happiness, but it is just contentment of "having what we think that we need in life." Sometimes it's just the ability to have the basics in life that brings us happiness that can't be bought or that it shows us that we may have the best life because we have the simple things in life. A roof over our head, food on the table, electricity to power our ac, gas in our cars or even just the ability to have our health to be able to walk around town. I think that when we take a step back to look at and focus on what we have and not just what we don't have in life, it may bring you a more elevated sense of happiness just through the simplicities of gratitude.

It's okay to take a simple step back and be happy for what we have in life.

Plain and simple are at times all we need to get by and that is okay too.

End of Day Reflection

Five Things I am grateful for:

1

2

3

4

5

What did I learn today?

1

2

3

TO DO TOMORROW

1

2

3

4

5

"Following your dreams and goals means you are going to have your ups and you are going to have your downs, but don't let the dream keep you down. Let it excite and fuel you for the endless doors of opportunities that are coming your way, and sure setbacks are going to happen, but you are further now from when you started. Look how far you have come in taking the first steps of action necessary to start your goals and deadlines to accomplish your dreams! You got this! I believe in you!"

"If I can look up, I can get back up!"
- Les Brown

When you have those downs when following your dreams don't let others tell you what you can and cannot do. It is during those times when you realize it's just a minor setback and things will improve, and they will get better! See yourself at that next level and put in the extra time you may need to improve! It's the journey to get to the ultimate destination that matters more than the actual destination itself. We never realize this until we reach that success that it's what you went through on the way that made you stronger and able to handle the success that you wanted. Never give up, never look back at what regrets you may hold, keep pushing forward and be happy with the idea that you found one less idea that you may need to get to where you are in life.

End of Day Reflection

Five Things I am grateful for:

1

2

3

4

5

What did I learn today?

1

2

3

TO DO TOMORROW

1

2

3

4

5

"Remember what may seem impossible isn't what it truly seems, "I'm/Possible"

This morning maybe was not your morning. Just because it wasn't a good morning, doesn't mean it can't be a good day, or good week, or a good weekend. Sometimes when bad things happen to us or when we encounter some misfortune, we will take it and carry around that bad energy for the rest of the day. Try to bounce back, stay positive, things will get better. Just because you have a bad week too, doesn't mean you will have a bad life.

NEGATIVITY HAS NO PLACE IN YOUR MIND. Just as you wouldn't allow someone who is negative and constantly bringing you down into your life.

There is no such thing as the impossible when you are consistently trying no matter what, when you persevere and never give up, that's when you get to that next level. When teaching a baby to walk, do you think it would ever learn if its parents weren't consistently trying to help the child along to keep getting up and trying again and again to try to walk?

End of Day Reflection

Five Things I am grateful for:

1

2

3

4

5

What did I learn today?

1

2

3

TO DO TOMORROW

1

2

3

4

5

January 25
Aquarius

"The way I see it there are two roads you can take in life with every choice you make, but in the end, no matter what, remember we are all going to die, just some sooner than others, so don't waste your life/time."

This may seem very morbid to hear this morning for you, but I would say this, if you knew you were going to die tomorrow you would spend every moment you could doing what you would want to do most to get things done and get to that next level. You would have a newfound sense of motivation within you, and you would accomplish what you may not have been able to accomplish otherwise. Motivation comes in all forms, shapes, sizes, and packages.

End of Day Reflection

Five Things I am grateful for:

1

2

3

4

5

What did I learn today?

1

2

3

TO DO TOMORROW

1

2

3

4

5

"Never live with regret - Try to take the chances, take advantage of every opportunity with careful reflection and logical thought and planning

Never fear asking about a new opportunity, take the chance, life is too short without having some risks with regrets.

We can only learn and grow through our mistakes and failures, so take the chance and realize that maybe things will work out.

"Sometimes the reason why you won't let go of something that is making you sad, is because it's the only thing making you happy." @morechrisgriffin - Hard Hitting Quotes Episode 50

End of Day Reflection

Five Things I am grateful for:

1

2

3

4

5

What did I learn today?

1

2

3

TO DO TOMORROW

1

2

3

4

5

"When a door closes, another one opens."

"There is always a way to get to your finish line. It's not, Can I? It's not, Is it possible? No, it's how, how do I get there? The dots exist, you must be the one to connect them, you must build bridges over the oceans of unknowns, the valleys comprised of the unforeseen, oh, there is a way! Remember that It's not the destination that is in question, but one's willingness to knock and knock and knock until the right door opens. Remember that you have everything you need, that you are armed with everything that is required. You have to just decide what is more important to you, the feeling of reaching the top of the mountain or the feeling of just staying in the shade at the bottom." – Eddie Pinero

The opportunities that we need to grow are literally all around us, you need to merely just reach out and grab them and ask about them from others around you!

Yes, sometimes we lose our jobs and whether we realize it or not, it's meant to be! Sometimes we can even lose ourselves along the way. However, in that process other doors of opportunity with better pay and benefits and good people come into our lives that show us how we can better and/or find ourselves or how we can get to where we want to be. You cannot look at the loss of a job and say, "Well I tried, and that was it," or think, "now I am nothing and nothing better or good is ever going to happen to me!" – Stop playing the "poor me game!' Stop playing the victim and realize this, you still have good things going on around you! You still have eyes to see, a mouth to talk, and ears to listen and if you don't, you still have a big heart and are still blessed to be alive today and to still be able to reach your dreams and goals. You just need to not let anything bring you down or get in your way and be open to new doors of opportunity and look around you and see what is still good and positive that is still going on around you!
NEVER LOSE HOPE!

End of Day Reflection

Five Things I am grateful for:

1

2

3

4

5

What did I learn today?

1

2

3

TO DO TOMORROW

1

2

3

4

5

January 28
Aquarius

"Accountability means that there is a need for you to accept responsibility for all of your successes and failures."

When making mistakes in life, remember it's a minor setback, something that you can learn and grow from, and you will figure out what you need to do by owning up to it along the way.

Something that is difficult to do but in principle people will respect you and admire you more for taking responsibility of the failures and the challenges and struggles that you have had to endure on the road to success. It is what makes those successes more meaningful. Sometimes in life, there is not a real path that is right to follow to success. There may not be guidelines or true steps that you must take to be successful and accomplish your dream. Sometimes you just must make your own path and decisions to what you think is the right way towards where you want to be in life and that isn't always the same path that the rest of society is taking either.

End of Day Reflection

Five Things I am grateful for:

1

2

3

4

5

What did I learn today?

1

2

3

TO DO TOMORROW

1

2

3

4

5

January 29
Aquarius

"Insanity is waking up every day doing the same thing over, and over again while expecting different results." - Albert Einstein

"If you are at all unhappy with your life, you must do something to change this, whether it's where you live, where you work, what you are studying, or who you are hanging out with. You cannot expect growth or positive change when you aren't taking the positive steps to grow and be a better person. The results are in the follow up and follow through."

A thought came to me when I read this, after spring always comes summer, after summer comes fall, and after fall then comes winter always. This much is certain.

If we are unhappy and we continue in the same routines daily without changing anything and keep expecting something new to happen, nothing ever will. It will just be more of the same thing. But you ought not to worry about the little things in life. Just as today is always the tomorrow we were worried about yesterday. A lot of the time the things that we worry about only affect the situations that we get ourselves into.

End of Day Reflection

Five Things I am grateful for:

1

2

3

4

5

What did I learn today?

1

2

3

TO DO TOMORROW

1

2

3

4

5

Everyone makes mistakes in life, but that doesn't mean they have to pay for them for the rest of their life. Sometimes GOOD people make BAD choices. It doesn't mean they are bad people; it just means that they are only human. Make sure you set goals and develop a life plan if you haven't already.

What are your short-term goals? Long term goals? Where do you see yourself in three years? five years? Ten years?

End of Day Reflection

Five Things I am grateful for:

1

2

3

4

5

What did I learn today?

1

2

3

TO DO TOMORROW

1

2

3

4

5

"ALWAYS be excited for tomorrow and make sure you always plan something for yourself for tomorrow to be excited for."

Having something to look forward to is important for your mental and emotional well-being. Always plan for things weeks in advance so that when the times are tough you have that thing to say to yourself that you know maybe, "you know today may be a bad day, but you know this is what I have to look forward to in the coming weeks."

Something to think about throughout the day – Be careful with the words that you speak, even the ones that you say in your own head. The story you tell yourself about your life is far more important than you may realize. When you say things like, "Bad things always happen to me," or "I'm always a failure," you are reinforcing that belief in yourself until you start living life through that lens. You might think it's harmless, but there is a certain magic when you start to think differently within about your life in a more positive light that things you never realized are possible until they become more possible. There is so much magic behind positive thought and positivity.

If used properly with intention, they can change your life for the better. When used carelessly, they can root themselves inside you and create a subconscious block that only grows stronger with time. Let go of needing to identify with an overly negative/victimizing mindset and mentality. Allow yourself the opportunity to be fluid and move with the flows of life, instead of against them. Be open to change, to evolving, to the potential of possibilities and watch how your life transforms.

End of Day Reflection

Five Things I am grateful for:

1

2

3

4

5

What did I learn today?

1

2

3

TO DO TOMORROW

1

2

3

4

5

February 1 — Aquarius

"Stay positive, you have made it a month into this year so far! Smile and be the joy for others in your life today!"

Things to Focus on this month: One thing to understand is, yes change is good to make when you are unhappy with the way your life is thus far, however too much change makes it difficult to stay focused on the task at hand of trying to accomplish your dreams and goals. Work on trying to understand emotions better and responding logically to them instead of reacting to them immediately. Try to work on Arrogance and realize that other people's opinions in your life may also be important or just as moving and motivating to learn from. Everyone has the need to feel important in life for what they are, who they are, and what they have accomplished but too much arrogance can be off putting to others. Sometimes it's how things are said around us regarding tone, voice volume, and the structure of our sentences that can make things to see like we are being misunderstood. Work on communication between you and other people in your life and take the walls down so people have a chance to get to know you. Lastly the last few things to work on are being rebellious, being detached, and being alienated.

Stay positive and see the good in those around you. If you stay positive and see the good in things around you, you will remain in a constant state of positivity and happiness. Continually seek and find the good and positivity in everything for as the Old African Proverb says, "If there is no enemy within, the enemy outside can do you no harm."

End of Day Reflection

Five Things I am grateful for:

1

2

3

4

5

What did I learn today?

1

2

3

TO DO TOMORROW

1

2

3

4

5

February 2
Aquarius

"A simple act of kindness, it's contagious, and it's a tool that costs nothing and lasts for miles!"

Before you assume things in life, learn the facts first. Before you judge, understand why. Before you hurt someone, feel. Before you speak, think, and place yourself in their shoes to understand what they are going through.

6 Hard truths you need to accept for being stronger:

1. Not many people really care about your matters. They ask and comment simply because they are curious. Don't let them affect the decisions you make.
2. You'll suck at everything in the beginning. But if you are persevering and patient, time will reward you with what you deserve.
3. No matter how good or bad your life is at this stage, always remember, "this time will pass away" and you can stay humble and motivated to continue your journey.
4. People close to you see things with more clarity than you do sometimes. Forgo your ego and take the good advice when you can.
5. You'll fail countless times before you succeed. But that doesn't matter. You only need to do the right thing when the opportunities come.
6. There are no answers to some questions. If you can't get them after trying, that means you need to let go.

End of Day Reflection

Five Things I am grateful for:

1

2

3

4

5

What did I learn today?

1

2

3

TO DO TOMORROW

1

2

3

4

5

"Pay it Forward - Be kind to those who don't have a sweet bone in their body."

Pick 5 people today to do something nice for ahead of time and then tell them to #payitforward

1

2

3

4

5

End of Day Reflection

Five Things I am grateful for:

1

2

3

4

5

What did I learn today?

1

2

3

TO DO TOMORROW

1

2

3

4

5

"Give to others without an expectation for a reward, payment, or recognition in return. Its more powerful to give in silence to make a difference in someone's life."

Now in this time, it is so difficult to do this for others due to our societies and communities becoming very self-centered at times to the point where you do something for someone and automatically people assume they want something from you in return or want payment of some kind. Kindness and giving is such a rare quality to have in these times and we need to be better as a society and more humane with each other.

I daresay it is so bad so much so that people become leery of the idea that someone would do something good, nice, or helpful without expecting anything in return at some point. It is your challenge from me to do this at least once a week at random. Help someone get to that one step further in accomplishing their own goal or dream. Teach someone something you know or show them how they can accomplish a certain task or skill or take the liberty to just do something nice for someone. Prove that our society isn't self-centered, and that there is still hope for humanity.

End of Day Reflection

Five Things I am grateful for:

1

2

3

4

5

What did I learn today?

1

2

3

TO DO TOMORROW

1

2

3

4

5

February 5
Aquarius

"Treat others the way you wish to be treated. Even if they treat you differently, don't let others change that kind and loving heart of yours."

It is a lesson that is a hard pill to swallow. Sometimes I have found this difficult to do. The perspective in which I try to view this as, there are already enough mean, nasty, and horrible people out there in the world, why would you want to be another one? If you treat others and those around you well, they will see for themselves the heart that you carry. When someone is mean to you or mistreats you, you won't need to speak or do ill of that person because others will see for themselves the person they are. Naturally we think negatively at times, so I think it is easy to think and do ill to others, but I challenge you to be unique and different and be that better person. Don't change who you are because of someone else's attitude or circumstances regurgitated on you. Nurture your mind and soul and be mindful of others and work on your own personal development constantly.

End of Day Reflection

Five Things I am grateful for:

1

2

3

4

5

What did I learn today?

1

2

3

TO DO TOMORROW

1

2

3

4

5

February 6
Aquarius

"See the goodness in the hearts of others around you."

With so much evil in the world, but that doesn't mean hiding indoors away from everyone in fear and it is easy to be blinded by nothing but evil and negativity. But at some point, you must trust in those around you that they too want a high quality of life and that you are still safe in this world too if you are aware of what's always going on around you. I have to say that there is goodness in every heart around you and deep within the hearts are a voice with their pain that they speak of around you. If you help to heal the pain and struggles of the people around you, you will see that they too will help you out eventually if times are tough for you. Stand strong, be strong and see that goodness in the hearts of those around you! I have always been inspired by the magic that people have within themselves to lend a helping hand or a kind heart to those who may need it. This is spreading good karma out in the world in some ways in my opinion. We need to be like this for others and we can make the world around us better.

People are in a rush to go nowhere usually that they forget to enjoy the here and now and take the time to enjoy some peace and the people around them. Today while you are off, go to a café and read or write or a bookstore and buy a book to read this week. Be spontaneous.

End of Day Reflection

Five Things I am grateful for:

1

2

3

4

5

What did I learn today?

1

2

3

TO DO TOMORROW

1

2

3

4

5

"Sometimes if you want something done a specific way, sometimes it's best if you do it yourself."

People make mistakes and they get forgetful. Sometimes it's easy to get distracted and off track. We are all only human. Sometimes you just need to double check what you expect. When doing so, it is easy to become mad and angry at someone when something wasn't done properly. Remember to share with that person the gift of patience and show them kindly how to handle or do it the next time. They will appreciate the kind manner and tone in which you handle the situation.

End of Day Reflection

Five Things I am grateful for:

1

2

3

4

5

What did I learn today?

1

2

3

TO DO TOMORROW

1

2

3

4

5

February 8
Aquarius

"Sometimes the answers you seek to life's difficult questions are right in front of you or they are located within."

Sometimes we walk through life blindly, waving around in the dark until we find the switch for the light that is in front of us. Sometimes while finding the light switch, we stumble and fall while searching in the dark. That is okay too, just remember to turn on the light and remember to get back up again. Don't let the scars and brises and scabs change the direction that you intend to go. Walk with purpose and good intentions and take in everything that is good and new to learn and grow from.

It is easy to let the small things in life get to you, when this happens take in a deep breath of air in silence and let it out slowly and think about something that brings you happiness, it could be the beach, the mountains, or the night sky. Remember to smile and that things are going to be okay!

End of Day Reflection

Five Things I am grateful for:

1

2

3

4

5

What did I learn today?

1

2

3

TO DO TOMORROW

1

2

3

4

5

February 9
Aquarius

"The doors of opportunity swing open more than once in life."

Sometimes, when one door of opportunity closes, another door opens and it's just a matter of us needing the patience to remember to wait for the opportunity to show itself behind the veil and then we can take advantage of the opportunity and learn and grow. Never be afraid of change in life. Yes, believe me, I know how scary things can be when it comes to changes, especially if it's something like moving from one state to another or countries apart. But look at the change as if it's something that you can experience and see differently. If you don't like the change after open mindedly taking on the said change for a year, go back to what you were more comfortable with if it's possible but at least you can say that you attempted the changes in your life and you have decided to only change what you can along the way.

I feel like you need to hear this today:

The best revenge is none.

Prove them wrong. Heal, and move on and do not become like those who have hurt you. Be the better person. Lead by example and don't let the opinions of others hurt you or change the person whom you are meant to be. Find that inner peace and happiness in knowing that you are better than the person who would take the same situation and be vengeful and angry. You know you don't need that type of drama in your life.

End of Day Reflection

Five Things I am grateful for:

1

2

3

4

5

What did I learn today?

1

2

3

TO DO TOMORROW

1

2

3

4

5

"Sometimes when we don't like someone, that isn't the issue, sometimes it's just an issue where we don't understand them and really know who they are, it means you have to get to know them, for them."

It is easy to judge those that are around us at face value, and to just look at them for who and what they are and not notice how significant they are. People are placed in our lives for a reason, a season, or a lifetime. There is no such thing as coincidences in life, there is purpose, and cause, and what is meant to be. Take the time to get to know those that are around you. Sometimes getting to know people is like trying to crack a nutshell, and sometimes the easiest nut shells to crack are often empty. The nutshells that are more difficult to crack, sometimes are the rarest of them all.

End of Day Reflection

Five Things I am grateful for:

1

2

3

4

5

What did I learn today?

1

2

3

TO DO TOMORROW

1

2

3

4

5

"Be Generous and you will be rewarded two-fold in life when you least expect it."

Gratitude and Generosity attract many people around you who sometimes end up leading you to unexpected places, and situations. Upon reflection of my own life, when there has been times of struggle and the need to figure things out, it is quite a humbling experience when people outreach to you, their help. You realize who is there for you and who will always have your back, in the same token, you learn also that you ought not to take advantage of the situations that you get into as well.

When you are generous to others, people never forget and then when times are tough for you, it is those same people who are understanding, caring, loving, and supportive of you when your cards in life are down. This is in essence the result of OQP (surrounding yourself with Only Quality People) and good friends and family. Never take people who are in your life for granted as they too can help or may need help too at times.

End of Day Reflection

Five Things I am grateful for:

1

2

3

4

5

What did I learn today?

1

2

3

TO DO TOMORROW

1

2

3

4

5

February 12
Aquarius

"In life, it is okay to want things but there is a difference between a need and a want."

There are times when you want something, and you only want it out of materialism or just because. This is not the same as needing something to survive and get by. In the same respect there are two different types of love, Nurture VS Survival types of love.

Nurture is loving someone out of the heart with emotion with care and pure love and affection. There is also the survival type of love in which there is no real emotion but its transactional giving your love (things) providing for the basic needs of your child/significant other to survive (i.e., roof over head, electric, food, clothes). Nurture at the end of the day is what we need to learn to give and be for each other.

End of Day Reflection

Five Things I am grateful for:

1

2

3

4

5

What did I learn today?

1

2

3

TO DO TOMORROW

1

2

3

4

5

February 13
Aquarius

"Be a light of hope to others around you."

The way I see it, there are already enough bad people in the world, why would you want to be one of them? Help others around you and help the world to conspire to help them achieve their dreams and goals without expecting anything in return.

"One thing I am learning is that you can be happy, hurting, and healing all at the same time. Healing isn't an overnight process; you don't decide you want to get better and wake up the next day feeling like a new person. It's a long journey, it's painful, and raw, and heavy, but it is also magical and exciting and inspiring, and you start to fall in love with parts of yourself you never thought you could. You'll have days where you feel like you can't go on, but you must…. Because eventually things that used to hurt won't hurt so much anymore and everything will feel so much lighter so if you are feeling overwhelmed and scared and tired of fighting it all the time, trust the process, trust that what is meant for you will find you and you will be ok." -@whateviedid

End of Day Reflection

Five Things I am grateful for:

1

2

3

4

5

What did I learn today?

1

2

3

TO DO TOMORROW

1

2

3

4

5

February 14
Aquarius

Happy Valentine's Day. Whether you have found the love of your life or not, no matter who they are, love is love. If you have not had a Valentine for today, it is okay. The right person will come into your life when the time that they are ready to, they are probably fixing themselves for you right now and you must do the same for them. When life is so short, I think that we forget the value of it at times and take for granted the precious moments that we have with and for others that are around us. Live today to the fullest and enjoy it in all its simplicity to the fullest. Take some time to work on yourself, go exercise at a park or go to the gym or go get some coffee, you never know whom you will meet! Be the Valentine light on someone's day. Pay it forward.

Don't live your life in the anxiety of what you don't have in life. Focus on what is in your life and the many accomplishments that you have completed in your life thus far, whatever happens, don't be hard on yourself for your failures of the past and don't let any depression get you lost.

End of Day Reflection

Five Things I am grateful for:

1

2

3

4

5

What did I learn today?

1

2

3

TO DO TOMORROW

1

2

3

4

5

February 15
Aquarius

"There are people in your life who need a hand to hold, a voice to hear, and a light to follow in hope and guidance and to be under care of your wing." -Anthony Parker

"You will find your people. The ones that make you feel like you belong. The ones that feel like sunshine. The ones that just get you. The ones you can dance all night with. The ones you can sit in silence with. The ones that lift you up. The ones that just want to be in your presence. The ones that make you feel loved. The ones that need you as much as you need them. The ones that feel your happiness, and sadness like it's their own. The ones that make you feel like you are enough just the way you are." - @ALLYISLIA

You are either going through something right now, about to go through something right now, or maybe you just got over something right now that was creating turmoil in your life, so you understand just as much as most what it's like to feel at the bottom. Be there for a friend today. Remember to tell them you value them, you value their friendship, and above all that you are here for them in whatever capacity that they may need.

"This is something that you need to hear. It is your fault when you hold on to someone that shows you time and time again that they are no good for you and you must take ownership of that. When someone shows you who they are, believe them. Remember it's not about what they say, it's about what they do and if their actions don't line up with their words, then it's probably best that you walk in the other direction. You can still respect them sure, but you must, and I mean must, respect yourself first. Love yourself so much that when someone else treats you wrong, you recognize it." - @morechrisgriffin

End of Day Reflection

Five Things I am grateful for:

1

2

3

4

5

What did I learn today?

1

2

3

TO DO TOMORROW

1

2

3

4

5

February 16
Aquarius

"I find it's better to trust others until given a reason not to. There is still hope, morals, and values, and integrity in and for humanity. "

Many of you go through life feeling like the world is against you or that the world owes you. Sometimes you must help others to get to where you want to be in life. Going through life with a hard shell, yes, it protects you but there are only a few who you need to have that hard shell of distrust to have against them. There was a time a few years ago when going through the journey of writing my book series that I had felt not the same as I had felt when the first few books came out. I had reached out to a fellow author whom I have trusted throughout my entire writing journey and told her what I was going through and releasing a book a year for a few years in a row and that's all that I had allowed myself time for. She had explained to me that I was going through a temporary moment of Burn out. It was then that I had come across a post in Instagram:

"When you go through a burnout, no one really understands unless they have gone through it. When you burn out, you care about your work or job but its so overwhelming that you just can't do it. It's not being lazy or procrastinating till the very end. It is months or years of constantly sacrificing yourself till you break. It's months or years of crying until you can't cry no more. Give yourself time for yourself and remember that something that once gave you "purpose," in life, can outgrow from your life. The longer you hang on to that life or idea, the longer you allow yourself to go through that pain. - @hearteningpoems. I had to learn something from this experience, though we have our hearts set on success and dreams and goals to spend years focusing on one thing, we lose time in life experiencing other things we ought to be doing like making memories and taking time for ourselves. I have learned that time management is important and that it's okay to have time to yourself and take breaks. We will reach our success and the end of our journey when we are meant to on our own time, not by a set time.

End of Day Reflection

Five Things I am grateful for:

1

2

3

4

5

What did I learn today?

1

2

3

TO DO TOMORROW

1

2

3

4

5

February 17
Aquarius

"I find that when there is a bad taste in your mouth, you spit it out - you don't constantly swallow it back down." - Amazing Grace Movie, Barbara Spooner talking to William Wilberforce

Sometimes when the times are bad, when you feel like you want to give up, when you feel like it isn't worth going through anymore… it's easy to throw in the towel. I wish I could tell you that it's going to get easier and that it's going to get better, sometimes you just need to find a new "why" your purpose. When you find your new "why" your reason to keep going, you find a way when there is no way. You find a way to get through and sometimes, when things are bad, it's better to talk to others around you. When you keep swallowing back in your struggles without reaching out for help, your mental and emotional health will decrease. When you get to the point where you can't take it anymore and when you keep pushing yourself, new doors of opportunity open and you can't give up on life.

End of Day Reflection

Five Things I am grateful for:

1

2

3

4

5

What did I learn today?

1

2

3

TO DO TOMORROW

1

2

3

4

5

February 18
Aquarius

"In meditation, sometimes it's in the silence that you find answers to your innermost feelings."

When you take the time to meditate on your life, when you are unsure about decisions that you must make, you find the answers that you are looking for within.

"Are you feeling behind in life? You need to know that you are not. There is no schedule or timeline that we must follow. It is all made up. Wherever you are right now is just where you need to be. Seven billion people can't do everything in the same scheduled order. We are different with a variety of needs and goals. Some get married early, some get married later in life, while some don't get married at all. What is early? What is late? Compared with whom? Compared with what? Some want children and others don't. Some want a career; others enjoy taking care of a house and children. Your life is not on anyone else's schedule. Everything is happening for you, not against you. Trust the timing of your life because the best is yet to come." - @lifeplanner.babe

End of Day Reflection

Five Things I am grateful for:

1

2

3

4

5

What did I learn today?

1

2

3

TO DO TOMORROW

1

2

3

4

5

Don't judge a book by its cover - you only learn more about it by flipping through its pages and giving it a chance.

When new people come into your life, it is easy to judge or complain about them without getting to know them. If you take the time to get to know them, and understand them with an open mind, you may learn more about them and about yourself along the way through them. There are people who come In and out of our lives and sometimes it's for the right reasons. Changes are hard to deal with, on the path while working on your dreams, and disappointment and failures happen along the way. These difficulties have not come to stay, they have come to pass.

End of Day Reflection

Five Things I am grateful for:

1

2

3

4

5

What did I learn today?

1

2

3

TO DO TOMORROW

1

2

3

4

5

Your destiny awaits you!

"No matter how bad it is, or how bad it gets, I am going to make it!" – Les Brown

We all have bad days and good days, and no matter what we will always pull through it. It is always better to be positive than negative and be an optimist than a pessimist.

"Let go of the chains of perfectionism; they are the shackles that hinder our flight towards greatness. Embrace the beauty of imperfection for it is within our own flaws that we find the courage to grow and the strength to soar like eagles. Embrace your journey for progress not perfection, by doing this it paves the path to fulfillment and accomplishment. When we release the need to be flawless, we unlock the potential to be truly extraordinary." – Logan Vadivel

End of Day Reflection

Five Things I am grateful for:

1

2

3

4

5

What did I learn today?

1

2

3

TO DO TOMORROW

1

2

3

4

5

February 21
Pisces

Sometimes people only learn from experience. When being told to do things by people around us you need to be weary of what is going on and the circumstances behind and around what you are told to do and how it might affect those around you in a more positive or negative way.

Take in the experiences that happen around you today and pay attention to everyone and everything from everyone's perspective. Learn from others and their mistakes.

Warriors Affirmation:

"If what you want me to do, is going to compromise my integrity, and therefore my inner peace, I am not interested in compliance. I'm not here to live a life others create for me. I'm here to co-create the life my soul dreams into BEING." - @jaymi.jai

End of Day Reflection

Five Things I am grateful for:

1

2

3

4

5

What did I learn today?

1

2

3

TO DO TOMORROW

1

2

3

4

5

There are some buttons in life that are okay to push.

Sometimes it takes many times for someone to say "no," to finally get that "yes" that you need. In sales it's called the batting average. In life, this may mean the ability to or not be able to get to that next level to accomplish your dreams and goals. People in life around you have always gotten many "nos" before they got to be successful in life. JK Rowling got denied many times before she got to publish the Harry Potter Books. The way you must look at it is, there may be a reasoning behind the no to find out what the intention or purpose is behind it. We all have goals and dreams that we want to accomplish but we allow the "nos" to guide us to supposed contentment but, the reason why we didn't get further with the dream or goal is we allowed the "no" to be a settled contentment in what the final answer is. There are always ways to work around this. Say you want to be an author and you keep getting rejection letters from various literary agents, you can accept them as a final answer, or you can keep submitting the manuscripts and adjust your cover letter to the agent or you could find other agents to submit the manuscript to or you can self-publish without dealing with a literary agent. Say you want to be a teacher but for whatever reason the school of the state you are in isn't accepting your application to be a college professor you can always go to other schools, in other states or other countries to teach the same thing. Never let yourself settle for what you think is, versus what things could be.

End of Day Reflection

Five Things I am grateful for:

1

2

3

4

5

What did I learn today?

1

2

3

TO DO TOMORROW

1

2

3

4

5

February 23
Pisces

No one ought to have the power over you to force you to believe something is impossible without you trying it first.

"What would you say is the biggest deception? What is the biggest lie you were ever told?"

"It's not that simple."

"Why not?"

"No, that is the biggest lie I was ever told. It's not that simple, it's a lie they tell you over, and over again."

"What's not simple?"

"Any of it. All of it. It's how they get you to give up. They say it's not that simple."

"So, what's the truth?"

"That it is. That if you just do the thing that they tell you that you can't do, then it's done, and you realize it *is* that simple."

End of Day Reflection

Five Things I am grateful for:

1

2

3

4

5

What did I learn today?

1

2

3

TO DO TOMORROW

1

2

3

4

5

February 24
Pisces

You may already have decided that the answer you seek may be a "no," but it's worth the risk to confirm your fear. Who knows they could say "yes."

"Align yourself with people that you can learn from, people who want more out of life, people who are stretching, and searching and seeking higher ground in life."- Les Brown

Sometimes people are just comfortable with where they are in life and don't want to ask the questions and do the things that it takes to get to that next level in life. Why not ask for a raise from your boss, or for a promotion, or ask to see if they are hiring where you want to work and where you see yourself in five years? They may not be hiring but you can volunteer or be an apprentice and eventually your time will come when the sun rises itself and shines on you! The question is are you going to jump on it when it does come, when the time comes for you to shine?

End of Day Reflection

Five Things I am grateful for:

1

2

3

4

5

What did I learn today?

1

2

3

TO DO TOMORROW

1

2

3

4

5

February 25
Pisces

> You can learn so much by listening to others and observing them in silence.

Sometimes we don't fully understand a person's situation until we take the time to understand why they are sad, why they are angry, why they are stressed, or why they are underperforming. By taking the time to step back and see what they are going through even possibly outside of the situation and listening to them, we will learn more and be more empathetic to what's going on at hand. When we force our scenarios on someone without taking the time to understand, we are minimizing their feelings and their opinions, undervaluing them and this also could affect their self-esteem. Be mindful as much as you can.

End of Day Reflection

Five Things I am grateful for:

1

2

3

4

5

What did I learn today?

1

2

3

TO DO TOMORROW

1

2

3

4

5

There is a Japanese legend that says,

"Crying is just a way your eyes speak, when your mouth can't explain how broken your heart is." - @copywrockett

"It is very hard to lose people you thought would never leave, but you will be okay because you have no choice. When we lose people that we love, we must find a way to keep going for the people we still have in our lives." – Good Doctor @themovietales

Stick up for what you believe in and for what you believe is right and just. Live in and with integrity. Never compromise, the moment you speak and decide the world listens and watches and observes. Whatever you do, please don't waste your time today comparing yourself to others. There is enough room for us all to be beautiful, intelligent, and successful in our own way.

End of Day Reflection

Five Things I am grateful for:

1

2

3

4

5

What did I learn today?

1

2

3

TO DO TOMORROW

1

2

3

4

5

February 27
Pisces

There is nothing wrong with being sad or angry, no matter who you are, it is okay to cry. This is what makes us human.

We forget as humans it is okay to have feelings and react to situations sometimes if it is in a healthy nonviolent manner and that isn't directed towards those around us. Bottling it up is not good for anyone. Live like a shaken water bottle being opened, not like a shaken soda can. It's easier to open emotionally in the end rather than being a shaken soda can!

End of Day Reflection

Five Things I am grateful for:

1

2

3

4

5

What did I learn today?

1

2

3

TO DO TOMORROW

1

2

3

4

5

February 28
Pisces

Sometimes when stressed it's easy to forget to take a moment to breathe. But when you do, and you close your eyes and breathe in deeply a few times, it relaxes your mind and body and allows you to move forward easier.

I think in life we forget to relax during stressful moments, and it potentially raises your blood pressure and our heart rate, and it physically affects us, and it can be debilitating for some. Take some time today and reflect on life in mediation. It works wonders for the soul!

End of Day Reflection

Five Things I am grateful for:

1

2

3

4

5

What did I learn today?

1

2

3

TO DO TOMORROW

1

2

3

4

5

March 1 — Pisces

Not everyone in life is going to agree with you and that is okay.

This is what makes us unique humans, having our own beliefs, values, personalities, thoughts, opinions, and experiences. But remember that while this is occurring this doesn't mean that anyone, not even you, can impose these thoughts and opinions on you or on others as, "THE ONLY RIGHT WAY" to do things or to believe. You are entitled to your own opinion and beliefs just as much as the next person. If everyone had the same beliefs the world would be a boring place to live in.

Things to work on this Month: Try to grow a thicker skin and not be too sensitive in general by being easily hurt by what people say, do, and react to around you. If you take things personally all the time, it will be hard for people to feel like they can bring up things to you if they feel like you will take it to heart. Work on not being moody all the time and feeling like you are a victim in life. Yes, things happen to us and around us, but this doesn't mean that you cannot do anything about your situation in life. You can choose to play victim where you are in life, or you can do something about it and change your circumstances. Allow yourself boundaries, don't be pulled into drama that you are not a part of. If you allow yourself to help everyone in need, you forget to take care of yourself, and this also opens you up to being taken advantage of. Do not run away from your problems in life. Try to work on confronting them head on and getting them resolved. Things are the way they are because you allow them to be. Tell people how you feel about things and don't be afraid to be open to people and tell them that you feel like you are being taken advantage of. Yes, confronting others in your life is a difficult task but also look at it like, if you don't tell them how things are, you will be stuck in the scenario forever and it may lead to your feeling internally miserable. People have feelings and emotions as well, but these emotions are easier dealt with when they are shared and confronted.

End of Day Reflection

Five Things I am grateful for:

1

2

3

4

5

What did I learn today?

1

2

3

TO DO TOMORROW

1

2

3

4

5

March 2

Today is the start of a new month. Think about your goals this month.

What are you doing to prepare yourself to ensure your success and continued success and growth? What do you want to do next month that you could start preparing for? Are you wanting to go on a trip next month? Would you start saving? Do you need to request the time off? Prepare yourself to do something fun this month as well. Having something to look forward to always helps keep you pushing forward! Are you at where you want to be in life yet? If not, DON'T GIVE UP!

The secret to finding strength in your lowest moments:

Create a list of all the things you've accomplished and overcome – write down your wins and keep adding to it overtime. When you feel defeated or depressed or sad in life, look at this list and remind yourself who you are, and what you have been able to do in your life.

End of Day Reflection

Five Things I am grateful for:

1

2

3

4

5

What did I learn today?

1

2

3

TO DO TOMORROW

1

2

3

4

5

March 3 Pisces

Find a new talent or hobby to get into. Meet new people.

How many people could you have the potential to have a good influence on in your life or around you? What goals or dreams could you help them accomplish through contacts and people that you know? Get to know someone new by starting a new talent or hobby that you wish to do on the side. You never know what your strengths and weaknesses are if you don't grasp and try the new opportunities to see if you are or aren't good at them. This is how you grow and get out of your comfort zone!

Sometimes we must be thankful for the closed doors, detours, and diversions that we have had in our lives. Because they have protected us from certain paths, places, and people who were not meant for us, and it nudged us in the right directions towards the right path along the way.

End of Day Reflection

Five Things I am grateful for:

1

2

3

4

5

What did I learn today?

1

2

3

TO DO TOMORROW

1

2

3

4

5

Success doesn't know cold or hot or late or early or tired, it just knows whether you showed up or not. People will find any excuse not to. Saying no is the easiest thing to do, rather than pushing themselves and learning and growing to that next level. Staying comfortable where you are is not going to get you anywhere. Complacency and repetition of the same thing day in and day out is the enemy of progress. Do not let yourself be fooled so that you can sleep in and still reach your goals in the end. Sleeping in, in the moment, feels like you are allowing your body to rest when its tired but if you aren't sick, you need to push yourself up early to accomplish more throughout the day.

Waking up this morning may have been difficult if it's rainy outside or cold out, but you know I just heard of a story called Running in the Rain – Motivational Video. Look it up on YouTube, it's powerful!

End of Day Reflection

Five Things I am grateful for:

1

2

3

4

5

What did I learn today?

1

2

3

TO DO TOMORROW

1

2

3

4

5

March 5 — Pisces

It takes courage and bravery for you to stand up for yourself and even more for when you stand up for someone else.

We all know what it's like to feel like the underdog, the one that gets made fun of or torn apart because of someone else's opinion, but that doesn't have to become your reality. Stand up for those who are oppressed and those who don't feel that they have a voice to stand up for themselves.

I am reminded of a story told by Sean Buranahiran. There is a famous analogy of a crow being the only bird that dares to peck at an eagle. The crow climbs on the eagle's back and pecks at its neck. Rather than responding, the eagle raises its wings and flies rather than fights. An Eagle can fly up to 10,000 feet using very little energy. The higher the eagle soars, the more difficult it becomes for the crow, and the crow falls off on its own. The same goes for the crows in your life and the life of those around you. Help them. If you are at a place where you expose yourself to the cawing of the crows, or you see someone else experiencing this, it's simply a sign for you to raise the bar and take yourself and the person being picked on, to the next level. Rather than responding with emotion, we rise. Rather than fighting, we fly. Rather than be demoralized, we demonstrate what it is to be great people, and must soar higher, like the eagle.

End of Day Reflection

Five Things I am grateful for:

1

2

3

4

5

What did I learn today?

1

2

3

TO DO TOMORROW

1

2

3

4

5

March 6
Pisces

There is nothing wrong with love in any form or shape.

Many times, in life, we get caught up in titles, labels, and traditional formalities and we lose the value behind love and its meaning. There is no way one can control how we love, only that Love is exactly what it is, love. When we use the words, "I love you too often, it also can lose its value and importance in a relationship as well. Using our actions to over empower the meaning of what love really is in its full capacity, when saying, "I love you, adds more value to it and shows through appreciation in its many forms to our significant other. Love in its simplest form is affection. Caring about the other person, spending time with that person, helping them do something or creating a memory with them. Sometimes it's expressed with physical touch and sometimes just by being there for them.

End of Day Reflection

Five Things I am grateful for:

1

2

3

4

5

What did I learn today?

1

2

3

TO DO TOMORROW

1

2

3

4

5

March 7 — Pisces

I wanted to share a story with you today about: The Happiest Bird in the World told by Sean Buranahiran: Once upon a time there was a crow that lived in a forest. One day he saw a beautiful white swan, a family was giving him food and taking pictures of him. So, he thought to himself, that swans must be the happiest bird in the world. So, he flew over to the swan and told him, "You are so white, and so beautiful and I am so dark. You must be the happiest bird in the world." The Swan replied, "I used to think that I was the happiest bird in the world, until I saw a parrot. The Parrot I saw had two colors and I only had one. You should go and ask the parrot what it feels like to be the happiest bird in the world. So, the crow flew over to the parrot and asked, "What does it feel like to be the happiest bird in the world?" The Parrot replied, "I used to think that I was the happiest bird in the world until I met the peacock, the peacock has many colors, and I only have two. You should go to the peacock and ask, "How does it feel to be the happiest bird in the world? The last time I saw him, he was at the zoo."

So, the crow flew over to the zoo, and he saw hundreds of people taking pictures of the peacock. He waited until everyone had left, and he flew over and asked, "Dear peacock, you are so beautiful, every day you have hundreds of people taking pictures of you, and when they see me, they chase me away. How does it feel to be the happiest bird in the world?" The peacock replied, "I always thought I was the happiest bird in the world, but because of this beauty, I am trapped in a cage.

With all this time by myself, I noticed that the only bird that is not placed in a cage is the crow. So, for the past few years, I have been thinking to myself, the crow must be the happiest bird in the world, free to roam wherever he wants. So, my friend, I must ask you, how does it feel to be the happiest bird in the world?" The cycle of comparing ourselves to other people is a never-ending cycle. The game where we compare ourselves to other people is a game that we could never win. In the end, the person that is satisfied with what they have is the happiest person in the world. I think it is okay to strive to improve the quality of life if you are doing it. If you are not seeing the value in what you have, I think that is a mistake. Think of three things you are grateful for: Health, time to spend with family and friends, time for your hobbies, chasing your dreams, don't compare your chapter one to somebody's chapter 20. If we are running in a race and we focus on the people who are running beside us, or ahead of us we may lose motivation and focus. You may slip and fall, just by looking at them. So, the best thing for you to do is focus on yourself and run at your own pace, because your finish line is not in the same place as everyone else's!

End of Day Reflection

Five Things I am grateful for:

1

2

3

4

5

What did I learn today?

1

2

3

4

5

TO DO TOMORROW

1

2

3

4

5

March 8
Pisces

Happiness and success aren't the same for everyone, that is okay, you do you.

  A concept that may be difficult for others to comprehend in which a good amount of understanding must be derived. What may make you happy, may make someone else miserable. Sometimes children feel that they must get involved with sports or special academic programs to get attention and acceptance or love from their parents. This must not be instilled in children because it also can affect their morale and overall self-esteem. If they are miserable in doing what they feel will gain them popularity or attention, how can they achieve their own version of success? How can this help encourage them to chase after their dreams and goals if they aren't chasing the dreams and goals that they wish to in life? Afterall, isn't the happiness of the child what the goal is in the end? I think that this important aspect needs to be realized not just in regard to parenting but also in our relationships as well. What one partner wants to do for fun may not be fun for the other. Compromise, understanding, communication, and mutual respect of each other are also important.

End of Day Reflection

Five Things I am grateful for:

1

2

3

4

5

What did I learn today?

1

2

3

TO DO TOMORROW

1

2

3

4

5

March 9
Pisces

    Friendship and money for me is like mixing oil and water, they never mix. You can't put monetary value on a loyal friendship. I admit there are some who do mix the two and take a tally as to how much that they spend on their friends…. but if you have been where I have been and have struggled you know what it's like to be the struggler and it doesn't make you any less of a person to be in this predicament. If anything, it makes you more humble along the way when someone can help you and when vice versa when you can be that hand to help.

    It is important for you to not only have friends, but also be there for each other for support. When going through the path of life, it can be lonely, and, sometimes, life happens, and having those friends nearby to just have someone to talk to without fear of judgment or retribution is helpful to get through the struggles in life. Money can be a tool for greed, but it can also, if used correctly, be used to help others recover and heal and overcome.

End of Day Reflection

Five Things I am grateful for:

1

2

3

4

5

What did I learn today?

1

2

3

TO DO TOMORROW

1

2

3

4

5

March 10 — Pisces

No one said life is easy, but it's worth it!

Today I want to share with you the analogy of Life and a bamboo tree as told by Sean Buranahiran.

There is a famous analogy of life compared to a bamboo tree. You see, the bamboo tree grows unlike any other tree in the world. You must water and fertilize it every day for five years. Here is where it gets weird. Nothing has happened for five years. You see nothing grow. It's like you are just watering the dirt. But in its fifth year, the bamboo tree will break through the ground, and it will grow up to eighty feet in six weeks. It's like you can see it growing right in front of your eyes. It's just like your life, you may be doing something and not seeing anything from your efforts, nothing changing, nothing is happening but trust me, deep inside of you, there is something happening. There is something changing. You are like the bamboo tree, digging its roots deep in the ground, so that when it rises, it will not fall, just like you. You are digging your roots deep in the ground, you are building the most important part of your life, which is yourself, which is the base. The base of a pyramid, the foundation. You are learning about yourself and other people, you are learning about what works, what doesn't work, you are learning about life, so don't worry. When the time is right everything will happen when it's supposed to. Everything will just come together, and you will grow eighty feet just like the bamboo tree, and everyone will see it in the end, how much hard work you put in. It will all be worth it in the end!

End of Day Reflection

Five Things I am grateful for:

1

2

3

4

5

What did I learn today?

1

2

3

TO DO TOMORROW

1

2

3

4

5

March 11 - Pisces

Sometimes slow and steady wins the race. We all want things from yesteryear and yes; I am quite guilty of my own impatience. Wanting things that are happening in the next year or two now. The thing that I must remind myself is, all good things come in good time. Whether we want them now or later, taking things one step at a time and handle things as they come and sometimes even ahead of time if they are foreseen is the best route to take.

If you are in a position of power and wish to promote someone. Maybe taking it slow and steady and see how they handle the responsibilities slowly you can see what type of person they are and how they get along with everyone first and get to know that person's personality on the good and bad days is the better route to go. Perhaps they have a lot of things going on at home and they don't mention it to anyone, and the added responsibility could be too much for that person. Perhaps that person you wish to promote wants to leave and they haven't said anything or maybe they are unhappy. Promoting that person when they are already unhappy is not the best thing and perhaps waiting and taking things slow would-be the best approach.

We are all in a rush to go nowhere and everywhere. The concept of time helps us and hurts us. It helps us because we can improve our running times, on reaching our goals by a goal date, making our appointments for doctors on time or even to work on time. But in the same respect I think time hurts us because of its warp speed. A lifetime flashes before our eyes and yet sometimes we forget to spend necessary time with family and friends before it is too late. Our days are numbered and at the same time, we don't know when it will end. Enjoy life in the moments and reflect on the past briefly without regret. Appreciate time as the arms on the clock reach out and grasp on to a new day.

End of Day Reflection

Five Things I am grateful for:

1

2

3

4

5

What did I learn today?

1

2

3

TO DO TOMORROW

1

2

3

4

5

March 12 — Pisces

The decisions that you make in your life are essential in determining your future.

You can say, I am eating right by eating a slice of cake and a soda, or you can say I am eating right by eating Greek yogurt and a protein shake. Both are arguably correct in the right perspective but in the end, they come down to the choices that you make in life. You can choose to stay up all night and watch a marathon of your favorite tv show or you could make sure you get eight hours of sleep the night before your big exam.

Something else that I feel you need to think about today:

You are stronger and more resilient than you give yourself credit for. I know that you have possibly been feeling doubtful about yourself lately and I want you to know that you are not alone. You can achieve great things, and you have so much potential within yourself. Today I want you to take a step back and look at all the amazing miraculous things that you have accomplished thus far. Remember all the times you have overcome obstacles and challenges and how much you have grown through those experiences. I also want you to know that it's okay to fail and make mistakes. Not everything is going to go our way but that is okay. It's natural to have setbacks along the way within our learning process. It's how you grow and improve and logically handle these experiences that matters more. Don't let fear of failure hold you back from pursuing your dreams. Temporary setbacks happen, and that is okay, that means you are one more step closer to where you want to be. Keeping yourself positive and pushing forward and never giving up MUST BE CONSTANTLY in the back of your mind. Remember you can attract more positivity and bees (people) with honey than you can with vinegar.

End of Day Reflection

Five Things I am grateful for:

1

2

3

4

5

What did I learn today?

1

2

3

TO DO TOMORROW

1

2

3

4

5

March 13
Pisces

Having a good moral and value compass will lead you in the right direction every time.

  We get these feelings inside of ourselves when we feel we shouldn't do what we are about to do, we should do something different than what is being presented to us. We get these gut feelings within ourselves that this doesn't feel good, and you get these bad feelings about a certain situation, and you don't prepare yourself. Then when we get these bad feelings of discomfort we give up and we turn around and then we stop. It takes courage to act, to follow through, or to start over again. Don't get comfortable, feel comfortable… do what others aren't willing to do today, so that you can have what others don't have tomorrow.
"Courage – going from failure to failure without losing enthusiasm." – Les Brown

  When you have something, you want to do, if you don't develop the courage to do what you want to do, you will lose your nerve, and other people will convince you that your dream doesn't have any value and you give up on your dream. If you have something special that you want to do, and you are filled with passion and you don't give up, eventually you will be successful.

End of Day Reflection

Five Things I am grateful for:

1

2

3

4

5

What did I learn today?

1

2

3

TO DO TOMORROW

1

2

3

4

5

March 14
Pisces

If you see something, do, and say something.

Sometimes we look at a person and say,

"That guy was stupid" – already being critical and judgmental of someone else without even meaning it.

Or we complain to others and say that "We hate our jobs because our manager is so horrible and stupid…."

When we complain you must realize the alternate reality is too funny….

Because if our manager was stupid, why did they sign your paycheck?"

Here was a guy that wasn't controlling his life because the manager controlled his paycheck. If you don't like the situation, you are in, you should do something about it, say something to someone about it. Sure, finding a new job is difficult and it would require change and challenge and meeting new people but, in the end, you might find happiness.

"Yard by yard is hard, but inch by inch is a cinch!" Robert Fuller

Yes, there are challenges that we face every day and there are times when you don't feel like there is that glimmer of hope at the end of the tunnel.

End of Day Reflection

Five Things I am grateful for:

1

2

3

4

5

What did I learn today?

1

2

3

TO DO TOMORROW

1

2

3

4

5

March 15
Pisces

Never give up on your dreams, there is no age requirement to accomplish them.

Some say, I am too old, or I am not old enough to accomplish my dreams. If you think this is true, it's right, but if you think this is false and that you can go and do what you are destined to do at your current age, I know you can! Looking back, you can see what you have accomplished. You have gotten through school, you are a mother, or you are a father, you have gotten your first job or got an "A" in your recent test or a "B," either way there is always something that you can be proud of that you have accomplished thus far. Don't look at your age and say it's not possible and give up because at the end of the day, the only true failure is when you do give up hope, or you stop trying. Look at the world of possibilities and opportunities that are going on around you today and live for today and look forward to something tomorrow. Continue to grow and learn and be better than you were yesterday!

End of Day Reflection

Five Things I am grateful for:

1

2

3

4

5

What did I learn today?

1

2

3

TO DO TOMORROW

1

2

3

4

5

Don't be afraid to get out there and travel and see new things and new cultures. Life is an adventure yet to be taken.

Did you know that the Amish only have an education up to eighth grade and they have one room schoolhouse classrooms? Did you know that they are predominantly living in PA, Ohio, and Indiana?

Do you know of the Seven Wonders of the World?

"(Switzerland — Honesty shopping, Tiny little shops in the middle of the Swiss Alps share the idealism of this society in the form of honesty shops. These are little shops that allow you to buy your fresh cheese, milk, bread, honey, and butter without anyone there to watch you indulge in the delicious dairy products of the area. In fact, most of the day, no one sees these shops because they are owned by farmers who are out taking care of the animals, so all you do is leave your money behind in a little basket. And what's amazing is that this form of consumer trust results in incredible customer loyalty and honesty among the communities. ALSO, IN Iceland — Christmas Eve books giving, we obsess over the eternal question of Christmas gifts; do we spend tons of money on new technology for our loved ones or just stick with the always-safe gift card? Will they read too much into a "Fitbit"? Iceland has solved this problem with the Christmas Eve tradition of giving a book. After everyone unwraps the books, they spend the evening reading together. Iceland has preserved the culture of books in this beautiful Christmas custom which many countries would do well to emulate!)
https://matadornetwork.com/read/10-interesting-customs-around-world/

End of Day Reflection

Five Things I am grateful for:

1

2

3

4

5

What did I learn today?

1

2

3

TO DO TOMORROW

1

2

3

4

5

March 17
Pisces

Trust is so powerful, don't lose it from others.

Trust is such an important factor when it comes to friendships, and relationships with those around you. The moment you lose that trust (Which can so easily be broken) it is difficult to restore. A thief doesn't announce who they are when they arrive in your life, they just take without notice or asking, and they would prefer you to think that they are honest people. This is not to say that everyone in your life is a thief or that everyone in your life is "a liar" or "out to get you."

Personally, I trust until I am given a few reasons not to trust a person seeing this through my own eyes, (this is also important not to let someone else's bad experience or judgment of someone cloud your judgment). It is easy to not trust others but at the same time being too trusting of others can be a bad thing as well. Your word at the end of the day is your bond of integrity with them regardless of the circumstances. We live in a world full of hate and evils but to trust others and love others as they are until given a reason not to otherwise will keep peace around you. We are all different in many ways, but we bleed the same and we all have hearts and feelings and emotions. Many a time, I have found it easier to be understanding of those around me. Some might call this "making excuses for others" but we don't know the full circumstance as to "why someone has been running late to work," or "why someone is having a bad day."

End of Day Reflection

Five Things I am grateful for:

1

2

3

4

5

What did I learn today?

1

2

3

TO DO TOMORROW

1

2

3

4

5

March 18 — Pisces

"Don't wish it was easier, wish you were better."
- Jim Rohn

Ah, this quote. The best example I can give for you to understand this quote is… Pick the worst subject in school that you ultimately and most grievously wanted to avoid at all costs. Mine was math. Math was difficult for me in school. I loved the other subjects, just not math. The reason in the end why I realized I hated the subject was because it was difficult to grasp and understand. If you wish it were easier, you wouldn't learn by struggling through the challenge. But if you were better and you tried your best to understand and love the subject, you would get through it easier and then it wouldn't be so bad after all. Anytime that you have a struggle or challenge in life, it's easy to say, I wish this was easier to handle or I wish I didn't have to do this part of things. But if you practiced or studied more or tried to gain a passion for the thing that you hated, you wouldn't mind it so much and you would overcome it.

It's easy to look back and get angry at yourself for certain decisions you have made in the past, but it's unfair to punish yourself for them. You can't blame yourself for not knowing then what you know now, and you made each decision for a reason based on the person you were at the time. As we grow up, we learn, and we grow up and we evolve. Maybe the person you are now would have done things differently back then, or maybe you are the person you are now because of the decisions you have made back then. Trust your journey, it is all going to make sense soon.

End of Day Reflection

Five Things I am grateful for:

1

2

3

4

5

What did I learn today?

1

2

3

TO DO TOMORROW

1

2

3

4

5

March 19
Pisces

Set a goal to build a life that you don't need a vacation from

Be and do what you want regardless of what others say or do to criticize you. Don't follow through with a career or a job or anything in life that you are not happy waking up every morning to do. If you are not happy, you are stressed, and you are miserable the rest of your life. A lot of times we feel the need to do and say and follow through with things, to make someone else impressed or pleased about us, as we disregard our own wants and needs. Don't live your life by living someone else's dreams. Be happy by following your heart and what you know will make you happy. If you don't build this kind of life for yourself, even your vacations will not feel like vacations.

Today, guide someone who may be lost in where they are in life and tell them to follow their dreams, goals, and aspirations whatever they may be and to wherever that may go and show them the path that they can take to be successful.

End of Day Reflection

Five Things I am grateful for:

1

2

3

4

5

What did I learn today?

1

2

3

TO DO TOMORROW

1

2

3

4

5

Life is too short to live with regrets and wishful thinking and shoulda coulda wouldves - Take control of your dreams and to where you want to be and find your own happiness regardless of what others say and want around you! I DARE YOU!

Where do you think that you will be in five years? Ten years? Twenty years? It is my advice that you always be thinking forward even when the times are bad. If you continue to plan for *that next big thing,* you will always have something to look forward to. Always have your dreams and goals in mind every day. Write them down and place them where you will see them every day and eventually if you are meeting the short-term goals to get you into that huge direction, you will get there. If your dreams don't scare you, they aren't big enough. DREAM BIG and DO great things and always strive towards these goals.

It is also my advice that you make short term goals that are achievable in 2 weeks, 3 months, 6 months and then make sure that they lead up to your one-year goal as well. When you achieve these goals, you will have a sense of accomplishment and you will find that you are establishing good daily habits to reach your goals as well.

End of Day Reflection

Five Things I am grateful for:

1

2

3

4

5

What did I learn today?

1

2

3

TO DO TOMORROW

1

2

3

4

5

"What is life without a little risk?"
- Sirius Black, Harry Potter Order of the Phoenix

  They say YOLO, right? But I also think that it's not that we live only once, we die only once, and we can choose to live every day or just sleep through our days. Life is precious and we must continue to live day after day. We do this because living and breathing and taking chances on things in life is important not only for us but for others as well. It is every day that we grow stronger and learn through our experiences. Don't let yourself be caught in a darkness of negativity; you don't have to feel alone, you just must reach out to those around you. Opportunities and choices are around us every day. What we choose to do with the options in front is us, that is what matters more, that shows what we truly are. Love yourself, love others, be successful, find joy in the simple things in life, and find that bit of happiness for your life, and when you find it hold on to it tightly and don't worry about what others say and think. Don't give up because you have survived 100% of your days so far! You are strong and you are special, and you are loved!

End of Day Reflection

Five Things I am grateful for:

1

2

3

4

5

What did I learn today?

1

2

3

TO DO TOMORROW

1

2

3

4

5

March 22
Aries

Practice makes it permanent. The more you practice at something the better one gets, and the more things become second nature and more casual.

I know we have all heard this phrase at least once whether in sports or in school or when we are being helped to do something that we aren't good at. This quote is so true. When attempting to do things the first time, even the best laid plans go awry. Things may not have gone right the first time but over time when using effort, you begin to understand how the thing that you are doing works and runs. You will also notice over time that as you constantly practice you get better at something you will begin to enjoy or like what you are doing and become an expert after repetition. This quote proves in many ways that if you don't give up at the first sign and stage of failure, and you pick yourself up and dust yourself off, you will get better over time. Never kick yourself over these failures, it's the journey to success and it's expected that people fall along the way a few times. That's how calluses are formed, and we get thicker skin!

End of Day Reflection

Five Things I am grateful for:

1

2

3

4

5

What did I learn today?

1

2

3

TO DO TOMORROW

1

2

3

4

5

March 23
Aries

No matter how good or bad your life is, remember to wake up with gratitude that you still have one.

Every day we expect to wake up, we expect to be healthy and continue with the plans that we make. Having expectations in your life isn't a bad thing, but you also must understand while having these expectations that sometimes things don't always go as planned and that is okay, in life there is no guarantees of tomorrow…

End of Day Reflection

Five Things I am grateful for:

1

2

3

4

5

What did I learn today?

1

2

3

TO DO TOMORROW

1

2

3

4

5

March 24
Aries

Nobody's perfect. We all make mistakes, which is why forgiveness and love are important to find inner peace. We have expectations that we place on each other and maybe they are higher than they should be. We need to allow for error in those around us. Be patient with those around you when they make a mistake. At some point, realize that it's not what happens to us, it's what we do with things after what happens to us around us that matters more. How you and others react and respond to situations. You can react with untamed emotion or respond with logic to things and the most logical response usually has the best outcomes.

We are only human at the end of the day. This quote brings back memories to the days I was working at a coffee shop. People would complain because there would be too much sugar or creamer or milk or not enough ice or too much ice, at the end of the day, I would remind myself, it is just coffee. Sometimes we make big deals out of little mistakes, and we learn from the mistakes. You can't let the little mistakes or the little things in life ruin your day or your week.

End of Day Reflection

Five Things I am grateful for:

1

2

3

4

5

What did I learn today?

1

2

3

TO DO TOMORROW

1

2

3

4

5

March 25
Aries

We make mistakes and we say the wrong things, we do the wrong things. We fall and we must remember to get back up. We then learn, grow, and move on.

My takeaway from this is life is too short to allow for the things that matter so little to prevent us from being able to move forward. Sometimes we say the wrong things or handle situations badly but to cut ties with someone completely may do more damage than hurt depending on who the person is. The choices that we make in life also affect those around us at times as well.

End of Day Reflection

Five Things I am grateful for:

1

2

3

4

5

What did I learn today?

1

2

3

TO DO TOMORROW

1

2

3

4

5

March 26
Aries

There are only ten bad people in the world, now they move around a lot though. Appreciate good people and ignore those who are more difficult to please as they are more upset about other things going on in their lives then they are directly of you and the good people, well they are hard to come by.

Personally, I have always felt there are far too many bad, mean, and nasty people in the world, especially when misery loves company, so why would I want to be one of those people?

End of Day Reflection

Five Things I am grateful for:

1

2

3

4

5

What did I learn today?

1

2

3

TO DO TOMORROW

1

2

3

4

5

March 27
Aries

No matter how big your house is, how recent your car is, or how big your bank account is, our graves will always be the same size. Stay humble.

   A lot of times in life, we get caught up in the material aspects of life, and we forget that in the end the only thing we have left with are the memories and the experiences that we have in life. That matters more than the things that we own and on top of that we can't take that material stuff with us in the end. This quote really keeps things in perspective because it also shows an even bigger importance of the differences between needs and wants in life, and it shows a different and more quality perspective of what is truly important when it comes to quantity and quality. We can have the next laptop or the next newest iPhone but what will matter more is even if we have the most basic phone and laptops, the difference and what will matter more is what we do with these things to improve our lives or the lives of others around us and what memories these items will create with others. I can truly say that my phone and laptop are just as important to me as my shoes. As my shoes help me walk around and experience things and create memories with others, so does my phone in connecting me to others and learning things and so does my laptop in helping me string together and connect these very words together for you to read to help you make a difference in your life. Today enjoy the basics and simplicities of life and use them to show you how you can make a difference in other people's lives.

End of Day Reflection

Five Things I am grateful for:

1

2

3

4

5

What did I learn today?

1

2

3

TO DO TOMORROW

1

2

3

4

5

March 28
Aries

When you are a good person, you don't lose people. They lose you.

Today with social media I think we take too much time to worry about the likes, the follows, and who and how many people subscribe to us that we let it get to us when we don't get these social responses. We worry too much about what others think about us and what everyone else is doing or thinking about us when in reality I think that we are too self-absorbed into ourselves sometimes and forget to really think about and check in on others. When you ask someone how are you they always respond with good and put on an act of a fake smile but if you really look into people you see that through the smiles and the social media posts of "living the dream" lifestyles they are really just like you, feeling around in the dark trying to find their way through the path of life as well. They too have their own demons that they are fighting and things that they too are struggling with. Social identity, family and relationship and financial problems. Figuring out when or how they are going to get their next meal or feed their own families. They depend on the paychecks they receive just to get by. Not everyone is saving. Not everyone has a backup plan. So today remember it's okay if you lose people around you, we are all going through our own cycles of life. Be there the best you can for those around you. Do you best to remind those around you that you are there for them and you can be there for them the best you can. It's okay to have a bad day and to not be doing well. It's better to have a job that cares about your mental health, and you are okay then to have a job that just only cares about the numbers at the end of the day.

Sometimes people come into our lives for a reason, or a season, and they are only meant to help us to get through a time or when we are about to go through a time, and they are not to be there for us for a lifetime.

End of Day Reflection

Five Things I am grateful for:

1

2

3

4

5

What did I learn today?

1

2

3

TO DO TOMORROW

1

2

3

4

5

March 29
Aries

"People who were raised on love see things differently than those who were raised on only survival." - Mindset Mentor Podcast

This quote is important when it comes to realizing relationships. If on the one hand someone is raised with love, and a great support system then this is a person in which the value of love is important, and nurture is important to that person. If they are raised for survival, and their parents only cared to ensure they had the money to pay for their child's survival needs and the need to worry about money and material things matter more to survive and get by rather than love and nurture.

End of Day Reflection

Five Things I am grateful for:

1

2

3

4

5

What did I learn today?

1

2

3

TO DO TOMORROW

1

2

3

4

5

March 30
Aries

There is always the right season and reason that things must be accomplished.

To everything there is a reason and a season and a right time and opportune moment with a purpose. Take advantage of all possibilities and opportunities that lie before you!

The person you will be in five years depends on the books you read, the people you surround yourself with, habits you adopt into your personal life, food you eat, and the conversations you engage in, choose wisely.

There are around you that you cannot control:

What others think of you, how others feel, other people's motives, External situations and what happens around you, the future, the past, and the beliefs and perceptions of others and what others say.

There are in your control:

Your positive attitude, your inner peace, what you eat and how you stay healthy, your relationships with your family and friends, your productivity, and finding creative and different ways to make money.

End of Day Reflection

Five Things I am grateful for:

1

2

3

4

5

What did I learn today?

1

2

3

TO DO TOMORROW

1

2

3

4

5

People come into our lives for a season, a reason, or a lifetime. It is our job to figure out for how long and their purpose for coming into our lives. Some come to heal, some come to help us move forward, and some come into our lives to restore us and support us to be there for us.

Not everyone is supposed to be in our lives forever, but those who do stay let them stay, and those who do go, let them go. Sometimes they are only supposed to be there for a reason or a season but that doesn't mean they are supposed to be there for a lifetime. Today reflect on the influences that are around you, who is there for you when you need help, and who is only there when the times are good. Those that are always there for you will remain in a special place in your heart. Keep them close and hold them tight.

End of Day Reflection

Five Things I am grateful for:

1

2

3

4

5

What did I learn today?

1

2

3

TO DO TOMORROW

1

2

3

4

5

April 1
Aries

Sometimes it isn't until after we lose someone important in our life that we realize how much of a difference or impact that they made on our lives until they are gone.

Today you need to understand that you matter, and that you are important. Your life is just as important as other people's lives. You are valuable, and there are people who love you. Without you in some people's lives, they wouldn't be where they are today because of the difference or impact that you have had on them.

Things to work on this month: Work on listening and being patient with those around you. Not everyone knows what you know about things and not everyone has the same level of intellect as you. Taking a step back and listening to those around you is an important factor in the skill of communication. You don't know what you don't know unless you give others the chance to show you what they know and what they don't know about things in life. You may learn something new from others around you. While making decisions in life is important, making rash or quick decisions without much contemplation is also something to avoid doing. This month keep in mind that if you come off as too bossy or demanding to others, you may make others feel like they don't have a choice to make decisions on their own and could even possibly make someone who is a little more sensitive feel emotionally hurt or feel uncomfortable around you. Take time to let things happen around you because good things come in good time.

End of Day Reflection

Five Things I am grateful for:

1

2

3

4

5

What did I learn today?

1

2

3

TO DO TOMORROW

1

2

3

4

5

April 2
Aries

The only person qualified to figure out your worth, is you…

Our Number one cheerleader in our lives is ourselves, you can be your greatest support, or you can be your own weakest link and not support yourself when things are bad in life. It really is true that "Your attitude on your life, determines your attitude." -Zig Ziglar. You are your own qualified, determinate, or indeterminate. There is an old African American Proverb that says, "When there is no enemy within, the enemy outside can do you no harm."

Today try to realize that you are worth it, your life is worth fighting for. The people in your life depend on you to help them through their day in one way or another. There are people in your life who love you just the way that you are, and even if you feel that there are people in your life who don't care about you, realize that you matter. That you are meant to make big impacts on the lives of those that are around you. Life is short as it is, so always try to make the most of what you have in life by focusing on what you have and not what you don't have.

"No one can make you feel inferior without your consent."- Eleanor Roosevelt

End of Day Reflection

Five Things I am grateful for:

1

2

3

4

5

What did I learn today?

1

2

3

TO DO TOMORROW

1

2

3

4

5

"No matter how dark and difficult things seem to get around you, find your happiness and hope and hold on to it by staying positive." – Anthony Parker

"Beware of destination addiction. The idea that happiness is the next place, the next job, or even with the next partner. Until you give up on the idea that happiness is somewhere else, it will never be where you are." - Robert Holden

I think that one of the hardest things to do for us sometimes is to be happy and realize that it's okay to live happy lives. We feel the need to please those around us by finding those social likes and feel-good comments by doing what others want us to do all the time just so that we can feel accepted. I think that the cost of doing this for the happiness of others around us instead of our own internal happiness is losing one's ability to realize that we ourselves can be happy where we are now if you make those decisions. I am not saying that we all need to become minimalists to find pleasure in the small little things in life. But expand on the theory, you want to be a teacher, but your father or mother or grandparents want you to carry the family business or to be a doctor. We have all heard this scenario at one time in our lives or another. The reaction of the son or daughter is they want to impress and gain the acceptance of the father or mother or uncle or grandparents, when they just want you to be happy doing what you want and not lead a miserable life.

"Happiness can be found in the darkest of times, if only one remembers to turn on the light." – Albus Dumbledore, Harry Potter Prisoner of Azkaban.

End of Day Reflection

Five Things I am grateful for:

1

2

3

4

5

What did I learn today?

1

2

3

TO DO TOMORROW

1

2

3

4

5

April 4
Aries

"We want people to be honest with us, but we struggle to be honest with people." - Jay Shetty

Honesty can be a double-edged sword, wanting the truth can also mean it can hurt us or help us grow to be emotionally stronger people.

"If you are feeling unable happy, try asking yourself some questions,

Why do I keep thinking about things that make me sad, instead of appreciating where I am and the good things that I have?

Why do I always think about the bad stuff that happened?

Why am I always so busy trying to ignore my sadness instead of learning to be happy with what's happening now?

It's not about fixing everything and making all the bad stuff go away. It's okay to accept things as they are sometimes. When you feel upset, take a deep breath, and try to understand why you are feeling that way. Why am I complaining so much? Why am I always thinking about what might happen in the future instead of enjoying the present moment?

Try to see things in a more positive light, and you might be surprised at how your feelings can change. Remember, happiness doesn't just come from changing what's happening around you; it's not dependent on others around you, it's also about finding inner peace and appreciating the good things that are happening now in your life." - @powercare.babe

End of Day Reflection

Five Things I am grateful for:

1

2

3

4

5

What did I learn today?

1

2

3

TO DO TOMORROW

1

2

3

4

5

"If you can't stop thinking about it, don't stop working for it."

Today reflect on what drives and motivates you. What are your ambitions that you want people to look back and say,

"Wow, (YOUR NAME) was put on this Earth for this specific purpose. This is what they were meant to accomplish in their life. This is what they were supposed to do to make a difference in the lives of those around them."

You can look at someone like Steve Jobs or anyone, and think upon reflection of their life, they were meant to be here. They were meant to change the way we see our perspective on life. Their accomplishments, their successes, their impact on society were important and great. We all want to be the next Steve Jobs or Robin Williams or the person you idolize but we can do that just by being the best of ourselves for those around us. We can impact those who are in need around us any day. We just need to make those choices to do so in life. We are all given the same number of hours in a day, no matter who you are, it matters how you intend to use those hours today? What do you choose to do today to make a difference?

End of Day Reflection

Five Things I am grateful for:

1

2

3

4

5

What did I learn today?

1

2

3

TO DO TOMORROW

1

2

3

4

5

April 6
Aries

"Your past is not holding you back. You are holding onto your past," [which is holding you back.] -Amanda Ray

While it is meaningful to look back and reflect on the past, you must realize that the past also hurts at times, but you have gotten through the past hurts to get where you are today. Sometimes the past of others telling you that you can't do it can hold you back upon reflection or make you think that you aren't good enough to do it. I am here today to tell you that you are worth it, it is worth it to keep looking forward no matter what happens around you. If you push forward from where you are now, there is no telling where you will be months or years from now. Be yourself and don't back down.

End of Day Reflection

Five Things I am grateful for:

1

2

3

4

5

What did I learn today?

1

2

3

TO DO TOMORROW

1

2

3

4

5

April 7
Aries

"If you want long term success in business, relationships, and life, you must get better at accepting uncomfortable truths as fast as possible. When you refuse to accept an uncomfortable truth, you are choosing to accept an uncomfortable future."
Steven Bartlett

These are just a few uncomfortable truths from:
https://www.rexpaxton.com/post/8-uncomfortable-truths-that-we-all-need-to-accept

1. Happiness is where you are now, or nowhere at all. It's not a new relationship, it's not a new job. It's not a completed goal, and it's not a new car. Until you give up on the idea that happiness is somewhere else, it will never be where you are.

2. Quitting is for winners. Contrary to popular opinion, quitting is for winners. Knowing when to quit, change direction, leave a toxic situation, demand more from life, give up on something that isn't working and move on, is a very important skill that people who win at life all seem to have. But don't quit because it's hard. Quit because it sucks.

3. If they really wanted to, they would. If you apply pressure, they'll do what you want them to. If you take the pressure off, you'll see what they'd rather do. Never waste your life fighting for what someone would rather do. Let them go. Move on. Do better.

4. Taking no risk is the biggest risk. You must risk failure to succeed. You must risk rejection to be accepted. You must risk heartbreak to love. If you're always avoiding risk, you're risking missing out on life.

5. Call yourself out. The most common reason why people keep making the same mistakes is because their insecure ego prevents them from taking responsibility for their own actions, their own toxic traits, and their own mistakes.

6. Closure is your choice. Closure isn't an apology, or justice, or answers. That's insecurity. If the situation made you feel awful, seeking closure by reopening it is insanity. Closure isn't something they can give you. Closure is moving on. Closure is your choice.

7. If you're happy alone, you'll be happier together. There is no type of affection that can fill the void of a person who doesn't love themselves already. There is no independence in

dependency. There is no personal security in attaching yourself to a secure person. Until you have a healthy relationship with yourself, you won't make healthy decisions about someone else.

8. It's not your job to fix damaged people. Your responsibility to help someone will never outweigh their responsibility to help themselves. But it's worth asking yourself why you resonated so strongly with someone that so desperately needed "fixing" in the first place. Often, our own toxic romantic and non-romantic attachments tell a story about an issue we have within ourselves.

End of Day Reflection

Three Things I am grateful for:

1

2

3

What did I learn today?

1

2

3

TO DO TOMORROW

1

2

3

If you want to avoid making the same mistakes twice, make more decisions based on past memories and less decisions based on your current emotions." Steven Bartlett

It is easy to let our emotions get the best of us and let them stubbornly dictate what we are going to do based on how we react to things. Whenever you run across this issue, take a step back and think about things from the other person's perspective. Maybe they have different reasons as to why they are doing what they are doing.

End of Day Reflection

Five Things I am grateful for:

1

2

3

4

5

What did I learn today?

1

2

3

TO DO TOMORROW

1

2

3

4

5

April 9
Aries

Reading is the best habit one can acquire. There is a reason why books are described as best friends. Never stop learning. Reading isn't something that everyone does every day but it's a great habit that also improves our vocabulary and our own writing. A book a day can help keep reality away. If you can stop at the bookstore or public library today to get some reading materials

Something else was on my mind today that I wanted you to know:

Reflect on this idea: Who am I?

It is a dangerous thing to not know who you are because you leave the door open for others to tell you who you are.

What do you want to be in your story of your own life?

What type of person are you?

It becomes easy to believe them when they say cruel things to you or about you, a part of you internalizing their words, forming judgements about yourself simply based on their perceptions, their own insecurities and fears they project onto you.

Who am I outside of what my family and social media says I am?

What do I agree with? What and who do I value most in my life? Today try to meditate on these thoughts."

Delve deep within yourself and get to know you as a person and take some time to meditate and explore the person who exists beyond the noise what people expect of you and watch how you never give another the power to dim your light of self-esteem again!

End of Day Reflection

Five Things I am grateful for:

1

2

3

4

5

What did I learn today?

1

2

3

TO DO TOMORROW

1

2

3

4

5

April 10
Aries

"Our prime purpose in this life is to help others, and if you can't help them, at least don't hurt them."
- Dalai Lama

This quote resonates with me because the way I see it, if there are already enough bad people in the world, why would I want to be one of them? I live by the quote, "Do unto others as they do unto you and turn the other cheek if wrong is done to you."

Something else to reflect on today:

YOU MATTER

Your name makes others smile. Your work moves people and inspires them. Right now, someone out there is complimenting you. The mere thought of you makes someone else's heart race. Your friends hold dear the moments you've shared. Someone might see a book in the store and think of you. Your work ethic and perseverance inspire and motivates others to keep going and you will get to where you want to be someday. Your presence is meaningful and leaves a lasting impact on the world every single day.

End of Day Reflection

Five Things I am grateful for:

1

2

3

4

5

What did I learn today?

1

2

3

TO DO TOMORROW

1

2

3

4

5

April 11
Aries

"A flower does not think of competing with the flower next to it, it just blooms." – Zen Shun

"No one is born with Self-confidence, Zero. For every single one of us our self-confidence was determined by how we were raised, the parents we had, the teachers we had, the bosses we have had, the jobs that we have had. My sister worked at her company for 17 years, and her boss had destroyed her self-confidence. She came out of that job, and she didn't realize until she got into her new job how afraid she was to make decisions because of her boss. It took her a while for her to get her confidence back. So, if somebody is insecure, we must prove to them over and over again, because we don't know where they came from, we don't know what kind of trouble they got in before for being honest or how they were raised. We must have total empathy and just prove to them that if they make a mistake, they are going to get helped not hurt. They are going to get supported not yelled at and the first time they won't believe you, they will think it's a game, they will think it's a con, it's a trick. The second time maybe, and we just must keep at it. I used to have somebody in my team who would regularly lie to me. Right? Because she would rather lie to me, than tell me she made a mistake, and if I saw the lie, I would ask so many questions to get her to say to me, I screwed up. I would be like well this doesn't make sense because I can't say you are lying to me. I would just say this doesn't make sense, this doesn't make sense and if this adds up to this then why is it that? And the lie would get bigger and bigger as she would yell at me about how I don't trust her, and then at the end I would be like, listen, it clearly doesn't add up and I'm okay if it doesn't add up or you made a mistake. But when you deceive me, I am going to ask you so many questions to get to the truth and it's going to get worse and worse. It happened many times until she finally got up the courage to say I made a mistake, and I would say cool thanks. Alan Mulally puts it brilliantly: he says, "You have a problem, you are not the problem." Right so if something goes wrong, we have a problem, but you are not the problem. We have told too many people that they are the problem and it's not the case, so we must tell people over and over that it's okay until it builds up their confidence again." - Simon Sinek

End of Day Reflection

Five Things I am grateful for:

1

2

3

4

5

What did I learn today?

1

2

3

TO DO TOMORROW

1

2

3

4

5

April 12
Aries

Be strong enough to walk away from what's hurting you and be patient enough to wait for the blessings you deserve.

"There are people that love you. Stop focusing on the ones that don't." - Sonya Tecki

It is difficult to leave toxic people and sometimes in life we become dependent on toxic people in our lives to get by, but it only enables them to harm us more. It is better to struggle in solitude than endure an even more bitter and toxic struggle with someone who enjoys hurting us or putting us down. You need to know your own worth in life, that you deserve nothing but the best, and you deserve to be living your best life yet!

End of Day Reflection

Five Things I am grateful for:

1

2

3

4

5

What did I learn today?

1

2

3

TO DO TOMORROW

1

2

3

4

5

April 13
Aries

Love was never meant to be easy. People fight, people make mistakes, people walk out, and then decide to run back. When it comes to real love, there is no limit to what you would do for one another, to protect, to provide, to profess. Nowadays it's a lot harder to stay together than to "fall apart," but I can promise you, love is worth every second of it. When you love, make sure it's the kind of love that is unconditional. That way, no matter what happens, no matter what comes your way, the love you have for one another will last a lifetime."
- Melissa Molomo

No relationship is perfect, in any relationship there are good days and bad days but what matters more is how you handle the relationships. Sometimes these are with people who are toxic or difficult and that is okay and other times it's just with people that we don't have a lot in common with and that is okay as well. Sometimes these are relationships that will last the rest of our lives. Just remember that if you are having a rough time in a relationship, there is a compromise that is also important to have. If you aren't in a relationship right now, that is also okay because if you aren't happy alone, you can't really be happy when you are with someone else. It's also important to have your own space as well. While in and out of relationships and be with your own circle of friends and family as well at the same time.

End of Day Reflection

Five Things I am grateful for:

1

2

3

4

5

What did I learn today?

1

2

3

TO DO TOMORROW

1

2

3

4

5

April 14
Aries

Sometimes everything hits you all at once. You lose a relationship, change jobs, old friends go, and new friends come. It's up one day and down the next. You have it altogether Monday but by Thursday you don't have a clue. Life is one big wave, and all we can do is flow, grow, and adapt.

It is good to make changes in life. To grow or get out of ruts in life that we get stuck in and aren't happy in, we must change and do something about it and sometimes this means moving, changing jobs, or cutting off people who we used to talk to. These are healthy changes that we can make in life that help us to deal with life in a better way.

Let us not hope for a mere chance to change our story; let us summon the courage to change it ourselves. Some will stand in our way, but we must not hide or minimize ourselves any longer. Let us believe faithfully that our dreams are worthy of any struggle and that it is our time to free ourselves and to rise to glory. – The Motivation Manifesto, Brendon Burchard

End of Day Reflection

Five Things I am grateful for:

1

2

3

4

5

What did I learn today?

1

2

3

TO DO TOMORROW

1

2

3

4

5

April 15 — Aries

"If you are not making someone else's life better, then you're wasting your time. Your life will become better by making other lives better." - Will Smith

Sometimes to find your own piece of happiness you must help and care about other people for them to help you and care about you. Sometimes it's what you do for others that enables them to want to help you out in turn. Also just being there for someone when they are struggling is meaningful to them as well. Personally, I feel that you may not be able to save everyone around you, but I try my best to help those who need it and have tried to help themselves out of their situations. Another thing to realize is that sometimes you can only help someone so much and there is a point where you cannot turn back either because of conflict or because of another reason and that is okay as well.

Hard Hitting Quotes Ep 65:

"A Best friend isn't the one that makes your problems disappear, a best friend is the one that doesn't disappear when you are facing your problems." - @morechrisgriffin

End of Day Reflection

Five Things I am grateful for:

1

2

3

4

5

What did I learn today?

1

2

3

TO DO TOMORROW

1

2

3

4

5

April 16
Aries

"A seed grows with no sound, but a tree falls with huge noise. Destruction has noise, but creation is quiet. This is the power of silence - grow silently."
- Confucius

Reflect on this and learn to appreciate the things that grow in silence around you. As you learn to appreciate the things that grow in silence you will begin to see there are hidden points of gratitude that you can have for the seemingly less meaningful things in life, and how big an impact that they can have on your life.

Today you need to know something:

I am so proud of you. Yes, you read that right. Despite the struggles so far that you have been through in your life, you have shown incredible strength, courage, and bravery, and you've made it up to today. I see your journey that you have made along the way to get to where you are right now in this moment and all those hard obstacles that you have overcome. You have endured through so much and I want you to know that I am here with you, every step of the way. I may not be right next to you, but I am there with you in spirit. I have seen that determination and your unwavering spirit, and your refusal to give up. It fills my heart with joy and admiration. You may not always realize it, but you are a shining example of resilience and courage. When the weight of the world feels heavy on your shoulders you continue to press on. You choose to keep going, even when it feels easier to quit. That takes incredible strength, and I want you to know that you matter, and you are strong and that YOU ARE LOVED so much by those around you!

End of Day Reflection

Five Things I am grateful for:

1

2

3

4

5

What did I learn today?

1

2

3

TO DO TOMORROW

1

2

3

4

5

April 17
Aries

"Real friends can never be lost."

The bonds of friendships that you make in life are important to have a great support system. In many ways, this is a support system that can be just as strong as you can have with your family. Today, spend time with your friends and take pictures of you with them this month. These pictures will become important memories in your future that you can look back upon.

"I feel alive today, because today is a blessing. In this moment, I can find misery or meaning, boredom, or motivation. I can expand the hatred in the world, or I can amplify love. In all the chaos, I can find stillness and joy within. All is well, and nothing has to happen to "give" me more happiness in life. I simply choose to be happy now, to be grateful now, to be a source of love, and light for others. I am whole. I am ready. [I can do this and accomplish anything that I set my mind to.] This is my day." – Brendon Burchard, Motivation Manifesto.

End of Day Reflection

Five Things I am grateful for:

1

2

3

4

5

What did I learn today?

1

2

3

TO DO TOMORROW

1

2

3

4

5

April 18
Aries

Just because you are struggling doesn't mean you are failing.
"You are not a victim, always a victor!"
– Joel Osteen

It just means that you have another reason and excuse to get back up again and keep pushing forward. Don't let this minor setback keep you from doing what you want to do most in your life. A struggle is merely a minor setback that your mind thinks is too difficult to maneuver around.

"I won't let others stoke fear in my heart. I choose to remain true to who I am and where my dreams direct me, no matter the hardship I might incur. – Motivation Manifesto, Brendon Burchard.

End of Day Reflection

Five Things I am grateful for:

1

2

3

4

5

What did I learn today?

1

2

3

TO DO TOMORROW

1

2

3

4

5

Sometimes quiet people really do have a lot to say. They're just being careful about why they open up."
- Susan Gale

  Sometimes we can learn more in silence than we can when we are talkative. When someone is talking, never say "I know," because they may have something to say that you didn't know, and they may never even tell you because they will think you already knew. Be patient with those around you because there is so much you can learn and so many conversations you could have with people. A quote that I always resonated with is, "You don't know what you don't know."

End of Day Reflection

Five Things I am grateful for:

1

2

3

4

5

What did I learn today?

1

2

3

TO DO TOMORROW

1

2

3

4

5

When you care about how other people perceive you, you'll only ever go as far as <u>they</u> want you to.

Open your mind and don't worry about what you think other people think about you because they don't think what you think that they think. Be yourself, stay positive and know that you make a huge positive impact on those that are around you.

End of Day Reflection

Five Things I am grateful for:

1

2

3

4

5

What did I learn today?

1

2

3

TO DO TOMORROW

1

2

3

4

5

April 21
Taurus

Find a heart that will love you at your worst, and arms that will hold you at your weakest.

When you can reciprocate this in a relationship, it is healthy and supportive. Within the realm of a relationship there are six factors that I can think of that are important off the top of my head: respect, open communication, honesty, trust, Loyalty, and positivity. Sure, one can't be positive all the time in all situations, but one can surely avoid negativity and have some hope and faith in a better positive outcome in certain or most situations.

End of Day Reflection

Five Things I am grateful for:

1

2

3

4

5

What did I learn today?

1

2

3

TO DO TOMORROW

1

2

3

4

5

April 22
Taurus

Hustle until your signature becomes an autograph.

Work hard and do what you love doing and share this with others around you. As you do, you will become known by others, and people will then want to have your autograph to be the best you that you can be.

"Why don't cows drink milk and chickens eat eggs? -No cows give milk and say I only drink 2% and no chicken goes I like them over easy.

They produce for someone else. – If you've got a gift to make money, that's not for you. If you have a gift to sing, or a gift to serve, that's for you to give to others. But you must stay connected to the vine of the people and connect to people in order to flourish. Fruit is the glory of the vines; it tells people you are connected to something.

"If there is something that you feel is good, something that you want to do because it means something to you. Try to do it. Because I think you can only do your best work because it's something you want to do, the way you think that it should be done. If you can take pride in it after you've done it, no matter what it is, then you can look at it and say, I did it and I think it looks damn good, that's what matters! "– Stan Lee

"Desire is a contract that you make with yourself to be unhappy until you get what you want. It is okay to desire something, but don't let it stop you from enjoying your journey, so let it go." - @cross.novia

End of Day Reflection

Five Things I am grateful for:

1

2

3

4

5

What did I learn today?

1

2

3

TO DO TOMORROW

1

2

3

4

5

"It is the set of the sails, not the direction of the wind that determines which way we will go." - Jim Rohn

   Sometimes things happen in our lives that are out of control and how we react or respond to those situations can have a positive or negative effect on us. The same winds of change hit us all, but if you can predict what can or will possibly happen you are prepared and can adjust your sails and decisions accordingly. The way I see it is "c'est la vie." ("That's Life") and you just must cope and deal with it as things change around you. There isn't exactly a manual for how things are supposed to happen in our lives and the proper ways to react or respond to situations, it all comes down to free will. Today don't let anything bring you down. DO what you think is best and don't stress over the things that can't be changed.

End of Day Reflection

Five Things I am grateful for:

1

2

3

4

5

What did I learn today?

1

2

3

TO DO TOMORROW

1

2

3

4

5

April 24
Taurus

"Make sure you're happy in real life, not just on the internet."
- Jay Shetty

We like to portray our life as positive and amazing and show off to others our experiences and changes in our lives and others are quick to compare their lives to what you are doing and sometimes there are rallies of support because of these changes that you make, and others cast a dark shadow of negativity and commentary on you because of jealousy or other reasons. It is better to live your life in happiness than to depend on other people's opinions around you to give you what you think is happiness but rather its criticism. Don't let other people's opinions of you bring you down or make you feel inadequate. You are the supplier of your own happiness, never forget that. This is a lesson that I learned recently on my own.

"You're going to realize it one day, that happiness was never about your job or your degree or being in a relationship.

Happiness was never about following in the footsteps of all of those who came before you, it was never about being like the others.

One day, you're going to see it – that happiness was always about discovery, hope, listening to your heart and following it wherever it chose to go.

Happiness was always about being kinder to yourself, it was always about embracing the person you were becoming.

One day, you will understand that happiness was always about learning how to live with yourself, that your happiness was never in the hands of others. It was always about you; it was always about you. "- @healandflowwithm and Martinasoderlind.se

End of Day Reflection

Five Things I am grateful for:

1

2

3

4

5

What did I learn today?

1

2

3

TO DO TOMORROW

1

2

3

4

5

"Working hard for something we don't care about is called stress, working hard for something we love is called passion."
- Simon Sinek

Today I reflect on what you define as happiness… Are you happy with where you are in your life right now? What do you define as being happy, like what are factors that make you feel happy? IF you aren't happy now, figure out why, and now, what are you going to do about it and by WHEN? If you don't give yourself a deadline for change, you won't change, and nothing will happen but the only thing that will continue is your own unhappiness.

End of Day Reflection

Five Things I am grateful for:

1

2

3

4

5

What did I learn today?

1

2

3

TO DO TOMORROW

1

2

3

4

5

April 26
Taurus

Loneliness doesn't come from being alone. It comes from the feeling that nobody cares.

There are people in your life who care about you and your well-being. You must realize that there are people in your life who would be torn apart if you weren't in their life anymore and that they depend on you. Being alone is okay, it lets you be able to do your own thing that you want to do.

End of Day Reflection

Five Things I am grateful for:

1

2

3

4

5

What did I learn today?

1

2

3

TO DO TOMORROW

1

2

3

4

5

April 27
Taurus

"You are virtually capable of any goal you thrive to go out and achieve. Have a giving nature that will set a foundation which in return will inspire others. The focus you should provide is an optimistic outlook that others will use in their path to success. The journey [for your success] can be made shorter if you pave the way for others. Be a leader, I know you have what it takes, it's time to put your skills into action." - Brian Fulginiti

If you always do what you have always done, you will always have what you have always gotten and not a thing more. If you do what you have never done before you will get things that you have not gotten before and be able to do things that you have never imagined possible due to your own mental limitations of what you had originally thought wasn't possible.

End of Day Reflection

Five Things I am grateful for:

1

2

3

4

5

What did I learn today?

1

2

3

TO DO TOMORROW

1

2

3

4

5

April 28
Taurus

"Being deeply loved by someone gives you strength, while loving someone deeply gives you courage."
- Lao Tzu

Today share your love with someone you love by doing something for them like taking them out to lunch or spending time with them. The time that we spend with others is important not only to them, but it is also something that is meaningful to you as well. Our time is so limited that we shouldn't take it for granted.

End of Day Reflection

Five Things I am grateful for:

1

2

3

4

5

What did I learn today?

1

2

3

TO DO TOMORROW

1

2

3

4

5

"A negative mindset will never give you a positive life." - Zig Ziglar

You can't be happy around negative people or by having a negative outlook or mindset on life. Negativity can drain you and others around you of good, happy positive energy and happiness to which there would be nothing left but misery. Stay Positive, Smile, Stay happy. Stay Humble.

End of Day Reflection

Five Things I am grateful for:

1

2

3

4

5

What did I learn today?

1

2

3

TO DO TOMORROW

1

2

3

4

5

"Your comfort zone or your goals. Choose what is most important." - Dany Castilho

   Sometimes you must get comfortable feeling uncomfortable in order to grow and be successful. Today try to do three things that will change you to do something that you normally wouldn't do that would be considered uncomfortable, whether it's talking to strangers and getting to know someone who you have never met or going out and doing something like going to the movies with a friend that you just met or travel to a town you have never been to near you. Get into this habit once a week until you get used to it and change it up a bit.

End of Day Reflection

Five Things I am grateful for:

1

2

3

4

5

What did I learn today?

1

2

3

TO DO TOMORROW

1

2

3

4

5

May 1
Taurus

"You and you alone can change your situation. Don't blame it on anything else or anyone else."

It is easy to say well I am in this situation because of this, or because of that circumstance or because I don't have a high paying job, that is why I am where I am. You can change that situation that you are in. It may take some discomfort but it's possible. Change the job or the friends that you hang around, or the influence that is in your life and you will notice how things change around your environment. Misery loves company.

Things to work on this Month: Work on not splurging/overindulging this month. Treating yourself out is good occasionally but also keep in mind that if you over do it, it might affect your finances or your health. Work on not being materialistic if you find that you are. Change is a good thing and can help you become a better person. Work on not being very possessive of things and people in your life. It is good to surround yourself with a good support system of people around you but also keep in mind that they may have other things going on in their life as well as with family and friends. Also work on being more open-minded and less stubborn about your decisions and the decisions others make around you. Don't be hard on yourself if things don't turn out the way that you want them to or planned them to. Sometimes the best laid plans go awry. Work on improving your self-esteem.

End of Day Reflection

Five Things I am grateful for:

1

2

3

4

5

What did I learn today?

1

2

3

TO DO TOMORROW

1

2

3

4

5

May 2
Taurus

"You can't tell anyone that they can't do something… The most powerful motivational speeches came from people who told me I couldn't do something. You know why? Because I was bound and determined that I could, tell me I can't, and I will show you that you chose the wrong one to tell me that I can't do something. If you have the proper mindset, I can't" will make you that much more determined to get to your goal. Let the "I can't fuel your fire! " - CT Fletcher

    I was once told that because of who I was and because I was lacking money and resources, and because I didn't know the right people and because of where I came from, that I would never be able to be where I am today. Sometimes when you have a vision and an obsession and a passion to do something it motivates and pushes you to a new limit and you eventually reach your goals in life. Don't ever let anyone tell you that you can't or that it's impossible. Find out what you need to do to accomplish your goals in life and do it one step at a time. Some people will cheer you on, and some people will hold you back, criticize you, or try to convince you it's a waste of time or that it's not going to happen, and they conspire against you in doing it. I am here to tell you that if this is something that you want to do and this is something that you would be willing to do every day and it will bring you happiness, then by all means DO IT! NO MATTER WHAT! DON'T STOP!

End of Day Reflection

Five Things I am grateful for:

1

2

3

4

5

What did I learn today?

1

2

3

TO DO TOMORROW

1

2

3

4

5

"When there are more tears than smiles, leave. When there are more fights than jokes, leave. When it hurts more than it feels good, leave. They don't have the right to destroy you just because you love them. Loving them doesn't mean you have to stay." - Jess Amelia

   Sometimes it is easy to feel "stuck" in certain situations and feel that you cannot leave or get out of them. You are in a situation that you are in and knowing when you need to leave is very important for your mental, emotional, and physical wellbeing and health. Many times, we feel the need to stay in the hopes that we will change the person we are around. This is not the case. You cannot hope to change someone who isn't seeing a fault in their ways or isn't willing to change. This is a very crucial lesson that even I myself have had to learn because having a big heart makes you care about those around you, and I have had to be told, I cannot be a soul saver for those who don't wish to be saved. You can love others around you and help them when needed, but you cannot enable others because it does more harm in the end than good. It is also okay to say no sometimes, especially if it comes down to doing something that we are uncomfortable with or would rather not do. Our actions speak louder than words as well. Saying No to doing something that is also against our own ideas and integrity is also important to staying true to yourself and who you are as a person.

End of Day Reflection

Five Things I am grateful for:

1

2

3

4

5

What did I learn today?

1

2

3

TO DO TOMORROW

1

2

3

4

5

May 4
Taurus

"People are fearful of their obsessions. There is a difference between obsession and passion. When you are passionate, everyone cheers you on and they are stoked for you. When you are obsessed, they are saying why are you so crazy, why can't this be enough… IF you aren't crazy, you aren't operating at the outer limits of your potential. Obsession is necessary. "– Tom Bilyeu

"Ryan Holiday, in one of his podcasts I was listening to, was talking about differentiating between passion and purpose. He called Passion temporary, a dopamine hit. It's the excitement before the project begins, the beginning of a journey, the honeymoon phase but passion alone falls short. Because anything worthwhile is hard, it tests us. It repeatedly presents us with those metaphorical cocoons we must fight through. We must earn our stripes, grow our wings and if we stop at passion, there's no reason to battle on to take the punches knowing that they will create for us a tomorrow full of infinite possibility and that's where we need purpose. That's what matters, a purpose to march towards, and a destination that's meaningful to remind us that those challenging times are not a burden. There is no poor me here. Our passions are the fires that sharpen the whispers to us, not only the importance of carrying on but the power contained within ourselves to do so. This world is not stacked against you, it is never a problem or an obstacle, nor is it the opportunity laid out at your feet. It's in those very times when we are uncomfortable, when we're unsure, when we don't know where to draw our strength and we need to remember that it comes within. It's an idea that is brought to life through courage, through understanding through the trials and tribulations through life. It doesn't intimidate or hold you back knowing that life has given you everything you need to blaze your trail. So don't be afraid to let it take you somewhere new." – Eddie Pinero

End of Day Reflection

Five Things I am grateful for:

1

2

3

4

5

What did I learn today?

1

2

3

TO DO TOMORROW

1

2

3

4

5

May 5
Taurus

"Part of my morning every day is to listen to the commencement speech Admiral McRaven gave at the University of Texas Where he is talking about 10 lessons that he learned during his time as a navy seal going through buds training. He positions them in a way that will really help anybody through life if they implement these concepts. It's an incredible speech and my favorite lesson of the 10 is around what he calls the sugar cookie. I want to delve into it a little deeper because it's such a perfect metaphor it's so relatable. So, for a quick overview basically during buds all the attendees were called to line up for a uniform inspection. All the instructors would know to walk by and check out their uniforms. They had to be perfect right as McRaven says uniform press, belt buckle shiny, no smudges on the shoes, but the point of the exercise that a lot of people really didn't understand is, that the uniforms were never going to be good enough, the inspectors or instructors would always find something wrong. The punishment was to go run down to the water with your clothes on and get soaking wet and then roll around in the sand and it sticks to you all day. That's why they call it the sugar cookie. And what he says is, you were never going to succeed. The perfect uniform was impossible, the instructors wouldn't allow it, but the interesting thing is that some people simply couldn't handle that idea. They didn't understand that no matter how well you prepare or perform, sometimes you are going to end up a sugar cookie, that is life. It's such a powerful concept, it's a life lesson that must be understood before someone can effectively make their way in the world. The idea that life simply isn't fair and those that refuse to accept that are pulled into this void of projecting out and looking to assign blame as opposed to continuing a march forward and reshaping the odds. Right, a tough lesson to learn. It's tough to work and work and not get that immediate validation that you hope for. It's tough that life drops obstacles before us that we weren't prepared for and don't feel equipped to take on. It's tough when people around you get rewarded or promoted or acknowledged for doing the same or less than you, and if you let it, it will eat you up, it will taint your view of the world. It can close the door to your own self-improvement and open it up for comparing contrasting, projecting blaming toxicity. You know it really hit home for me. When McRaven

says look, some people just couldn't understand that no matter what they did, they were going to be a sugar cookie. They couldn't rise above the clear unfairness they didn't realize that they were being prepared for the reality of life. Not the gentle predictable fair world that we often feel is owed to us. So, the ones who made it out of the class took their hits, they learned to deal with their discomfort, they learned to expect more out of themselves. Right there simply was no room for the victim mentality there. Those who wouldn't help themselves got weeded out, left behind. It really is the perfect metaphor for life."
– Eddie Pinero

End of Day Reflection

Five Things I am grateful for:

1

2

3

4

5

What did I learn today?

1

2

3

TO DO TOMORROW

1

2

3

4

5

May 6
Taurus

"Stay Positive and remember what it is to live a life full in gratitude, doing this consistently is extremely important." – Anthony Parker

"Growth also appears to have a cyclical nature. When we have an obstacle, we must push, we must fight, we grow, sometimes without realizing it, we achieve a result and by default this transformation that in one or another makes us something new. But then it becomes easy to level out right and that's the challenge it creates during this period of stagnation. It's like we made the jump, and it becomes easy to stay there and that's why I have found value in when life is not providing resistance to manufacture some. Because that's the only way to grow, progress is happiness. Victor Franklin Man's Search for meaning says Purpose is defined from struggle. If things are too calm or simple or quiet, life begins to lack meaning and that's never a spot we want to be in. Life is about the pursuit of something, you just must figure out what that blank will be. You get to decide which mountain to climb. There's a story about a butterfly making its way out of a cocoon and making a little hole and starting to attempt to push its way out. Someone walks by and they see it struggling and open the cocoon up to help the butterfly out, thinking that they did this great deed. But in doing so, that butterfly has lost its ability to use its wings to fly. Why? Because the strength that was necessary to fly, would have been forged when he fought its way out. The butterfly was deprived of the very thing it needed to become something more. And that's the point, it's easy to get lost in the now and seek to eliminate everything that doesn't make the moment more comfortable to remove that which doesn't make things easier but whether we're talking about collectively or the complacency in our individual lives we must remember that avoiding discomfort isn't the answer. When your biggest problem is that your feelings are hurt by someone's comments or opinions on social media, you've lost track of yourself, you may be living in a world lacking the resistance necessary for growth. Maybe it's time to ask - ``What matters?'' – Eddie Pinero, youtube.com

End of Day Reflection

Five Things I am grateful for:

1

2

3

4

5

What did I learn today?

1

2

3

TO DO TOMORROW

1

2

3

4

5

May 7
Taurus

"Carry out a random act of kindness, with no expectation of reward, safe in the knowledge that one day, someone might do the same for you." - Princess Diana

It is the simple things that you can do in life that have the power to make someone smile and be the most meaningful to you and the other person. Sometimes we take for granted the little things in life and it is these things that have the most meaning and significance to us. The little strolls in the parks or around the malls without friends. The ability to take a friend out to the movies or spend time with them at a restaurant. The little things that make all the difference.

End of Day Reflection

Five Things I am grateful for:

1

2

3

4

5

What did I learn today?

1

2

3

TO DO TOMORROW

1

2

3

4

5

"Sometimes you must hurt in order to know, fall in order to grow, lose in order to gain, because most of life's greatest lessons are learned through pain." – Pain

We have all been there, we have all fallen and lost hope when things are difficult and when things don't work out in the way in which you intended. We can all wish and say we shoulda coulda woulda but when things pass and happen, sometimes there is no going back. The best that we can do is our best in life and hope that people are understanding around us from our perspective. Sometimes we must walk a mile in someone else's shoes to see what they are dealing with and going through.

End of Day Reflection

Five Things I am grateful for:

1

2

3

4

5

What did I learn today?

1

2

3

TO DO TOMORROW

1

2

3

4

5

"Daydreaming about something that we want to do instead of putting it into action will not get you far. The idea is great, but it isn't as powerful as taking the necessary actions to reach the end goal, which is just as important. Take a small step at a time to achieve that goal and you will find that you will have an inner happiness and peace within." – Anthony Parker

"In a perfect world hard work is always rewarded. The correct actions always have positive consequences but that's not always reflective of reality. As the saying goes, it's not your fault where you start or when things you can't control present themselves and make your life challenging you didn't choose that hand, not your fault. But guess what, where you go from here is your responsibility. It is your responsibility to move beyond the cosmic injustice you can do nothing about and create a better situation, a better outcome, a better world. How many times in life do we find ourselves looking in the mirror, now saying hey I did everything I was supposed to do, why am I being punished? Why is this happening to me? Why did I take that "L"? On paper every box was checked. I've asked the question, we have all asked the question and every time we do, we are placed at a crossroads of sorts. Do we go one way, let it derail us, distort our worldview? Do we let it alter how we perceive ourselves? Or do we go the other way and realize that life is a marriage of highs and lows and to make something of it. And to make something of it, we shouldn't feel slighted by the challenges but accept them and to let them make us better. You should also understand that the universe is indifferent to your agenda. All it does is present an obstacle course in front of you and allows you to navigate as you see fit. Will you focus on the negative? Will you have resentment towards life's injustices? Because a lot of people do. A lot of people can't get past it. So, they hide from the struggle that will ultimately become their strength. See I'd much rather work to be the type of person who finds the positive, who carries on, who doesn't take hardship personally, because it isn't a personal thing. In fact, let's remove the emotion from it altogether. Let's focus on getting through. A good friend of mine says, if you are on a hiking trail and you get bitten by the snake are you going to chase it into the woods so you can kill it and get your vengeance? Or are you going to go to the hospital and get the medical help you need? Are you going to focus on what's necessary for your betterment to move on to grow? Every time that you accept responsibility for a situation, every time you point at yourself that can make something good happen, you move forward, and you stack the odds in your favor, you position yourself for something bigger and better and it doesn't mean that it will happen overnight or even that you are entitled to an outcome, but those who remain empowered by life's trials and tribulations they usually find a way. Not because they deserved it, but because they simply did not stop, they did not waste time blaming the universe, and instead created something of value. Accept your defeats and then you can learn from them. The best thing to do is when looking back at yourself through the mirror, understand that sometimes we don't get the ideal hand in life, but it will always be up to you and how you play it out. There is always a win, always a positive side to situations that happen in our lives and to remember that is to create a world of your making."- Eddie Pinero

End of Day Reflection

Five Things I am grateful for:

1

2

3

4

5

What did I learn today?

1

2

3

TO DO TOMORROW

1

2

3

4

5

> If you do not heal from what hurt you, you will bleed on people who didn't cut you." – Unknown

This quote is very true when it comes to starting new relationships after getting out of bad ones. Or when we meet a new friend after losing a bad friend. We tend to think things will happen to us again from someone else and we lose trust and faith in others around us. The one thing to understand is that some people come into our lives to heal and help us move forward. We grow stronger through the rough experiences that we have, and we learn from them, we forgive others who have wronged us, and you don't forget and move forward. It is always a better outcome for us to cut ties with those who have wronged us or learn not to go back to those situations when we have them with others, but at the same time it is not fair to project those same thoughts that this will happen again with someone else. If you have suffered in an unhealthy relationship or friendship with someone else, you need to know that there are only a few bad people in the world, they just move around a lot. Give others a chance to prove to you that they are different and never assume that others will treat you wrongly. Try to not compare others to earlier friendships/relationships or bring them up in the new friendship or relationship. Not all people are the same. If you don't try to heal yourself from the earlier relationship before starting the new relationship it will be harder for you to move forward. If you don't heal you literally will push this reaction from the earlier relationship onto the next person and you won't be able to heal or change and realize that not everyone is out to hurt, you. It's not that the world around you has changed, it's the fact that you have had an experience with someone else that has made you see the world differently. Not everyone in the world is toxic and not all experiences that you have with others are going to be the same and if you take a second to stop and realize that, give others the chance to be different, you may be surprised by the new outcome.

End of Day Reflection

Five Things I am grateful for:

1

2

3

4

5

What did I learn today?

1

2

3

TO DO TOMORROW

1

2

3

4

5

May 11
Taurus

"See the opportunities that are around you today when most will simply walk by. No word is as deceitful as the word "Impossible." Possibilities multiply and become realized when you look around and see with your imagination VS reality. There are two things that define your world: your perception of the world, and how you act on that perception. Never ask yourself if something can be done, the question is how... how you are going to do it. It is the unknowns in life that point us to the unconventional things that we want most in life. Live a life without walls, a life where you are the author, and your story can be shared with the world." – Eddie Pinero

Nothing is impossible when you realize that the very word impossible means I'm Possible. Seeing things in a negative light versus a positive light are two very different perspectives and both can affect us in two entirely different ways. If you choose to see things in a negative light, you can see how things 'affect' you and how things cannot be possible and sometimes this negativity can easily project onto others. This drains the life out of those around you, even when it may not be your intention. Choosing to nitpick at others, criticize others, or judge others based on their actions and inactions sometimes brings temporary happiness to you when you feel you are superior to others, but at the same time it brings them down to your level in character. In most cases when one acts like this, it pushes people away from you and you become lonely because it is difficult for others to be around negativity. Being positive and encouraging others and complimenting others and being a positive impact on someone's life will attract more people to you socially and people will want to be around you and socialize. As the old saying goes, "you can attract more bees with honey than you can with vinegar." If you are the recipient of negativity, it is sometimes harder to turn the other cheek or be around someone who is like this, and it is a toxic environment to surround yourself in when you are constantly being put down. If you find yourself in such a scenario when you are around someone like this, it is okay to separate yourself from them and realize that once someone is like this, it is hard for them to change and most of the time, they are stuck in these ways and won't change, even if you highlight this negativity for the other person because 'old habits stick to us sometimes.

End of Day Reflection

Five Things I am grateful for:

1

2

3

4

5

What did I learn today?

1

2

3

TO DO TOMORROW

1

2

3

4

5

May 12
Taurus

You cannot save people that you cannot reach.

There are people who are very stubborn around us, and they are stuck in their ways and opinions. You may wish to help them and "unstuck" them, but you cannot save everyone in your life. Sometimes it is necessary for those who are even the most stubborn to live their life and learn through their mistakes. When they fall on their back, they will learn to look up and get back up even stronger. I have had to learn this lesson on both sides of this aisle. People would tell me, I am doing something wrong, or that I am "with the wrong person" and I wouldn't listen until I saw for myself how things are. We learn and grow with our experiences and yes when you are struggling you want to help them out and you feel empathetic to their situation but sometimes helping them is enabling them as well and isn't really helping them learn how to get out of their situation as well. The situations that we surround ourselves in are there for us to overcome and show others that we are unbreakable. You have survived 100% of the days you have lived through so far. If you are reading this today, you know that within you are stronger than you think and that you can withstand anything that is set in front of you.

End of Day Reflection

Five Things I am grateful for:

1

2

3

4

5

What did I learn today?

1

2

3

TO DO TOMORROW

1

2

3

4

5

May 13
Taurus

"You are too concerned with what was and what will be. There is a saying: Yesterday is history, tomorrow is a mystery, but today is a gift. That is why it is called the present. One often meets his destiny on the road he takes to avoid it." – Master Oogway, Kung Fu Panda

   We are all destined to do great things, whether they are good or bad is entirely up to you. You may wish for things to go a certain way today but remember that you are only in control of your actions and inactions, reactions, and responses. The best laid plans often go awry. As the saying goes, "Man plans, God laughs." This is okay, things will go as they are meant to be and sometimes things are better if they aren't forced on others. Be the best you that you know how to be in all areas of your life and enjoy it to the best of your abilities as tomorrow is never guaranteed. Sometimes the inevitable happens and it's out of our control and we just need to learn to accept things and people for who they are and who they choose to be regardless of our opinions of them. Love others as they are, and you will find a great inner peace.

End of Day Reflection

Five Things I am grateful for:

1

2

3

4

5

What did I learn today?

1

2

3

TO DO TOMORROW

1

2

3

4

5

Some people find friends in their families, but some friends become our family.

"Your soul is attracted to people the same way flowers are attracted to the sun, surround yourself with those who want to see you grow. - Pavana

One does not choose one's family, all families have their dysfunctionalities, but you can pick your friends. You are the average of the five most people you hang around with, so choose your friends wisely.

End of Day Reflection

Five Things I am grateful for:

1

2

3

4

5

What did I learn today?

1

2

3

TO DO TOMORROW

1

2

3

4

5

If you love someone, you tell them. Even if you are scared that it's not the right thing, even if you are scared that it will cause problems, even if you are scared that it will burn your life to the ground, you say it and you say it out loud, and then you go from there.

A warrior's destiny is greater than his wounds."
- Brendan Burchard

A chance not taken is an opportunity lost. Our destinies in life are shaped by the very fabric and outcomes of life decisions that we make every day.

It is not worth fearing what is, what could be, or what will come. We can prepare for it and hope for the best outcome and adjust to the changes and grow stronger from them, even if we don't like the outcome.

End of Day Reflection

Five Things I am grateful for:

1

2

3

4

5

What did I learn today?

1

2

3

TO DO TOMORROW

1

2

3

4

5

May 16
Taurus

No matter what happens to you, you will never lose – your value.

A Professor stands in the front of the class and says, who wants this $20 bill? Everyone raises their hand and says yes. The professor then crumples the $20 bill and then says, who still wants this $20 bill, everyone raises their hand and says yes. The professor then puts it on the ground and then stomps it on the ground and moves his foot on top of the dollar bill. Then the professor picks it off the ground and says who wants this dollar bill and everyone raises their hand and says yes, they still want it.

Then the professor says, "I just showed you a very important lesson, no matter what I did with this money, you still wanted it because it never lost its worth. It is still worth $20. Well, there are many times in our lives when we feel like life has crumbled us up, put us on the ground and into the dirt. We may make some bad decisions or must deal with some poor circumstances, sometimes life can make us feel worthless. But no matter what has happened, no matter what will happen, you will never lose your worth, you will never lose your value. Don't ever forget that.

End of Day Reflection

Five Things I am grateful for:

1

2

3

4

5

What did I learn today?

1

2

3

TO DO TOMORROW

1

2

3

4

5

May 17
Taurus

"Treat yourself like you are someone that you are responsible for helping." – Jordan Peterson

SO many of us are amazing at being there for others through tough times, for pain, attending to their wounds, offering advice, and helping them change. But in the end, we sort of neglect and avoid helping ourselves. That is because we are the one going through it and when a wound is our own and not someone else's then we really feel it. And it is really challenging to feel it and then also to heal and help us. That is the most selfless thing that we can do, because the more we help ourselves the more that we can truly help other people. – @infiniteseeking

End of Day Reflection

Five Things I am grateful for:

1

2

3

4

5

What did I learn today?

1

2

3

TO DO TOMORROW

1

2

3

4

5

May 18 — Taurus

Thoughts are not facts. How do we know this? Because the types of thoughts that you have are influenced by how we feel at the time. Here is how it can be life changing. Once you learn that your thoughts don't always reflect reality, you realize that a thought only has power over you if you buy into it. So, if a thought is causing you distress, it makes sense to check it out, whether it's a true reflection of reality or not. You can learn to do this with a friend, or a therapist, or learn to do it by yourself.

- @drjuliesmith

When it comes to sharing ideas and what I call the "Sales Pitches of Life" we begin to think for others – "No they don't want to join me, no they don't want this, no they will laugh at me at this idea, they won't want to support me."

We have these internal thoughts and begin to think that this is a reality when this is not the case. Yes, people around us tend to judge us, but this isn't a strong enough reason not to share our ideas, dreams, aspirations, and goals with others.

"Never limit yourself because of others' limited imagination; never limit others because of your own limited imagination." – Mae Jemison

End of Day Reflection

Five Things I am grateful for:

1

2

3

4

5

What did I learn today?

1

2

3

TO DO TOMORROW

1

2

3

4

5

May 19
Taurus

You have the patience, the strength, and the passion to achieve your ambition, your goals, and your dreams. All you need to do now is try.

The only true failure that you have in life is when you really stop trying. Sometimes to find that inner peace, the external and internal feelings of success and happiness when finding your true purpose in life is only a matter of being patient with time. It takes time, an action plan and follow through with severe perseverance to get to that next level where you want to be. As the old saying goes, "Rome wasn't built overnight." Sometimes the things that come to us easy aren't worth it.

The true concept of success I believe can be achieved the moment you are born and the moment you find out why you were born. Within us all, we have great forces of nature that can either help us or hurt us on our journey in accomplishing our goal. Sometimes it's a matter of taking things around us from another perspective, outside of the box.

My question to you is, do you know what you want? Do you know where you want to be in life?

What are you passionate about? When you woke up this morning, what did you most want to do? What was it that helped you wake up? Was it that you wanted to be a writer? Was it that you wanted to be a teacher at a school? Whatever it is, the first thing in the morning that you envision yourself doing every morning is what you are supposed to be doing. FIND YOUR WHY! What motivates you every day? Who motivates you daily? Be around people who want to support you and see you be successful.

End of Day Reflection

Five Things I am grateful for:

1

2

3

4

5

What did I learn today?

1

2

3

TO DO TOMORROW

1

2

3

4

5

May 20
Taurus

"Show the world you are grateful, and life opens another realm to you." - Brendan Burchard

People want to help those who help themselves. If someone sees that you are "fighting the good fight" towards your goals and you are putting in the effort, if you ever need help and you ask for help, they may be more willing to help you if they see you are trying to help better yourself too. Gratitude also opens gates and windows and doors to more opportunities in life as well.

When someone sees that you are appreciative of those around you and what you have around you, they feel pulled towards that energy and positivity. You can have the world tumbling around you, but you will end up on top if you show gratitude and humility and humbleness to those around you.

End of Day Reflection

Five Things I am grateful for:

1

2

3

4

5

What did I learn today?

1

2

3

TO DO TOMORROW

1

2

3

4

5

"The prettiest smiles hold the deepest secrets. The prettiest eyes have cried the most tears, and the kindest hearts have felt the most pain." Anonymous

I think we forget that everyone around us at one time or another is either going through something, about to go through something, or has just gotten over something. We are all in these situations and sometimes in our own worlds that we forget to really take a step back and say, what was going on in hers or his life that was affecting her or him to act like that way towards us. Sometimes when someone is angry or emotional it's not meant to be directed towards us. Sometimes it's pushed onto us because it is a reaction to what is going on in the moment for the other person and something that they are mentally thinking about or going through either at school or home.

End of Day Reflection

Five Things I am grateful for:

1

2

3

4

5

What did I learn today?

1

2

3

TO DO TOMORROW

1

2

3

4

5

"Our lives begin to end the day we become silent about things that matter." -Martin Luther King

  Even today his quote is very relevant, there are a lot of injustices and inequalities that happen around us all the time. We need to be outspoken about things that we don't feel is right or ought to be. Humanity at times forgets to look after each other while being self – absorbed into themselves and this is when things can be overlooked or not seen properly. There are always ways in which we can choose to handle certain things, certain situations and turn these moments into teaching moments for our children and sometimes even our own friends.
  There was a moment in my life when I myself had to speak out because of how a friend of mine was treating our server. My friend felt that they were above that person and, in some ways, yes, my friend was a little better off financially than this server possibly was. It was at that moment that I had to stop the conversation between my friend and I because I disapproved of the way in which he was treating our server as this hit home for me. I was once a server myself and I had to take a step back and teach my friend that sometimes it is how you treat others that matters more. The circumstances surrounding that server was unknown to him and I and I am sure this server had worked a good long shift that day and may or may not have made money and almost certainly didn't get a break while fetching this, that, and the other for their tables. The fact that my friend had disregarded this and said this is what the server is paid for, I had to explain that the server is probably only paid $2 to $3 dollars per hour and depends on tips. I had a lot of respect for that server and what they had to put up with and when being explained this situation my friend understood and apologized for his behavior.
  In the end what matters more is how you treat others around you.

End of Day Reflection

Five Things I am grateful for:

1

2

3

4

5

What did I learn today?

1

2

3

TO DO TOMORROW

1

2

3

4

5

"That's the spirit - One part brave, three parts fool."
- Christopher Paolini

This quote is originally from the movie, Eragon. What I can say about this quote is that there are times in our lives when we want to be the brave knight in shining armor for others and for our circumstances that we get ourselves in, but to do so, we must remember that you can't go running into a situation without thinking and without proper planning. This goes for all matters in our lives, a fool run into a circumstance and situation without planning what could or should or would happen and what to do in those situations. Always think of Plan B, C, and D. Just in case, and don't live with the expectations of others around you. If you do, you will always be disappointed and never satisfied. When you don't have expectations, you will always find yourself pleasantly surprised by the most random people that you come across.

End of Day Reflection

Five Things I am grateful for:

1

2

3

4

5

What did I learn today?

1

2

3

TO DO TOMORROW

1

2

3

4

5

"When there is no enemy within, the enemy outside can do you no harm." - Ancient African Proverb

Facing the Enemies Within by Jim Rohn - We are not born with courage, but neither are we born with fear. Maybe some of your fears are brought on by your own experiences, by what someone has told you, by what you've read in the papers. Some fears are valid, like walking alone in a bad part of town at two o'clock in the morning. But once you learn to avoid that situation, you won't need to live in fear of it. Fears, even the most basic ones, can destroy our ambitions.

Fear can destroy fortunes. Fear can destroy relationships. Fear, if left unchecked, can destroy our lives. Fear is one of the many enemies lurking inside us. Let me tell you about five of the other enemies we face from within. The first enemy that you've got to destroy before it destroys you is indifference. What a tragic disease this is. "Ho-hum, let it slide. I'll just drift along." Here's one problem with drifting: you can't drift your way to the top of the mountain. The second enemy we face is indecision. Indecision is the thief of opportunity and enterprise. It will steal your chances for a better future. Take a sword to this enemy.

The third enemy inside is doubt. Sure, there's room for healthy skepticism. You can't believe everything. But you also can't let doubt take over. Many people doubt the past, doubt the future, doubt each other, doubt the government, doubt the possibilities, and doubt the opportunities. Worst of all, they doubt themselves. I'm telling you; doubt will destroy your life and your chances of success. It will empty both your bank account and your heart. Doubt is an enemy Go after it. Get rid of it. The fourth enemy within is worried. We've all got to worry some.

Just don't let it conquer you. Instead, let it alarm you. Worrying can be useful. If you step off the curb in New York City and a taxi is coming, you've got to worry. But you can't let worry loose like a mad dog that drives you into a small corner. Here's what you've got to do with your worries: drive them into a small corner. Whatever is out to get you, you've got to get it. Whatever is pushing on you, you've got to push back. The fifth interior enemy is over-caution. It is the timid approach to life. Timidity is not a virtue; it's an illness. If you let it go, it'll conquer you. Timid people don't get promoted. They don't advance and grow and become powerful in the marketplace. You've got to avoid over-caution. Do battle with the enemy. Do battle with your fears. Build your courage to fight what's holding you back, what's keeping you from your goals and dreams. Be courageous in your life and in your pursuit of the things you want and the person you want to become. To Your Success, Jim Rohn

End of Day Reflection

Three Things I am grateful for:

1

2

3

What did I learn today?

1

2

3

TO DO TOMORROW

1

2

3

May 25
Gemini

Few thoughts for today:

• Sometimes our self-thought is self-taught, you become what you think about. A negative person will never become a positive person and therefore if you are always thinking badly about yourself, you are always only ever seeing that part of yourself and your self-esteem will self-destruct. You must know that you are an amazing person, you deserve to be happy and live a positive life. You deserve to be able to accomplish your hopes, your dreams, and your goals.

• Who has more? The person who has everything or the person who wants nothing.

I call a person who has everything but thinks that they have nothing I would say is ungrateful. I say this because at the end of the day, I think if you have your health, strength, love of family or friends, a roof over your head and food in your belly, you are rich beyond comparison.

• "Kindness is the language which the deaf can hear and the blind can see." - Mark Twain

• A simple and random act of kindness. This is something that anyone can do, and it wouldn't cost you anything and yet it can be noticed by all.

End of Day Reflection

Five Things I am grateful for:

1

2

3

4

5

What did I learn today?

1

2

3

TO DO TOMORROW

1

2

3

4

5

May 26
Gemini

"Great relationships aren't great because they have no problems. They are great because both people care enough about the other to make it work."

It is easy to give up on the relationships that you are in, and it is easy at times to walk away and say, "I'm done."

I myself have done this, in reflection it can be a regret, or it can be a healthy decision depending on the scenario. An empathetic person can easily be caught up in a toxic relationship and in certain situations you can feel it is difficult to walk away. At the end of the day, I believe it is better to walk away early from a toxic relationship than to believe you can change the other person when indeed you cannot expect to get into a relationship with someone who doesn't want to change or won't. I believe it is all around healthier to get into a relationship knowing you must accept the person for who they are with all of their flaws and imperfections. Over time, I do believe that people can change, but they have to want the change and realize that they need to change themselves for themselves, even if we don't like the people, they associate themselves with or how they think. You must be willing to see the person as they are and be okay with the idea that they may not change after all. Another personal take on relationships that I can say is that yes, they do take work, but they also take compromise. Sometimes the other person envisions doing something with you that you may not feel comfortable with, like going mini golfing for example. You may not be good at it, but they want to share the experience with you. Enjoy the experiences that you have in your life with others because they become memories that we can look back on and laugh at or reminisce about.

End of Day Reflection

Five Things I am grateful for:

1

2

3

4

5

What did I learn today?

1

2

3

TO DO TOMORROW

1

2

3

4

5

May 27 — Gemini

You have survived 100% of your struggles so far.

It is easy to be caught up in our current situations and say, "It's over, the world is crumbling around us because it is not going according to plan. Or because we don't have the money for food or for rent or we get "stuck" in our situations, and we feel there is no getting out.

It may seem dark around you at the moment and what you are going through you may feel like there is no getting out, but now is the time to look back at your life and think about other times when you were "struggling to get by" or when you felt that the cards were against you. What did you do then? How did you overcome it? Who was there for you the last time? Who could you meet with to get you through it? You have gotten through all your life's struggles throughout your past. Why? Because you are strong, you are capable, and you are an overcomer. You are filled with opportunities and there are opportunities all around you! Don't give up and don't look down. Keep your head held up high and know that you are going to get through this! Stay positive!

"The longer I live, the more I realize the impact of attitude on life. Attitude, to me, is more important than facts. It is more important than the past, than education, than money, than circumstances, than failures, than successes, than what other people think, say, or do. It is more important than appearance, giftedness, or skill. It will make or break a company… a church… a home. The remarkable thing is we have a choice every day regarding the attitude we will embrace for that day. We cannot change the inevitable. The only thing we can do is play on the one string we have, and that is our attitude…. I am convinced that life is ten percent what happens to me, and ninety-nine percent how I react to it. and so, it is with you… we are in charge of our attitudes." - Dr. Charles Swindoll

End of Day Reflection

Five Things I am grateful for:

1

2

3

4

5

What did I learn today?

1

2

3

TO DO TOMORROW

1

2

3

4

5

May 28
Gemini

"Be the change you want to see in the world! You may be looking around the world today in disappointment by seeing all the homelessness, the crime, the suffering, and the despair around you. Maybe perhaps even close to home. At the end of the day, if you have the resources or the ability to help those in need, the best thing that we can do is help when and where we can. We may not be capable of "reducing crime" or helping someone who doesn't want to be helped but we can try to do something about it. It is easy to lose faith in the world when seeing all the damage and destruction around us, but we gotta have hope for those who do have the resources and ability to help others. With the want of change, you must remember to have courage, courage to try something new, to expand your horizons, and take advantage of new opportunities that may arise. Courage. It is a word that conjures up images of great and dramatic actions. And yet I realize that we all have the opportunity to be courageous every day, in small and large ways. And it is when we choose to be courageous that we change our lives and the lives of those around us. Courage changes lives. Yes, it changes lives. First, the day you begin to stare down your fears and worries, and instead act courageously, your life will change. You will be set free to fly like you never have before. You will accomplish things you once only dreamed of. You will experience things you thought were only for others - the courageous ones. You will realize that your fears were baseless and just paper tigers, a mirage. You will begin to live your dreams. You will become a person of character! You will also change the lives of others. Simply put, courageous people pull others along with them. Everybody benefits from courageous people.

Here are some quick tips for acting courageously:

1. Know what you want. Courage is about choice. If you are to act courageously, you need to know what the right choice is. Be clear about your dream and vision.

2. Do not worry. I heard recently that worry is the wrong use of the imagination. That is perhaps the best definition I have ever heard. Worry is just thinking about all the bad

possibilities, isn't it? Well, courage is just thinking about all the great possibilities and then acting upon them!

3. Do your homework. It helps to get the facts. It helps because then you can make an informed decision that will put your heart and mind to rest. There will probably be a downside, but we understand it, choose alternatives, and act decisively instead of those.

And finally, #4 Act. Do you know what you want? Have you thought of the possibilities? Have you done your homework? The next step is to take the first step, and ACT!

End of Day Reflection

Five Things I am grateful for:

1

2

3

4

5

What did I learn today?

1

2

3

TO DO TOMORROW

1

2

3

4

May 29
Gemini

"Confidence isn't walking into a room thinking you're better than everyone, it's walking in and not having to compare yourself to anyone at all." - Rob Dial

Because of the influences of social media and technology around us, sometimes I feel that others feel the need to one up with each other. Or show which one of us is "living the best life." But I fear that it not only hurts others' self-confidence, but it also hurts their self-esteem in some ways, seeing others doing what they wish they could and thinking that they themselves can't do what they are doing because of where they are in their life. Though it isn't your job to worry about the personal development of others you can reach out a hand to those who are quick to criticize or judge in negativity/jealousy. Another piece of advice I can give is, be true to yourself and live with integrity, showing yourself with your flaws and strengths, to open yourself up to be vulnerable at times. Not to show others that you are weak but that you are human as well.

End of Day Reflection

Five Things I am grateful for:

1

2

3

4

5

What did I learn today?

1

2

3

TO DO TOMORROW

1

2

3

4

5

May 30
Gemini

"There is an old Cherokee legend that talks about the inner conflict that is constantly occurring in the hearts and minds of all humans. Inside of us all there truly is a strong fight going on. It is a conflict of two wolves within. One is manifested with negative energy. It is made of anger, envy, sorrow, pride, jealousy, inferiority, self-doubt, and evil. The other is manifested with joy, faith, hope, compassion, positivity, and truth - all that is good. The question is which one wins? The answer is, the one that you feed."

At the end of the day, you must realize that everyone at one time or another has had to struggle, to go without, or not have what we need or want the most. There are times when we are surrounded by the characteristics of those of the first wolf. I must say that even I myself have known what it is to go through what I call "the struggle" in life. Sometimes when going through struggles we are resilient, we overcome, and we don't let it define who we are, and we let this struggle fuel us with strength within. When going through these struggles, I must say that it's okay to ask for help, and to admit defeat and we will overcome it with help from others around us. In the end, it's the journey to success, rather than the success itself that matters more in order to find our purpose, our calling, and our true happiness.

End of Day Reflection

Five Things I am grateful for:

1

2

3

4

5

What did I learn today?

1

2

3

TO DO TOMORROW

1

2

3

4

5

"Love happens from your heart and cannot be forced. True love is to have good intentions to someone you love. Closeness is the reason why we fall in love with somebody, this is based on the reality that even friends turn into lovers." - Anonymous.

Sometimes we feel societal pressures and the need to find a significant other in fear of the idea of being alone. I think we should normalize that it is okay to be single in order to find and do what we are passionate about and figure ourselves out and see what and who we really are and what we want in our companion. It is true that this is something that cannot be forced.

End of Day Reflection

Five Things I am grateful for:

1

2

3

4

5

What did I learn today?

1

2

3

TO DO TOMORROW

1

2

3

4

5

June 1
Gemini

"Always be excited for tomorrow and make sure you always plan for something for yourself for tomorrow to be excited about/for. Lastly, don't forget to dream. Don't be afraid to envision a dream or goal that seems scary/almost impossible to obtain. If your dreams don't scare you, they aren't big enough."

If you have something constantly to be excited for you will always have a positive state of mind. Second, too many times people go through life thinking that the dreams that they have are impossible because they are feeling like they are too old, or because of their current circumstances, it's not possible. I want to tell you that the voice telling you this in your mind is not you, do not believe it! Your dreams and goals can be obtained at any age. Fear, our own inner fears scare us into believing that it's impossible. Your fears are only fears but there is no truth to these claims. Do not let these fears determine where or how you may or may not be able to accomplish them. Don't let these setbacks that are only temporary hold you back. Things to work on this Month: Work on not being so talkative. Being talkative is important in communication but too much of it will not allow for others to have a say in things edgewise around you or share their own views and opinions. Learn to listen to those around you; you may indeed learn something you never knew before. Keep yourself from exaggeration of circumstances around you. People will like you just as you are for who you are. Trying to exaggerate situations and circumstances around you will not earn you more importance or leave people thinking that you are more interesting. Nor will they think any less of you if you don't dramatize a situation. I always tell people, keep it at 100% honesty, this is always the best policy, the truth always comes out. You don't always need to be the center of attention in life, and it's okay to allow people to talk about themselves around you as well. By doing this it pushes more connections of people around you to make with others and allows for people to get to know others as well in a group conversation environment.

End of Day Reflection

Five Things I am grateful for:

1

2

3

4

5

What did I learn today?

1

2

3

TO DO TOMORROW

1

2

3

4

5

June 2
Gemini

"Loneliness is dangerous, it's addicting. Once you see how peaceful it is you don't want to deal with people." -Rob Dial

Contrary to this, I personally don't mind company, and I don't mind being near people from time to time. I also don't mind being alone in my thoughts and writing. As a matter of fact, I am sitting alone by myself as I write this in a cafe. Being here listening to music is peaceful. Just as sitting on the beach listening to the waves is peaceful to me as well. Everyone has what I call their happy place and comfort happy foods. I feel I have a healthy mix of being an introvert and extroverted-ness within me. Sometimes I feel the need to have company and be around others and sometimes I enjoy being alone in my room watching movies with biscuits and tea. Sometimes it's good to take time for yourself for an evening drive or alone to listen to music. It helps to de-stress and have a few moments of peace in your life.

Today take some time for yourself today, you deserve it!

End of Day Reflection

Five Things I am grateful for:

1

2

3

4

5

What did I learn today?

1

2

3

TO DO TOMORROW

1

2

3

4

5

June 3
Gemini

"The scars you acquire while exercising courage will never make you feel inferior." -- D.A. Battista

"Courage is a special kind of knowledge: the knowledge of how to fear what ought to be feared and how not to fear what ought not to be feared." -- David Ben-Gurion

"Courage is fear that has said its prayers." -- Dorothy Bernard

Don't be afraid to meet someone new within your usual routines. There is always a reason why we meet new people that come into our lives. There are times when it must be the courage found within us that needs to be taken up in order to meet, get to know, and understand others who may come from different walks of life and to make new friends.

Remember, a stranger is merely a person whom we have never met yet. We as a people, in a community should never fear the unknown. It is the unknown that helps us grow into stronger, better, more loving, and understanding people of empathy. Meet one new person today and try to make a new friend. This is your challenge for today. Get to know someone who you don't know and learn about them and their dreams and goals.

End of Day Reflection

Five Things I am grateful for:

1

2

3

4

5

What did I learn today?

1

2

3

TO DO TOMORROW

1

2

3

4

5

June 4
Gemini

"The greatest mistake you can make in life is to be continually fearing that you will make one." - Elbert Hubbard.

When we meditate and think about what our life's dreams, goals, and ambitions are. When we think about what our true purpose is, or what we could be doing right now to find what we define as our success or our happiness, we don't do it. Why? A few reasons, FEAR to change your life, fear of disappointment, and fear of pain. Moments of self-doubt don't give up on your dreams whatever happens. Rough times come, but they don't come into your life to stay, they come to pass. When you stop pushing yourself, when you stop growing and trying to grow and learn to become a better person then you were yesterday, (as I, myself strive to do) you just complain about things as they are, and you don't do anything about it because you've grown comfortable. Most people stop working on their dreams, why?

Because of fear of failure - What if I try to accomplish my dreams and goals to find happiness and self-success and I fail, and they don't work out?

Then also because of The Fear of Success - What if I do become successful and I can't handle it?

If you continue to think, what if? - You will never know, and you may never find that purpose in life, that inner peace, or that happiness.

Sometimes you must take risks in life to find love, happiness, or success.

End of Day Reflection

Five Things I am grateful for:

1

2

3

4

5

What did I learn today?

1

2

3

TO DO TOMORROW

1

2

3

4

5

June 5
Gemini

"One often meets his destiny on the road he takes to avoid it."
- Jean de la Fontaine

"Every human has what it takes, the ability to get through whatever it is that they are going through, if they only push through it. SO, PUSH THROUGH IT! Tragedy and trials come to everybody, only the strong survive! Y'all running from obstacles, when it's the obstacles that are going to bring you to that next level! Every opportunity is the last opportunity." Eric Thomas

Be comfortable being uncomfortable and with fear and failure. TODAY, I challenge you to put aside a half an hour today and think about who you are, what are your likes and dislikes. Spend time doing what you enjoy doing once a week. Get to know yourself better. Change parts of yourself that you don't like whether it's bad habits, people, and things that stress you out or make you upset. Have mental health days for yourself once a week.

End of Day Reflection

Five Things I am grateful for:

1

2

3

4

5

What did I learn today?

1

2

3

TO DO TOMORROW

1

2

3

4

5

June 6
Gemini

Success doesn't know tired, cold, early, too dark, or too difficult, it just knows whether you showed up or not. Change your mindset and try to find the positive in the small things. Try to find the positive for others and the small steps needed to be taken to be successful! Not everyone is going to support you and that is okay. Change your crowd to one that continues to cheer you on.

I realize that trying to surround yourself with positive people and getting rid of the negative people in your life is probably going to be difficult. Sometimes the negative people are within our own families. In these situations, perhaps we need to just limit communication to those who bring us down. As the fictional character Charlie Chan once said, "The mind is like a parachute, it only functions when it is open."

End of Day Reflection

Five Things I am grateful for:

1

2

3

4

5

What did I learn today?

1

2

3

TO DO TOMORROW

1

2

3

4

5

June 7
Gemini

"Let go of the illusion of control. There are things that you cannot "make" happen. A flower and tree both bloom on their own and in their own time. Though you may wish for the tree or flower to turn into a fruit tree or a flower tree, if it is not what it is, there can be nothing done. There are things that we can control in life, we can control the type of plants we wish to plant in life, and we can control when the fruit falls off the tree, and when and where to plant the tree." - Anonymous.

Every time someone wants to control something outside of their ability, two things happen: either it enlightens them, or it ends them. We can control our behavior, emotions, hard work, manners, etc. It is within our nature to exceed our limits or want to be better.

End of Day Reflection

Five Things I am grateful for:

1

2

3

4

5

What did I learn today?

1

2

3

TO DO TOMORROW

1

2

3

4

5

"If you always do what you've always done, you will always get what you've always got." - James P Lewis

Sometimes by changing different aspects of your life slightly things can improve around you. The small little changes that we make in our lives like going to a cafe in the morning or changing the location or type of job you work, you meet new people and experience new, sometimes better/different circumstances in which they improve your mental health/quality of life. Don't fear changes in your life to adapt to them. "Great progress is often the result of subtle change of seeing something a little bit differently than you did just a moment before. It is not that the world around you has changed, it's that your thoughts about the world have." - Eddie Pinero

End of Day Reflection

Five Things I am grateful for:

1

2

3

4

5

What did I learn today?

1

2

3

TO DO TOMORROW

1

2

3

4

5

June 9
Gemini

"I am not afraid to die, I just don't want to be there when it happens." - Woody Allen

I think that this has a lot to do with fear and our inner fears of the unknown. That uneasy feeling when you are during a struggle in life that you get. That feeling inside the pit of your stomach of uneasiness.

The "What is going to happen to me now feeling" we all know the tales of old biblically that explain what life could be like after life on Earth. A story of the kingdom of heaven. To envision such a place of love, happiness, positivity is unimaginable to be in existence, a place where we all want to go and visit and be a part of but don't want to die to get there knowing once we leave, there is no coming back to our same bodies, lives, etc. A point I want to make from this is simply something that we will come to eventually understand. Tomorrow is never guaranteed, life is short, we don't know when our time will come, so don't live a life others want you to live or in regret. But rather live the life you want for yourself, find and be in that happiness and share it with others.

End of Day Reflection

Five Things I am grateful for:

1

2

3

4

5

What did I learn today?

1

2

3

TO DO TOMORROW

1

2

3

4

5

June 10
Gemini

"Nothing is so common as the wish to be remarkable." - William Shakespeare

Every morning when you wake up, have a reason to wake up, wake up with a sense of driven purpose. Everyone wants to have the ability to do and be something remarkable, to have made a significant difference in the world. Some of us want this but get lazy and use excuses and fear to get out of doing what it takes to be remarkable, to make a difference and be successful. We can all say/do all we can but at the end of the day, it's the small steps that we take along the way that matter more.

To be remarkable, maybe we must do something common in nature to have such an impact. Holding the door for someone who is/has been having a bad day. The small gestures of kindness to be that significant driving force/influence on someone so they change their perception/attitude for the day.

Sometimes it's paying it forward, taking the seemingly small steps to make a difference.

"It is not our abilities that show what we truly are, it is our choices." - Albus Dumbledore.

End of Day Reflection

Five Things I am grateful for:

1

2

3

4

5

What did I learn today?

1

2

3

TO DO TOMORROW

1

2

3

4

5

June 11
Gemini

"Where there is no struggle, there is no strength." - Oprah Winfrey

I find that when there is struggle there is always a fight or flight response directly to what we are going through at the time. During times of great struggle, sure there is also pain and suffering during the times I call, "Adulting" we all, at the end of the day must face the human nature of pain and suffering but it doesn't mean you have to face dark times alone. These times are only temporary, temporary setbacks made to ensure you come out of the struggle that much stronger than when you were before you were going through it. Without struggle, without pain, without setbacks, there cannot be room for growth. Sometimes, to get by and to get past these setbacks, we need to change, change the situation we are in, change the jobs or our environment or even the very influences from the people we surround ourselves with. Doing this takes much strength and courage as I have experienced such changes, but these troubling times sometimes call for more drastic changes/approaches to what we are going through. "The only way you are going to get through to the other side of this journey is you have got to suffer to grow. To grow you must suffer, and some people get it and some of you won't. Life without challenge is a life without growth, embrace the pain and the struggle to grow." David Goggins

End of Day Reflection

Five Things I am grateful for:

1

2

3

4

5

What did I learn today?

1

2

3

TO DO TOMORROW

1

2

3

4

5

"You gain strength, courage, and confidence by every experience in which you really stop to look fear in the face." - Eleanor Roosevelt

For every experience that we have in life, we gain true wisdom and knowledge from it. It is because of experiences that we have in life, we can learn and grow from them and help others by sharing experiences with them.

When we have new experiences in life, we grow from them but also with that knowledge we can also use it to combat our very own fears that we get internally.

We shouldn't go through life afraid of our own shadows but rather see our shadows grow taller and bigger as we begin to feel excited to see our inner and our outer selves grow stronger, and our personal growth grows as we get older and wiser.

End of Day Reflection

Five Things I am grateful for:

1

2

3

4

5

What did I learn today?

1

2

3

TO DO TOMORROW

1

2

3

4

5

June 13
Gemini

"Sometimes the words we leave unspoken are the most important ones that should have been said." - Unknown

By holding back from saying how we truly feel or should have said can lead to living a life of regret and unknown possibilities. This fear sometimes prevents us from living to our full potential. It is never good to live a life of regret because it will lead to you living a miserable life and you will begin to be unhappy about things going on around you because you live in these regrets. Think about how things are in your life right now.

End of Day Reflection

Five Things I am grateful for:

1

2

3

4

5

What did I learn today?

1

2

3

TO DO TOMORROW

1

2

3

4

5

"Sometimes when we want things to go our way in life, we have to be the change that we want to see in others. Loving, living, and leading by example."

This is especially true for those who are especially stubborn in our lives. By leading by example, it's easier for others to see you do what you need them to do, so their thought process goes, "Well, if they can do it, so can I," or "Today I want to help them out with something they always do, so will do it for once for them."

We all like to believe that there are people who have faith in humanity and act on goodness for the sake of humanity and others in their lives. In my experience it's better to have faith/hope in others and eventually people will surprise you.

End of Day Reflection

Five Things I am grateful for:

1

2

3

4

5

What did I learn today?

1

2

3

TO DO TOMORROW

1

2

3

4

5

June 15
Gemini

"Value not the things you have in life, but rather who you have in life." - Unknown

   Material things of this world are it; they are only of this world. You cannot take the diamond ring, the Gucci clothes, the Swiss watches, or the fancy Lexus, Mercedes, or BMWs with you when you leave this Earth. We all leave the same way in a coffin, or ashes to ashes. What matters more is the people, experiences, and memories that you share with others and your talents. This has more significance and meaning once the money's gone and spent, you may or may not get it back in your future but the experience and memories that you share with others last a lifetime to look back upon. Use money that you have for good to create a world in which you wish to share with others. When you do you will realize how much more worth it was to create memories with others. Our time is limited so don't waste it living it selfishly.

End of Day Reflection

Five Things I am grateful for:

1

2

3

4

5

What did I learn today?

1

2

3

TO DO TOMORROW

1

2

3

4

5

June 16
Gemini

"Fairy tales do not tell children that dragons exist. Children already know dragons exist. Fairy tales tell children that dragons can be killed."- G.K. Chesterton.

There is plenty of good and evil in this world. The nice thing is there are always ways to overcome our struggles and ways to handle the more difficult people that we come across. We may see evil doers lurking in the darkness, but you should also remember, you don't have to be alone.

"Nothing is easier than to denounce the evildoer, nothing more difficult than understanding him." - Fydor Dostoevsky

"There is a fight going on inside of us all." - Prince EA

End of Day Reflection

Five Things I am grateful for:

1

2

3

4

5

What did I learn today?

1

2

3

TO DO TOMORROW

1

2

3

4

5

June 17
Gemini

"Well, boy, better get used to death, this happens every day on the streets around here. Just be happy you are alive… You gotta tough life as it is out there, it's not all sunshine and daisies, and roses. If you want something in life, you gotta fight for it. You gotta prove not just to others, but to yourself, that you want and deserve success! … Kids today need to know how bad life is out there, and how fragile it is, and that life needs to be respected. You can't be naive in life. It is better to be strong and know what you need to do to survive and what you are up against." - Susie Que, Grey Matter Series Volume 1 Story of Mark Trogmyer in the World of the Unknown, pg. 18, by Anthony Parker.

Take your time and enjoy your day today. Life has beauty to it even in its relatively shortness to it. If you don't take a step back to enjoy it, you will miss all its beauty along the way and the stresses of life can hold you back from experiencing it in the way that it should be. Don't be afraid to take risks and chances in life, when you do, and you take advantage of all of life's opportunities you learn and grow so much!

End of Day Reflection

Five Things I am grateful for:

1

2

3

4

5

What did I learn today?

1

2

3

TO DO TOMORROW

1

2

3

4

5

June 18
Gemini

" The most authentic thing about us is our capacity to create, to overcome, to endure, to transform, to love, and to be greater than our suffering." - Ben Okri

Upon reflection, I noticed that in the bookstore you will find hundreds of books about how to be happy, how to be peaceful by finding your inner self. and how to be successful and how to motivate others, but rarely will you find books on how to fail and on failure. If you know how to fail, then you learn how to recover from great pain, struggles, and suffering. It is my personal belief that you may then find you will find your success in life. The point of being successful is not the success itself, but rather the journey that you took to find success and to be the exact definition of what you and others see as success. Think of ways in which today you can overcome obstacles that may be standing in your way and be great through overcoming them.

End of Day Reflection

Five Things I am grateful for:

1

2

3

4

5

What did I learn today?

1

2

3

TO DO TOMORROW

1

2

3

4

5

"Hope is the thing that feathers, that perches in the soul, and sings the tune without words, and never stops at all." - Emily Dickinson

Hope is metaphorically transformed into a strong willed, stubborn bird that lives within us all. There is so much power behind hope and living your life in positivity in what is to come, no matter what, and it doesn't require much if others were to live this life as well like this.

Living positively will steer others to want to be constantly around you. It empowers others as well to be encouraging and positive leaders of others around them as well. It is like the old saying, "You can attract more bees with honey then you can with vinegar." Besides, it costs nothing to be friendly, helpful, caring, and to smile while being supportive of others.

End of Day Reflection

Five Things I am grateful for:

1

2

3

4

5

What did I learn today?

1

2

3

TO DO TOMORROW

1

2

3

4

5

June 20
Gemini

"Nothing revives the past so completely as a smell that was once associated with it." - Vladimir Nabokov

Our sense of smell during times of our past is most sensitive in both good and bad times. Sometimes it's certain smells that bring us memories of those we lost/love. Perhaps your grandfather used to smoke tobacco, or your parents had a certain smell attached to them in certain memories. Having these memories be triggered by smell can also bring about times of nostalgia and that's normal and natural. If these are bad memories to certain smells, work on attaching these smells to good memories to be made, overcome, and find a way to let it empower you. For me, even certain songs remind me of relationships of my past and perhaps one of the ways I overcame that setback was to recreate new memories with those same songs.

End of Day Reflection

Five Things I am grateful for:

1

2

3

4

5

What did I learn today?

1

2

3

TO DO TOMORROW

1

2

3

4

5

"The right word may be effective, but no word was ever as effective as a rightly timed pause." - Mark Twain

There is so much power behind the pen when stringing the proper words together - also power behind the correctly/properly timed pause to make a point - a difference - or impact. Sometimes it isn't just the words that we say within conversation that we use but what also matters more is the way, context, and emotions that we use to say it. There are moments when we need to decide in life, which is better to tell someone something whether it's a call, in person, or a text. The way to think about it is. People read text messages based on the mood that they are currently in. If someone is mad, frustrated, sad, overwhelmed, depressed, or stressed, this is the way in which they will read incoming messages. Most of the time it is better to talk to people in public and or over a phone call, so nothing gets miscommunicated or seen as being rude to us or others.

Think carefully about what you want to say and how you want to say things to people. Sometimes our intentions may be pure in thought and we believe what we are going to do is right, or for the best behind what we want to do or say. Try to remember to put yourself in their shoes when considering the formality in which you wish to communicate with people.

End of Day Reflection

Five Things I am grateful for:

1

2

3

4

5

What did I learn today?

1

2

3

TO DO TOMORROW

1

2

3

4

5

"Surround yourself with people who see your value and remind you of it!" Sean Buranahiran

Being you, you may not be able to pick your family, but you are responsible for the people whom you choose to call your friends and the people who you choose to just be acquaintances with. If you surround yourself with a strong support system who are empathetic, kind, respectful to you and to others around you, wise, and positive people. You will grow so much and be able to overcome anything if you do!

If, however, you surround yourself with negative, complaining, abusive people, who just see you as a walking bank atm, or are just using you, and are only being around you when times are good, they probably aren't good company to keep. Choose your friends wisely. If they are more knowledgeable and higher minded than you, that's okay as long as you are a good listener/support and are positive around them, things will be great for you to grow with them.

The wisest thing you should consider is…

"I don't know what I don't know, and I am going to try being open minded enough to accept new perspectives, ideas, and learn from experience, it will help me gain a better understanding of those around me and to know myself better."

End of Day Reflection

Five Things I am grateful for:

1

2

3

4

5

What did I learn today?

1

2

3

TO DO TOMORROW

1

2

3

4

5

"The easiest way to make the change that you are desperately seeking is by changing your perspective on the life you are already now living." - Steve Bartlett

When you internally reflect on how you really are:

Physically, Emotionally, Financially, Healthwise, Socially, Mentally, Spiritually, Environmentally, and Occupationally….

Dissect how you feel about these different areas of your life. What is going on? Where are you in your life in these situations? Are these good situations? When you look from the outside in, does it look like you feel happy? Successful? Healthy? and okay? Or are you just telling others you are okay without analyzing where you are at in life and how to fix/see where you want to be?

Once you start changing the small intricate details of things going on in your life that aren't good, you will slowly begin to see yourself happy, healthy, and feel successful and not as stressed out.

End of Day Reflection

Five Things I am grateful for:

1

2

3

4

5

What did I learn today?

1

2

3

TO DO TOMORROW

1

2

3

4

5

"Anything is possible for those with a dream, a plan, and the determination necessary to make it happen, no matter what. In life you have two choices, do what is necessary to do it or not."

There is no time limit, age restriction, nor exact calendar date when we are all supposed to be successful or accomplishing our dreams. The common misconception is "Oh I have to have my life put together by 30, and already be a millionaire." The truth is 40 is the new 30, 50 is the new 40 and it is never too late.

1. What are your dreams?
2. What is needed to make them happen?
3. Research the steps necessary to be and do what you want to most do in life.
4. Come up with an action plan.
5. DO IT!

People who can't do the first three things rarely finish the action plan necessary to accomplish it.

I wanted to be an author/writer - the books never write themselves. You gotta just get into gear, set the time aside and stubbornly stick to a healthy habitual regiment needed to accomplish the end result.

End of Day Reflection

Five Things I am grateful for:

1

2

3

4

5

What did I learn today?

1

2

3

TO DO TOMORROW

1

2

3

4

5

"It is better to walk alone, then with a crowd going in the wrong direction." - Herman Siu

The best thing you can do is find your own path to what you think is success. Ask people who are already where you want to be in life to be your mentor so you can do what they have done and be where they are in life. Also remember that sometimes everyone's path to success isn't the same. Sometimes you must ignore others who are not supportive or not encouraging you while you are on this path and sometimes you will find yourself alone and that is okay too. Many try and fail; many try and fail and give up - that is why there are so many dead carcasses on the path to success. But this is also why cemeteries are filled with unaccomplished dreams and goals of the past.

*The key to failure, try - fail - try - find another way to fail - try again - you make a mistake, keep trying again and at that last moment, a few more inches, a few more seconds, a few more miles, then you will eventually find that success."

End of Day Reflection

Five Things I am grateful for:

1

2

3

4

5

What did I learn today?

1

2

3

TO DO TOMORROW

1

2

3

4

5

"Time decides who you meet in your life, your heart decides who you want in your life, and your behavior decides who will stay in your life." - Ziad K Abdelnour

Those who you deem special in your life, will always remain in your heart. Life is too short to take it for granted. Choose your battles wisely and don't be afraid to give others second chances. Don't be afraid to try something new. Be proud to be different.

End of Day Reflection

Five Things I am grateful for:

1

2

3

4

5

What did I learn today?

1

2

3

TO DO TOMORROW

1

2

3

4

5

Imagination is more important than knowledge."

-Albert Einstein

Imagine the endless possibilities that could happen if you acted on your imagination to create new/different things. Don't be afraid of your imagination. Dream what has yet to be done and be what/who you want to be. Dare to dream, dare to live. I dare you to be creative today, be artistic, create something that has yet to be invented. Be original and innovative in everything you do. I find when working listening to music helps me be more productive, particularly instrumental music. "They say music is the bridge between Earth and Heaven." - Forbidden Kingdom.

End of Day Reflection

Five Things I am grateful for:

1

2

3

4

5

What did I learn today?

1

2

3

TO DO TOMORROW

1

2

3

4

5

"Sometimes it takes only one person to change your life. One who is there for you, encourages you, and believes in you. If you haven't met this person yet, be this person for someone else." - Jim Kwik.

Sometimes to be successful all it takes is some words of encouragement, support, acts of kindness, or just love to help get someone from being just someone to feeling/being remarkable. Don't be afraid to encourage others to be successful in a sincere honest way.

End of Day Reflection

Five Things I am grateful for:

1

2

3

4

5

What did I learn today?

1

2

3

TO DO TOMORROW

1

2

3

4

5

"The weak can never forget. Forgiveness is the attribute of the strong." - Mahatma Gandhi

The weak can never forget, especially when it comes to the fights of life. They remember the pain, suffering, and struggles and the overwhelming feelings of defeat when they are beaten. Because they remember, they fight that much harder to prevent that from happening again and forgive themselves for not being strong enough at first. We need to fight our best fights strongly but sometimes we must remember while in these rings of struggle, in the fight called life - You are not alone. Never be afraid or too proud to ask for help. Pride is dangerous - it prevents others from doing kindness for us and it only enables an even harder hardship. "Asking for help doesn't make you weak - it makes you and everyone around you human."

End of Day Reflection

Five Things I am grateful for:

1

2

3

4

5

What did I learn today?

1

2

3

TO DO TOMORROW

1

2

3

4

5

June 30
Cancer

Greed is the root of all evil. Money blinds us and can make people try to turn relationships/friendships into transactional relationships.

For me, I see friendships and money like oil and water, I never put a numerical value on a friendship/relationship. Sure, like everyone there is a line that needs to be drawn sometimes as to how much "help" we can give someone without making ourselves fall into deep holes of debt. I have found that when mixing the two ideas of money and friendship it has an effect of preventing people from thinking you sincerely care and genuinely want to help. Give of yourself generously and it will come back in two folds during times of hardship when you ask help of others. Every day, I myself, try to be a better person than I was yesterday. Along the way, you will find that giving can also attract people who may only attempt to use you. As long as you learn the lesson along that way, sometimes enabling people isn't a good thing. Those people move on and realize there is only so much that you can do for them eventually. Sometimes you can only carry one person on your back and even then, they become heavy and you both fall.

End of Day Reflection

Five Things I am grateful for:

1

2

3

4

5

What did I learn today?

1

2

3

TO DO TOMORROW

1

2

3

4

5

July 1
Cancer

"My boundaries were not created to offend you. They were created to honor me." - Unknown

Healthy boundaries in life are good to have. Lines drawn as guidelines between you and others. Balance between the peace in your life within the chaos that may be going on around you. Make sure that even within the realm of the relationships that you are in, that YOU have "you time," time in which you can unwind, relax, and enjoy some peace. Be there for you. Because at the end of the day, no one is going to care more about your health, your success, your wellbeing, and your situation that you are in, more than you. You do you - by doing what is best for you, regardless of what other's opinions are of those around you.

Things to work on this Month: Work on being more independent and a more direct person in conversation with your intentions and feelings. We miss out on opportunities of growth within ourselves if we don't work on our own weaknesses on our own. People in our lives come and go and not everyone is meant to be in our lives for a lifetime or many seasons. People come into our lives for a reason, a season, or a lifetime and sometimes they leave us like leaves on a tree in the winter. But more people come back the following season. Do not fear be alone, being alone allows you to work on yourself and to improve yourself. It is okay to be a sensitive person but don't dwell on the mistakes of others around you in the past. Yes, people are human, and they make mistakes but holding it over their head for the scars that they made will not allow you to grow as a person or fully be able to move on. It is okay to let go of the past.

End of Day Reflection

Five Things I am grateful for:

1

2

3

4

5

What did I learn today?

1

2

3

TO DO TOMORROW

1

2

3

4

5

July 2 — Cancer

"No one will hit you harder than life itself. It doesn't matter how hard you hit back. It's about how hard you get hit and keep moving forward. How much can you take and suffer and keep moving forward. That's how winning is done." - Sylvester Stallone.

Ask yourself. If I fall today and fail at whatever I am trying to accomplish - or if my car breaks down - or if I lose my job tomorrow - Are you prepared? What's your next plan of action?

Everyone falls and everyone fails sometimes at the things that they are attempting to do at some point of their life. My question to you is, if/when you fail, when that happens are you ready? It is also easy to say, I am/would give up. There wouldn't be any point in trying anymore. It would be easy to say, yep, I am going to throw in the towel and just live off the streets and beg for money. I am not suggesting it's better to be overreactive to the point where you don't try - or reacting to anything and everything going on around you. But what I am saying is come up with an action plan of some sort of what you are going to do, mentally and emotionally prepare for the worst of what could happen and have faith and hope for the best at the same time.

When going through what I call "the struggle," I have found that sometimes we must reach out a hand and ask for a hand to hold or to hang on to so that we can get through the temporary setbacks that we get in life. This is sometimes easier said than done, but sometimes we need to try to mentally strengthen our resolve and think positively but remember if life knocks you down, get back up and push forward. Never look back in regret. - Changes that occur in our lives are sometimes for the better, even if at the time we don't see it right away.

End of Day Reflection

Five Things I am grateful for:

1

2

3

4

5

What did I learn today?

1

2

3

TO DO TOMORROW

1

2

3

4

5

"Envision where you want to be and the dreams and goals that you want to accomplish. Research and do the sacrifices necessary now to put it into action. Do the steps necessary to get to that <u>next level</u> in life. Don't be afraid to go the extra mile required. If you are afraid, you are going in the right direction. The road to success can make you feel lonely, and it can be dark. Never look back, keep going, keep moving forward. If your dreams and goals in life don't scare you enough, you aren't going in the right direction. It is so easy to get lost in your fears of the unknown and not know if you are going in the right direction and you may not even notice much change over the next few days while taking these necessary steps and that is okay, Rome was not built in a day. Nothing remotely successful has ever been hugely successful overnight. Success takes time and sometimes years to accomplish. If you can go that extra mile, then you can go even farther than you realize and thought you could."

Yes, I put this in twice, I need you to get into the habit of revisiting the thoughts and goals of your dreams regularly and relook into the steps necessary because then you will get to that success that you want. Occasionally you've slept since the last time you did this, and situations and circumstances change daily. Create that bucket list - 20 things you want to do before you leave this Earth, life is too short not to try to accomplish them!

End of Day Reflection

Five Things I am grateful for:

1

2

3

4

5

What did I learn today?

1

2

3

TO DO TOMORROW

1

2

3

4

5

July 4 — Cancer

"Sometimes bad things happen to good people. What needs to be realized is that it's a matter of perspective. - Bad things happen to us (taking on a sort of ("victim mentality") or - Bad things get to happen to us (taking on a sort of ("let's try to overcome this challenge") type of perception. When these challenges arise, look at these as new opportunities to overcome adversity, for changes to happen in your life for new experience and new people to come into your life to make a difference in your life that you otherwise wouldn't have had."

Yes, you are probably going through something right now, or you are about to go through something right now, or you just got over something that just happened to you. - This is a minor setback. It won't last forever, and you are not alone. Do not forget that there is always hope when there is faith and don't be afraid to reach out to people that you know occasionally and check in on them and catch up and make sure that they are okay as well.

End of Day Reflection

Five Things I am grateful for:

1

2

3

4

5

What did I learn today?

1

2

3

TO DO TOMORROW

1

2

3

4

5

July 5 — Cancer

"People build too many walls and not enough bridges." - Unknown

   When you put walls up you prevent others from being able to be there for you and get to know you. You enclose yourself to possibly even people who are toxic for you in your life without you even realizing it. It could close your mind and prevent you from opening up to anyone. I think that people would do a much better service to others if they listened to people around them and hear what the struggles and pains of others are so we can reach out to them and learn to understand them better. I think that God gave us two ears for the reason for us to use them and listen to what is going on in the hearts and minds around us instead of telling people how they should be hurting because their words and actions may not match their beliefs, opinions, etc.

   When you build bridges, it has a life altering effect on you. It enables you to meet and have conversations with people you would never have thought possible. When doing this you can form unrealized bonds of love, trust, and it encourages a team/open community relationship/friendship. Build bridges with others and help connect people together to others that you know because perhaps by doing so, you could help them accomplish their own hopes and dreams through other people that you may get to know and meet.

End of Day Reflection

Five Things I am grateful for:

1

2

3

4

5

What did I learn today?

1

2

3

TO DO TOMORROW

1

2

3

4

5

July 6
Cancer

"Do the best you can until you know better. Fake it until you make it. Then when you know better, do better." - Unknown

At the end of the day, the best is all we can do to strive for. We are only human and someone giving 120% of their 120% may only look like someone else's 80% effort. Nobody is perfect even if perfectionism is the thing that we all strive for. Today all you can do is your best by giving your best effort. By striving to do our absolute best, we can all collectively contribute for the betterment of all.

End of Day Reflection

Five Things I am grateful for:

1

2

3

4

5

What did I learn today?

1

2

3

TO DO TOMORROW

1

2

3

4

5

July 7
Cancer

"It is better to know and be disappointed than to never know and always wonder." - Oscar Wilde.

This is especially true if you find someone that you may want to get to know and possibly date. If you never ask you will never really know for sure if you ask at least you know.

This quote even works in the working environment if you don't know what to do or how to do something you may never learn or know if you don't ask. It is always better to know and possibly be disappointed to know if you have been doing your job wrong than to continue to do it wrong and make two times the work for everyone. You don't know what you don't know, and people cannot read your mind if you don't understand something or if you need help if you don't ask for it. Always be constantly striving to learn and grow.

End of Day Reflection

Five Things I am grateful for:

1

2

3

4

5

What did I learn today?

1

2

3

TO DO TOMORROW

1

2

3

4

5

"I am not what happened to me. I am what I choose to become." - Carl Jung

"You may have failed at something today, yesterday, last week, or last year but if you didn't learn from it and get back up and keep moving forward from it, that would be your only setback."

"We all fall and scramble to our knees occasionally. Life happens and we fear the unknown of what could happen next, and we blame and call ourselves or each other's failures for making mistakes. YOU are not a failure. Yes, a failure or mistake may have happened, but you are not defined by the errors you make in life. You are beautiful, successful in surviving 100% of the days you have been through so far. You are blessed and I know you have the confidence and the perseverance and the stamina to never give up, to never give in and to show others. You are going to make it! You are not defined by your actions/inactions. Those mistakes may be thought as failures, but they are merely EVENTS NOT A PERSON not you…. Your self-talk is self-taught - what you may think others are thinking is not the case. Think highly about yourself - raise your standards - be the person you want to be. The best version of yourself and you will be successful.

End of Day Reflection

Five Things I am grateful for:

1

2

3

4

5

What did I learn today?

1

2

3

TO DO TOMORROW

1

2

3

4

5

July 9 — Cancer

"The ultimate reason setting goals is to entice you to become the person it takes to achieve them." - Jim Rohn.

A goal is the selling point for New Years Resolutions. If you can also see it as a steppingstone towards a bigger dream. Have the vision and the enthusiasm to put forth the action required to accomplish these dreams/goals.

It's one thing to say you want the dream,

It's another to say I will put forth all action necessary to accomplish it.

As the old saying goes, I will adjust to it. Actions and inactions speak louder than words.

"A picture is also worth 10,000 words." - Charlie Chan

End of Day Reflection

Five Things I am grateful for:

1

2

3

4

5

What did I learn today?

1

2

3

TO DO TOMORROW

1

2

3

4

5

"If you have a dream don't just sit there. Gather your courage, self-motivate yourself enough to realize why you want to accomplish your dream. Believe that you <u>WILL</u> do it! You will succeed and leave no stone unturned, no box unchecked, no "T" uncrossed, no missing dots on top of your "i's" to do what is necessary to make it a reality." - Anthony S. Parker

I can sit here in Starbucks and say… "It would be nice to be an author of over 100+ NY Times Bestselling books."

It would be nice to say my car has been paid off.

It would be nice to be able to say I own my own home and it paid off.

It would be nice but…

Books must be written, edited, copyrighted, and published by an author. They must be submitted to the qualifications that NY Times requires books to be in to be considered a NY Times Bestseller. The credit needs to be good to qualify for a house.

The car can only be paid off with the cash earned from working a good paying job.

Wishing it VS Willing it to happen. There are necessary steps needed to be taken to start to accomplish these dreams and the action is crucial and critical to follow through consistently to get to where you want to be.

End of Day Reflection

Five Things I am grateful for:

1

2

3

4

5

What did I learn today?

1

2

3

TO DO TOMORROW

1

2

3

4

5

"Stay positive, even if it feels like things are falling apart."
- Anthony S Parker

   This is much easier to say than acted upon. The first thing that needs to be done is realize when you react to things going on around you, it produces contagious negative energy that can be absorbed by those around you. It causes you to emotionally react to the situations we are in, versus being able to logically, and positively respond to the situation, and figure out what to do next. What's the next step necessary that is needed to happen to positively move through and over the issues at hand?

   When you do this - Life is easier to take in smaller chunks step by step. Asking for help is also something that not everyone is good at, but it's necessary to reach our goals, and dreams sometimes and we should all frequently refer to it. There is no shame in asking others for help, it's only natural for human beings as they say we live in communities and sometimes it takes a community to help us and be a support for us all.

End of Day Reflection

Five Things I am grateful for:

1

2

3

4

5

What did I learn today?

1

2

3

TO DO TOMORROW

1

2

3

4

5

"Sometimes it takes being away from someone for a while for them to realize how much they really needed you in their life, but it can also take a while for you to realize how much of a toxic burden they were for you as well. Always focus on creating healthy boundaries. This is indeed a great lesson that we all need to learn even in a relationship with our significant others." - Anthony S. Parker

People come into our lives for a reason, a season, or a lifetime. Sometimes people come into our lives and hurt us, use us, abuse us, or make our situations with them toxic. These "toxic" people we are meant to learn from end up not deserving to be a part of our lives. Many times, it's the toxic people who need to learn and grow from their mistakes.

These are the times when you need to raise your standards after you figure out who the toxic people who are hurting you in your life are. Realize that "I deserve OQP (Only Quality People) in my life!" These are people who support you and help you and love you for who you are and look out for you. These are people who are there for you when you need a shoulder to cry on, a person to hug, or a person to listen to you when you are upset. These are people who want nothing but the best for you and help you grow into a stronger, more enduring person. If you want people to leave your life, let them go so that they can grow. Never beg anyone to stay in your life, sometimes if they are meant to go, they aren't meant to stay. Please realize this, even if it hurts, as it's only advice that is meant to help you in the end.

End of Day Reflection

Five Things I am grateful for:

1

2

3

4

5

What did I learn today?

1

2

3

TO DO TOMORROW

1

2

3

4

5

July 13
Cancer

"Your Past does not have to define your future."

Our past is exactly that, our past. To move forward and onward with your life, never look back in regret. You need to go through what you have gone through in your past to get you to where you are today. Grow stronger by learning from the past, but never waste time thinking the past mistakes/failures are what define who you are today. You have survived through 100% of the days that you have gone through up to today. Not one moment is a moment when you should think, because this happened, or because I should have done this differently. The world is going to end, or the time of hope has passed. You are exactly where you are meant to be in life. Looking positively forward towards a brighter future with hope. Sure, you may not be exactly where you wanted to be in your life as a few weeks ago you had hoped today you would be, but you are steadily getting to do and get to where you want to be in life as long as you keep putting forth the necessary action.

Today recognize upon reflection what changes you can make to ensure life is better in quality and ensure what is possibly making you unhappy in your life is no more. Change what you can control in your life, but while also realizing that there are things in your life that are things you cannot control and there is nothing you can do to change them. For example, you cannot make someone like you, or what to talk to you about. You cannot force someone into your life, and you cannot force yourself into a job that isn't available. But you can introduce yourself to people to find the right person for your significant other, you can apply for jobs that are available and if the interviews go well, you could get a job in the field or with the title that you feel would help accomplish your goals or dreams and do what makes you happy. These are things within our control that if you just try and put in a little effort, they can make a world of a difference.

End of Day Reflection

Five Things I am grateful for:

1

2

3

4

5

What did I learn today?

1

2

3

TO DO TOMORROW

1

2

3

4

5

"A man has died here Fudge and he won't be the last, we must take action." - Dumbledore

I will not, In times like these in the wizard world look to its leaders for strength, Dumbledore!" - Cornelius

Then for once show them some!" - Dumbledore

The Triwizard Tournament will not be canceled, I will not be seen as a coward…" - Cornelius Fudge

"A true leader does what is right, no matter what people think…." - Albus Dumbledore, Harry Potter Goblet of Fire.

Our brains are magnetically attracted to negativity and what is easiest to do. We must try to be the aura of positivity and put in the extra mile, and the extra attempt at goodness, the extra work in life to achieve higher levels of quality in life and those that are around us.

"Don't wish life was easier, wish you were better." - Jim Rohn.

You cannot go through life believing that life should be easier or that the world owes you. THE WORLD OWES YOU NOTHING! That is not how that works. No one said when we are born that life is going to be easy or that it won't be full of challenges. From the moment we are born, we need help eating, and getting around, dressing ourselves, etc. But through time we learn to walk, we learn how to eat, and we learn how to properly dress ourselves, over time we learn and grow into the people we are today. We grow stronger through the struggles that are placed in front of us in our lives and we learn to adapt when people say, "No" to us.

It is within these struggles that we incur in life that by doing what is right, with integrity, and perseverance, that defines who we are, and we find our own humanity.

End of Day Reflection

Five Things I am grateful for:

1

2

3

4

5

What did I learn today?

1

2

3

TO DO TOMORROW

1

2

3

4

5

July 15
Cancer

> "The greatest weapon against stress is our ability to choose one thought over another." – William James

"Stress can be a tough thing to overcome. Many of us have found ourselves allowing negative thoughts to rob us of a peaceful night of sleep. After a while, the tossing and turning and feelings of stress and negativity continue to build. The next thing you know, it seems that you just can't get back to sleep no matter how hard you try. While the above scenario can be extremely frustrating there are ways for us to alleviate such stress. Here's a technique I have used with great success. If I find myself tossing and turning in bed from one issue or the other, I make this simple declaration to myself, "If you are not going to get out of bed and do something about the issue right now then stop thinking about it." Sometimes I have to say this to myself several times, but it works. One effective way to stop thinking about any issues that may be causing you stress is to, as Willam James said, "choose one thought over another". Thought substitution is a powerful method for combatting stress by replacing the negative thought that may be associated with stress. When dealing with stress though, substitution is simply a way of distracting your mind and taking it off the negative path it has taken. You can reflect upon something pleasant such as that tranquil vacation you spent at the beach or that relaxing afternoon at the art museum. One of the most common ways to implement thought substitution is with a change of scenery. With me, for instance, my Sunday morning walks along the river never fail to soothe and relax me. Now a walk along the river may not be your cup of tea. What change of scenery or activity would help you to relax and feel more at peace? Whatever that change of scenery or activity is, take some time to enjoy it." - Tony

The Greatest Weapon Against Stress Is Our Ability To Choose One Thought Over Another | Effective Self Improvement
https://www.effectiveselfimprovement.com/inspirational-quotes/the-greatest-weapon-against-stress-is-our-ability-to-choose-one-thought-over-another/

End of Day Reflection

Five Things I am grateful for:

1

2

3

4

5

What did I learn today?

1

2

3

TO DO TOMORROW

1

2

3

4

5

July 16
Cancer

"Choose your battles wisely because if you choose them all, you will be too tired to win the really important ones." - Unknown

When in the heat of the moment and seeing other people do things that may perhaps annoy you or do things you may not understand right away. When in these situations it's best not to allow these situations to make you react to them easily. Think of why they are doing what they are doing. Like a chess game, thinking about the reasoning why they are moving the pieces. When you react to why your pawn is taken on the board you may see there are other ulterior motives as to why they are making the moves that they are making.

Choose your battles, choose your arguments carefully. Fight for things that matter more to you. When choosing arguments, I look into the logic of it. Does the other person have reasoning as to why they are doing what they are doing? When taking yourself into the other person's shoes, you get to understand them better. If you cannot find the reason, then you can logically argue about what's going on.

There are true battles that happen around us, especially when it comes to our feelings and love that are worth the fight. When you know that you still have feelings for that special person in your life and it's been a healthy nontoxic relationship sometimes, fighting for the relationship to work out and sacrificing the necessary things needed for the other person is necessary within reason.

End of Day Reflection

Five Things I am grateful for:

1

2

3

4

5

What did I learn today?

1

2

3

TO DO TOMORROW

1

2

3

4

5

July 17
Cancer

"If it can be solved, there is no need to worry, if it cannot be solved, then worry is of no use." - Dalai Lama.

Worrying for no reason is something that we as humans are at times good at. As I have put this before, if there is something that is going to happen, that could happen, or we are worried it has already happened... it's out of our control and we need to have hope and faith that things will work out in the end one way or another. At this point, if we cannot control it, we ought not to worry about it and realize that this is perhaps someone else's headache to handle if it comes up and perhaps, we can help in the aftermath. You cannot live your life in constant worry, it is a miserable life to lead full of negativity and falsehoods at times. Be there for those around you as much as you can. Also, another piece of wisdom that has been even harder for me to understand is that sometimes when we "try to help" in situations we enable others instead of showing them how they are able to help themselves.

One beautiful afternoon, a young man was taking a stroll around his garden when he noticed a cocoon of a butterfly on a leaf. Thrilled to see an amazing transformation of nature, he sat and watched the butterfly for several hours as it struggled to force its body through a little hole in its cocoon. After a while the butterfly seemed to stop making any progress. It was struggling so hard to get out! It looked like it couldn't break free! It looked desperate! It appeared as if it had gotten as far as it could, and it could go no further. The kindhearted man decided to help the butterfly. He got a pair of scissors and tweaked the cocoon to make a larger opening for the butterfly. The butterfly emerged easily without any struggle. But unlike any other butterflies in his garden, it had a swollen body with small and withered wings. The man was happy that he made the butterfly come out of its cocoon without much struggle. He continued to watch the butterfly, expecting that, at any moment, the wings would dry out, enlarge, and expand to support the swollen body, which would contract in time. Unfortunately, neither its wings expanded, nor the swollen body reduced. The butterfly crawled around with shriveled wings and swollen body, never able to fly all through its life. Although with good intention the man hindered the growth of the butterfly. The continuous effort from the butterfly to come out of its cocoon would force out the fluid stored in the body to convert it into the wings. What the man, in haste to help the butterfly, did not understand was that the restricting cocoon and the struggle were the key to the butterfly's beautiful body and wings. Sometimes struggles and challenges are exactly what we need to grow in our lives. Like, the struggle to get out of the cocoon gives butterflies its beautiful wings, struggles in our life makes us stronger and gives us wings to fly. Trying to "help it along," only hurt the outcome for the butterfly.

End of Day Reflection

Three Things I am grateful for:

1

2

3

What did I learn today?

1

2

3

TO DO TOMORROW

1

2

3

4

5

July 18
Cancer

"Everywhere you go, you will see people settling around you. They settle for average jobs, average relationships, average degrees, leading to average lives. I don't know about you, but I absolutely refuse to settle for anything less than my highest potential. I will not settle. I can't deal with having regrets in my life. I want to know what is in store for me, what opportunities lie ahead that I can take advantage of to continue to grow and be a better person. I want to ensure that I give everything I have to live my best life. I want to be constantly better than I was yesterday, last week, and last year. Constantly growing, raising the standards, and quality of my own life.".

Having this mindset, you will find that you will be leaving yourself completely open to new possibilities. Yes, you may have gotten stuck in the 9-5 rut of going to work and school but there is still time afterwards to do something you are passionate about or research other things that you want to learn about that are even outside of your career field. You are not limited to only learning the things you went to school for there is a whole world of a wealth of knowledge on different things. Go to your local library and pick a topic that you want to become knowledgeable about to strike conversations with people with. Always be continually learning and growing and challenging yourself, this is my challenge for you today.

End of Day Reflection

Five Things I am grateful for:

1

2

3

4

5

What did I learn today?

1

2

3

TO DO TOMORROW

1

2

3

4

5

July 19
Cancer

"Don't be afraid of being outnumbered. Eagles fly alone. Pigeons flock together."

Sometimes when doing something that no one else is doing you have to inherit an, "I don't care what you think attitude." By focusing on things that you love, or things that you have a passion or love of doing, sometimes it isn't a "money making activity" or it doesn't seem like it's going to "make you a lot of money" not everyone understands it. This is okay if it brings joy to your heart that matters more.

"Joy in heart is more profitable than money in the bank." - Charlie Chan in a Paris movie.

There are things that happen in our lives that are worth more than any amount of money. For me, even if a lot of people don't read or use this journal, what will bring me joy is even if I don't make money from selling this book, it brings me joy from those who benefited from doing this journal. It may make people smile realizing how much their lives improve from reading my books or who enjoy reading the books. Hearing people be happy about reading what I have to say makes more of an impact on my life then any amount of money earned. You have to do what makes you happy and be with those who make you happy otherwise you are living a lie, you aren't being true to yourself, and inside you will feel miserable. Misery loves company so be careful. You cannot focus on what people say about you when doing things you love, just keep going at it!

End of Day Reflection

Five Things I am grateful for:

1

2

3

4

5

What did I learn today?

1

2

3

TO DO TOMORROW

1

2

3

4

5

July 20 — Cancer

"You must make your dreams a priority in order for it to become your life." - Bob Proctor.

If your dreams and goals are not a priority, you will become a priority to someone else's dreams and goals, and no one will take you seriously. If you show others that you are working on something, and they are supportive, then you have good people in your life who will continue to support you and help you thrive in doing what makes you happy.

If you show others that you wish to accomplish these dreams and goals that you have, speaking it into existence and acting upon them, the world around you will conspire to help you achieve them provided you are surrounded by OQP (Only Quality people).

Share your dreams and goals with people in your life today. Have these honest conversations and see if anyone in your life has ideas of how you can accomplish them, maybe someone knows someone in their life who is already where you want to be in your life. The worst that can happen is they say they don't know anyone, but they will be supportive of you. If not, you can move forward, and they can stay in your life and be a support or watch you from the outside accomplish your dreams and goals.

True quality people will be there for you during the bad times and the good times.

End of Day Reflection

Five Things I am grateful for:

1

2

3

4

5

What did I learn today?

1

2

3

TO DO TOMORROW

1

2

3

4

5

"Time keeps moving forward, even when you aren't ready for it. The question is, what are you going to do with the time you have left?" - Anthony S. Parker

Our time is limited here on Earth. As I sit here today, I am reflecting on a dear friend of mine who I lost before he was supposed to. When thinking of this person, I can only think about everything that they are missing out on. Every opportunity that has happened around me and every new experience that has happened to me and that I cannot share with this person what's going on or ask for help or guidance. It hurts me to think about the opportunities that they would have had with their family to repair things had they stayed the course, and nothing happened to my friend whom I lost. This person was a great person, who made a difference in my life. I wouldn't have wished ill harm to come to them and I'd give anything to bring them back and talk to them. Perhaps you have lost a loved one in your life before they were supposed to leave this world? Perhaps this loss of a friend or family member has shown you how fragile our lives really are. How precious the time that we have left is here.

When coming to reflect on this reality here today, it has shown me that I need to push even harder at trying to accomplish my own dreams and goals. It has shown me that if someone around me shares their own dreams and goals with me that I want to help them reach that reality in their lifetime here as well. Life is too short to take things for granted and spend time with those that we love and to be honest with others and ourselves about our feelings for them at the time of occurrence when it happens that we come to these realities. If you live in regret and constant wonder of what is or what could have been you are also in effect preventing other opportunities to arise.

End of Day Reflection

Five Things I am grateful for:

1

2

3

4

5

What did I learn today?

1

2

3

TO DO TOMORROW

1

2

3

4

5

July 22
Cancer

"Anything is possible for those with a dream, a plan, and the determination and resolve to make it happen no matter what gets in your way!" - Anthony S. Parker

You cannot give up hope and trust in the process. We all face moments of hardship, of struggle, life happens around us and people leave our lives and come into our lives constantly and even sometimes our circumstances improve or strain dramatically. When you "roll with the punches in life" and you have that consistency of constantly working on your dreams and goals, eventually through hard work, it will happen. People may look down on you or say, "Why even try? or Just give up!" see that is the easy way out. Giving up and believing in that lie. You though, are unique, you are special, and what you do is significant to the lives of those around you. You may not realize what your dreams are or when your dreams and goals are going to happen but within this process, it will happen eventually. It may not be this month, next year, or five years from now, but if you keep working at what you are most passionate about, people will notice, and you will get there! We all have this gnawing at the back of our minds of negativity but don't succumb to these thoughts and feelings. Know you are stronger, and you will persevere!

Imagine yourself accomplishing your hopes and dreams and goals today. Imagine how you will feel, and what it will look like!

No matter what happens today, realize that YOU GOT THIS!

End of Day Reflection

Five Things I am grateful for:

1

2

3

4

5

What did I learn today?

1

2

3

TO DO TOMORROW

1

2

3

4

5

"When it rains, look for rainbows. When it's dark outside, look for stars." - Unknown

Be a positive person for those around you, even if things feel gloomy around you, when doing so, you will make a world of a difference! If you are having a bad day today, don't let anything bring you down today. Perhaps you are going through a rough time right now. Just know that you are not alone. You have family and friends around you to support you. Maybe today isn't meant to be your day today but make it your job to make someone else's day. Pay for someone's meal behind you today, (No matter the cost). Go to the grocery store and pay for someone's groceries behind you. Never stop spreading love, and kindness around you.

Maybe today you are having a good day, smile and contagiously spread it to those around you. Give people compliments.

End of Day Reflection

Five Things I am grateful for:

1

2

3

4

5

What did I learn today?

1

2

3

TO DO TOMORROW

1

2

3

4

5

July 24
Leo

"You learn nothing from life if you think that you are right all the time."

Saying "I know, I know" all the time will prevent people from telling you things that you may not know. Another thing to consider is, you may learn something from someone if you occasionally say, "You know, you may be right about this."

It's okay to tell people that the ideas that they have to offer are great ideas. Encourage those around you today. The inches we need are all around us, we are too slow, or too fast, or too short, or too tall, there is always a learning curve around us.

By being beams of encouragement to others around us, even in a home, school, or working environment, you are able to boost people's confidence around you and it will also encourage innovation and creativity as well.

End of Day Reflection

Five Things I am grateful for:

1

2

3

4

5

What did I learn today?

1

2

3

TO DO TOMORROW

1

2

3

4

5

July 25
Leo

"Nothing is permanent. Don't stress yourself too much because no matter how bad the situation seems now, it will change, it is a minor setback and it will improve, it will come to pass." - Anthony S Parker

Life happens. People change. People's decisions change. Financial situations arise. People lose their jobs. People die. Friends and family moved away.

Things are out of our control. We may wish for things to have happened differently or for things to have stayed the same, but we all learn and grow, and things happen.

Today we need to remember that yes, the struggle is real, we can make changes in our lives to improve our situations. Changing jobs to higher paying ones, getting more education to grow and qualify for more jobs, come up with side hustles to make more money. Go to therapy for the grieving process instead of muddling about our situations in alcohol or drugs. Do more to be better and grow with the struggles that have arisen around you. Don't let these temporary setbacks in your life tear at you.

End of Day Reflection

Five Things I am grateful for:

1

2

3

4

5

What did I learn today?

1

2

3

TO DO TOMORROW

1

2

3

4

5

July 26 - Leo

"Logic will get you from A to B. Imagination will take you everywhere else." - Albert Einstein

At the core this is so true. I can logically think about the books I am working on and think what logically makes sense chronologically, but when writing about make-believe lands and destinations, the story doesn't have a set path, and anything is possible!

When in reflection of this quote with regards to our own lives, yes logic is important in accomplishing what we most want to accomplish. However, when it comes to playing with children, they can activate our sense of creativity within us, and we can grow even more.

Spend some time with those of the younger generation today. Activate those thoughts of creativity and learn that anything is possible in potentiality in your own life!

End of Day Reflection

Five Things I am grateful for:

1

2

3

4

5

What did I learn today?

1

2

3

TO DO TOMORROW

1

2

3

4

5

July 27
Leo

"You don't know what you don't know."

There is so much wisdom out there today! There are people who I follow on YouTube and on social media who share so much wisdom on life and finances and motivational stuff that I follow. Since doing so, it has led to seeing things from different perspectives and has opened my mind up in ways in which I never would have thought possible. On YouTube look up "motivational videos."

Every morning I challenge you to listen to one of these a day. There are multiple accounts that come up with varying lengths, if it hasn't hurt me, it will help you!

End of Day Reflection

Five Things I am grateful for:

1

2

3

4

5

What did I learn today?

1

2

3

TO DO TOMORROW

1

2

3

4

5

July 28
Leo

"Your attitude, not your aptitude will determine your altitude." - Zig Ziglar.

The way in which you emotionally handle situations that you come across in your life will determine if you are fit for leadership or stressful job positions by those around you. It is better to be emotionally strong and be able to maturely talk about your feelings on things with others in a professional manner within a working environment.

Also, when dealing with life situations that arise, you can either take things with a victim mentality or you can say, "Let's overcome this and get others involved to help the situation improve."

End of Day Reflection

Five Things I am grateful for:

1

2

3

4

5

What did I learn today?

1

2

3

TO DO TOMORROW

1

2

3

4

5

July 29 — Leo

"Negativity is the cause of Stinkin Thinkin!" - Zig Ziglar

At the root of all negative energy, in the background is negative thinking. It's easy for everyone to think negatively about things that happen to us, or around us, it's so easy to complain but the only way to overcome this is to find the positive in all situations that we find ourselves in. Be optimistic about the opportunities that arise and for those around you. By doing this you will see a different perspective. When thinking about things in a positive light, we have the ability to evolve into even greater things. Think about this logic. Say someone says that they got fired from their job. You can immediately think and say, "What did you do wrong? How did you get fired?

Or alternatively you can say… What did you learn? Let's find you a better paying job that is going to be a better opportunity for you with better hours or that may be even closer for you to get to, or a better working environment.

You can immediately try putting someone down and tearing down their ego by telling them they are a failure and antagonize the situation or you can choose to change the thought process of those around you by encouraging them or helping them along to show them that life isn't over, and that there is hope and better opportunities knocking. By attacking someone's chances of having hope after this terrible event effectively you are not stimulating the idea of positivity by showing faith in them or encouraging them. Change isn't always a bad thing, sometimes it's for the better even if the environment that they were working in isn't good, or if the job wasn't helping you grow as a person, or they weren't paying you enough. All of these are circumstances that need to be considered as well.

I challenge you to constantly be encouraging and positively engaging in all your conversations in the future.

End of Day Reflection

Five Things I am grateful for:

1

2

3

4

5

What did I learn today?

1

2

3

TO DO TOMORROW

1

2

3

4

5

"A journey of a thousand miles begins with a single step."
- Lao Tzu

At the crux of having a dream, the one thing that is considered is what do I need to do to accomplish it? It can be daunting when realizing that to be a writer you must think of a plan and then map out the story line or come up with multiple drafts and do a lot of editing.

It's easy to say, "Yeah this is too much!" or "I'm giving up, it was a nice idea, but I can't do it."

You MUST take the first step and continue to push on. When realizing the steps needed to overcome the composition of life's difficulties, don't let the steps bring you to believe the lie that it's not possible. Believe that it is possible and take these first steps and create a habit daily that will help you to accomplish your dreams and goals. Eventually you will see that finish line and it will be a breath of fresh air. Remember to start these steps today if you haven't already.

This also means that when it comes to needing to get things done, do not procrastinate in doing them.

"Waiting for tomorrow is a waste of today." - Charlie Chan in Egypt movie, 1935.

End of Day Reflection

Five Things I am grateful for:

1

2

3

4

5

What did I learn today?

1

2

3

TO DO TOMORROW

1

2

3

4

5

July 31 — Leo

"If you want a wild bird to sing, do not put him in a cage."
- Charlie Chan in London movie, 1934

This quote was said when a Sargent wanted to arrest someone for trespassing during a murder investigation when the Detective Charlie Chan knew this person was possibly not even guilty for the murder in question. The detective had said if you want the bird "Murderer" to sing basically give him the free reign to hang himself.

This was an interesting quote that I was thinking about the other day when I was thinking about how life is. Sometimes we put ourselves in cages of averages or "normal day to day activities" without giving ourselves free reign to change how our lives are. We feel that if we reach outside of our comfort zone, we will not be able to handle it. I mean I was thinking you know, I work from home, but I can access work from anywhere on my laptop. What if I went to the cafe to work instead of staying at home? How would life be different? How else would I have the opportunity to meet others? Who else would I have an impact on as a person if I decided to change it up a bit? We need to reach outside of these cages of comfort that we come across in life to stretch our wings and grow into stronger birds. I think the winds of changes in our lives would push us in different directions and we would grow so much more and faster as a person by being open-minded to change.

End of Day Reflection

Five Things I am grateful for:

1

2

3

4

5

What did I learn today?

1

2

3

TO DO TOMORROW

1

2

3

4

5

August 1
Leo

"Sometimes there are no words, no clever quotes to neatly sum up what's happened that day, sometimes the day just ends."

It can be stressful going through the daily day to day activities of school, work, dinner, soccer games, and schedules of the rest of the family in a week. At the end of it all we just want to relax and decompress from it all and we are just left at the end of the day just sitting down and taking a deep breath from the stresses of the day and we just forget to just appreciate these moments. Life can be overwhelming and hectic but also remember that time keeps passing us by and we cannot control it all, but you can take a step back and enjoy it all. Today, appreciate the small things around you.

Things to work on this month: Work on your Ego, if you have a big ego, it's okay to cut it back a few notches. Try not to be too dominating of others around you. People have their own values, opinions, and ways in which they like to do things and if they are indeed what you think is the wrong way to do things, sometimes you must let people fall in order, so they learn. Being too controlling of people and things going on around you can be off putting and it will make people scared to make decisions on their own. Work on not being too Vain and cut back on showing off too much to others if this is something you find yourself doing. Trying to get the approval of others can be difficult but no one likes it when someone is showing off.

End of Day Reflection

Five Things I am grateful for:

1

2

3

4

5

What did I learn today?

1

2

3

TO DO TOMORROW

1

2

3

4

5

August 2
Leo

"In the eighteenth century, there was something that spread across Europe and eventually made its way to America called Puerperal Fever, also known as the Black death of child bed. Basically, what was happening was women were giving birth and they would die within 48 hours of giving birth. This Black Death of Childbirth was the ravage of Europe and it got worse, and worse, and worse, over the course of a century. In some hospitals it was as high as 70% of women giving birth who would die because of giving birth. But this was the renaissance, this was the time of empirical data and science, and we had thrown away things like tradition and mysticism. These were men of science, and these were doctors. These doctors and men of science wanted to study and find the reason for this black death of childbirth. So, they got to work studying the corpses of the women who had died. In the morning they would do the autopsies, and, in the afternoon, they would deliver babies and finish their rounds. It wasn't until somewhere in the middle of the eighteenth century that Doctor Oliver Windell Holmes, father of supreme court justice Oliver Wendell Holmes realized that all these doctors conducting autopsies in the morning weren't washing their hands before they delivered babies in the afternoon. He pointed it out and said, "Guys, you're the problem. They ignored him and called him crazy for 30 years. Until finally somebody realized that if they simply washed their hands that it would go away and that's exactly what happened. When they started sterilizing their instruments and washing their hands the black death of the child bed disappeared. The lesson here is sometimes you're the problem. We have seen this happen all too recently with our new men of science and empirical studiers and men of finance who are smarter than the rest of us until the thing collapsed and they blamed everyone else except themselves. My point is to take accountability for your actions. You can take all the credit in the world for the things you do right, if you also take responsibility for the things, you do wrong. It must be a balanced equation. You don't get it one way and not the other. You get to take credit when you also take accountability." - Simon Sinek.

End of Day Reflection

Five Things I am grateful for:

1

2

3

4

5

What did I learn today?

1

2

3

TO DO TOMORROW

1

2

3

4

5

August 3
Leo

"A few months ago, I stayed at the Four Seasons in Las Vegas. It is a wonderful hotel. The reason it is a wonderful hotel is not because of the fancy beds, any hotel can go out and buy fancy beds, no the reason it is a wonderful hotel is because of the people who work there. If you walk past someone in the four seasons and they say hello to you. You get the feeling that they wanted to say hello to you. It's not that somebody told them that you have to say hello to all the customers, to say hello to all the guests. Right? You feel that they care. Now in their lobby they have a coffee stand. One afternoon I went to buy a cup of coffee and there was a barista by the name of Noah who was serving me. Noah was fantastic. He was friendly and fun, and he was engaging with me. I had so much fun buying a cup of coffee, I think I gave 100% tip. He was a wonderful person. So as is my nature, I asked him, Do you like your job? " Without skipping a beat, he says, "I love my job." So, I followed up and said, "What is it that the four seasons is doing, that would make you say to me, "I love my job." Without skipping a beat, he said, "Throughout the day, managers will walk past me, and ask me, "How are you doing? and Is there anything that I need to do my job better?" He says, "Not just my manager, any manager." Then he said something magical, "I also work at Caesars Palace. At Caesars Palace the managers are trying to make sure that you are doing everything right. They catch us when we do things wrong. He said "When I go to work there, I like to keep my head under the radar and just get through the day so I can get my paycheck. He says, "Here at the four seasons, I feel I can be myself." If we create the right environment we will get people like Noah at the four seasons, if we create the wrong environment, we will get people like Noah at Caesars Palace." -Simon Sinek

From the outside looking in, you can see how the different styles of management work on the employees, Micromanagement VS Macro Management. When micromanaging and telling the employee constantly what do to do and constantly criticizing their abilities, it shows them you have a lack of trust in their abilities, and it will not only create toxic "walking on eggshells" type of environment but it will also make it more difficult for the employees to be themselves and create a more warming environment. Trying to be a manager that engages with the employees and customers and helps them out as much as they need allows for a more productive and energetic type of shift for everyone. If you are or aren't at a leadership type of position, I recommend you read, Five Levels of Leadership by John Maxwell as I found it mind opening and instructive.

End of Day Reflection

Five Things I am grateful for:

1

2

3

4

5

What did I learn today?

1

2

3

TO DO TOMORROW

1

2

3

4

5

August 4
Leo

"So, a friend of mine and I went for a run in Central Park, the road runner's organization. On the weekends, they host races. It's very common at the end of the race they will have a sponsor who will give away something, apples or bagels or something. On this day, they had bagels at the end of the race, and they had picnic tables set up and on one side there was a group of volunteers and on the table, there were boxes of bagels and on the other side there were runners all lined up waiting to get a free bagel. So I said to my friend and said, "Let's get a bagel." and he said "Eh, the line is too long." and I said, "Free bagel." and he said, "I don't want to wait in line." and I was like, "FREE BAGEL!" and he said, "Nah, it's too long." and that's when I realized that there are two ways to see the world. Some people see the thing that they want, and some people see the thing that prevents them from getting the thing that they want. I could only see the bagels and he could only see the line. So, I walked up to the line, and I leaned in between two people and put my hand in the box and pulled out two bagels and no one got mad at me. Because the rule is, you can go after whatever you want. You just cannot deny anyone else to go after whatever they want. Now I had to sacrifice my choice. I didn't get to choose which bagel I got, I got whatever I pulled out, I just didn't have to wait in line. So, the point is you don't have to wait in line, you don't have to do it the way everybody else has done it. You can do it your way, you can break the rules, you just can't get in the way of someone else getting what they want."

- Simon Sinek

End of Day Reflection

Five Things I am grateful for:

1

2

3

4

5

What did I learn today?

1

2

3

TO DO TOMORROW

1

2

3

4

5

August 5
Leo

"No Matter how dark the moment, love, and hope are always possible."- George Chakiris

When in the moment of stress and struggles in your life, always remember to have hope in the seemingly impossible around you and love others that are around you even tighter. It's during these moments that we grab onto people who are around us even tighter that we can find the strength and overcome even more when we have people/ a support system to be there for us.

Create and strengthen your support system and spend time with others that are in your life, grab a coffee or lunch and be there for people today, they may need you whether they realize it or not.

End of Day Reflection

Five Things I am grateful for:

1

2

3

4

5

What did I learn today?

1

2

3

TO DO TOMORROW

1

2

3

4

5

August 6
Leo

"We all die. The goal isn't to live forever, the goal is to create something that will." - Chuck Palahnik

"In other eyes, my life is the essence of success, but aside from work, I have a little joy. And in the end, wealth is just a fact of life to which I am accustomed. At this moment, lying on the bed, sick, and remembering all my life, I realize that all my recognition and wealth that I have is meaningless in the face of imminent death. You can hire someone to drive a car for you, make money for you - but you cannot rent someone to carry the disease for you. One can find material things, but there is one thing that cannot be found when it is lost - life. Your true inner happiness does not come from the material things of this world. Whether you are flying first class, or economy class - if the plane crashes, you crash with it. No one wants to die. Even people who want to go to heaven don't want to die to get there. and yet death is the destination that we all share. No one has ever escaped it. and that is as it should be, because Death is very likely the single best invention in life. It is life's change agent. It clears out the old to make room for the new. Right now, the new is you, but someday not too long from now, you will gradually become old and be cleared away. Sorry to be so dramatic but it is quite true." - Steve Jobs

Today don't take it for granted, take risks of what you think will make you happy, change things up a bit, live for you not for anyone else. Take an afternoon off this week and sit in a park and read a book by some water. Or take a trip to the mountains or the beach, a place that would relax you and enjoy life because we don't know when our last day on this Earth will be. Take time to spend some time with others around you.

End of Day Reflection

Five Things I am grateful for:

1

2

3

4

5

What did I learn today?

1

2

3

TO DO TOMORROW

1

2

3

4

5

August 7
Leo

"Life is not about waiting for the storms to pass; it's about learning how to dance in the rain."

A lot of times when we are down and out in life, we give up or we start thinking negatively about our circumstances and we start trying to feel like we have fallen victim to our situations. I have to say that through experience I can say that it is within these times that we must learn to "roll with the punches" that hit us and learn to weather through the storms of dramas that occur around us and learn how to cope and learn and take the best out of these situations. Crying over milk that has already been spilt doesn't resolve the issue. The question to ask ourselves is, what are we going to do about it? What are you going to do now to get yourself back up on your own two feet to walk through the waves? What can you do about things right now? Is there anyone around you who you can ask for help? Are there any resources around you that you can go to for help? Sometimes we just need to suck up our pride and ask for help even though that isn't easy, these are difficult but meaningful learning curves that we can overcome and use to handle coping with challenges that arise in our lives.

End of Day Reflection

Five Things I am grateful for:

1

2

3

4

5

What did I learn today?

1

2

3

TO DO TOMORROW

1

2

3

4

5

August 8
Leo

"Life is like an onion, you peel it off one layer at a time, and sometimes you weep." - Carl Sandburg

When learning the story of what someone has been through sometimes though inspirational and powerful, we cry when hearing what they have had to overcome to get to where they are today. People are so strong to overcome a lot and adapt to what is happening around them. We go through difficult and seemingly impossible feats of struggle and pain and suffering and it's amazing to hear stories of how simple acts of kindness can go a long way in the face of darkness in someone else's life. People always need help but sometimes aren't always able to ask for it when needed. When you see these acts of kindness occurring sometimes, we weep, and our hearts go out to those who are in need.

End of Day Reflection

Five Things I am grateful for:

1

2

3

4

5

What did I learn today?

1

2

3

TO DO TOMORROW

1

2

3

4

5

August 9
Leo

"Today, is the tomorrow that you were worried about yesterday."

This is so true, you have made it through today so far and you are still alive and breathing, just another thing to be grateful for. We ought not to take life for granted and we can learn and grow from many experiences that have happened around us. Sometimes we get worried for no reason about things that could or might happen and yet these worries may not be anything to have needed to be worried about yesterday. It's not always worth worrying over the things that in life we have no control over. You are strong, you are an overcomer, and you are built with a strong foundation of fortitude and courage and bravery. Take pride in your achievements of everything that you have accomplished up to today. No one is holding you back from accomplishing so many great things this year and you are doing it, you are making it happen, and you are striving through experiences that you never thought were possible to overcome. _Today I stand here to tell you that you are a magnet for positive energy, and you are going to overcome so much this year! HAVE COURAGE! Be Brave and nothing will stand in your way.

End of Day Reflection

Five Things I am grateful for:

1

2

3

4

5

What did I learn today?

1

2

3

TO DO TOMORROW

1

2

3

4

5

August 10
Leo

"Life in a way is like a strategic chess game, one false move and you may be done before you know it.

When things come up in our lives, we need to reflect on things like vision boards and observe them daily to come back to the path of following our reason why we have our dreams and goals and things that we hope to accomplish. Reaching out to the dreams and grabbing them even when we are scared to accomplish them is important and when you have these feelings of fear or uneasiness it's okay to grab hold onto things and people who are around you tighter.

End of Day Reflection

Five Things I am grateful for:

1

2

3

4

5

What did I learn today?

1

2

3

TO DO TOMORROW

1

2

3

4

5

August 11
Leo

"A book has so much power to it that just reading it can change your life and very possibly your opinion/perspective/mindset. Be careful of the literature that you bring into your life."

By reading a good book you can get lost in a world that you have never known or been to. You will learn of people and places and cultures that will open your mindset and help you possibly see more things in a positive light.

End of Day Reflection

Five Things I am grateful for:

1

2

3

4

5

What did I learn today?

1

2

3

TO DO TOMORROW

1

2

3

4

5

August 12
Leo

"Follow your heart, listen to your inner voice, stop caring about what others think." - Roy T Bennett

At the end of the day, you must be happy with your life and life decisions. No one else should be living your life for you as an 18-year-old adult. As an adult at this age, you are responsible for your own actions and inactions. You must ensure that you are doing what you most want to do in life to accomplish your own hopes, dreams, and goals, regardless of what others think or say that they want you to do. As an adult you can do or not do what you most want to do. You are not stuck in your situations. Sure, you may feel like you have been dealt some bad cards, but this doesn't mean you are stuck. You ought to do what you can do with the cards you have in life that are given to you. But do so in a responsible manner. What I mean is, if you choose to stay up late partying or socializing when you know you have a huge exam to do the next morning or have prior commitments, it's very important to prioritize responsibly. In school we aren't taught about money and nor are we taught about what I call "adulting scenarios" some of us are coddled by our parents so when things hit the fan, and something happens to our parents we aren't aware of the life of bills and work life necessary to sustain monthly bills and it all comes as a shock to us/kids/parents. As parents in their teenage years or even around the age of 12-14 is the perfect age to let them be aware of what's involved in adult life like this, so they are prepared for life.

End of Day Reflection

Five Things I am grateful for:

1

2

3

4

5

What did I learn today?

1

2

3

TO DO TOMORROW

1

2

3

4

5

August 13
Leo

"Appreciate those who do not give up on you."

- Unknown

At the end of the day, the support system of people that you are surrounding yourself with is going to help you with the results that you are expecting in your life, whether they are positive or negative people, it's just like the saying goes, whether you think you can or whether you think you can't both are normally right. Are you envisioning that you are a dying person inside or a living person inside. Both are correct whether you see this in a perspective of you are nearing death's door or that you are living and breathing right now to the best of your ability. Being and remaining positive is extremely crucial to trying to achieve your goals, dreams, and to be successful. Never give someone else the satisfaction of being correct in bringing you down. Never let the negative energy of those that happen to be around you influence whether you try or give up. Don't give up on your dreams.

End of Day Reflection

Five Things I am grateful for:

1

2

3

4

5

What did I learn today?

1

2

3

TO DO TOMORROW

1

2

3

4

5

"Hope is being able to see that there is a light despite all of the darkness." - Desmond Tutu

It is easy to feel alone and vulnerable in the darkness, but you must be strong and persevere. Yes, "the struggle in life is real" as I always say, but to see you defy all odds and to overcome all that is placed before you will inspire those around you. It's the journey to finding success and accomplishing the goals that matters more, these are the reasons that make both accomplishing and wanting the success that much more worth it in the end. When you fight for something that you are passionate about you have the reason that is worth fighting for. This strengthens you and those around you. Sure, everyone in the end will be proud of you for your accomplishments and maybe even possibly jealous but, to be honest, they will not understand the sacrifices and the uphill battles you had to fight to be where you end up unless they traveled the path with you towards the same goals. Within that darkness is the ability to see that through hope and faith you can accomplish great things in life.

End of Day Reflection

Five Things I am grateful for:

1

2

3

4

5

What did I learn today?

1

2

3

TO DO TOMORROW

1

2

3

4

5

"Change your thoughts and you will change your life."

I am sure if you have been using the journal every day and writing at night the things you are most grateful for, your perspective on life and those that are around you have probably changed and you see things and people in a different way then you did in the beginning of the year, and this is absolutely normal.

End of Day Reflection

Five Things I am grateful for:

1

2

3

4

5

What did I learn today?

1

2

3

TO DO TOMORROW

1

2

3

4

5

August 16
Leo

"You cannot control what happens to you, but you can control your attitude towards what happens to you, and in that, you will be mastering change rather than allowing it to master you." - Brian Tracy

It is natural that when things happen around us, we tend to emotionally react to things first without considering the thoughts and feelings of those around us first and without putting ourselves in the shoes of those around us. When in the moment try to remain positive and remember that even the best laid plans go awry. We cannot control everything around us so if you give up on trying to control things you can learn to appreciate when things happen around you smoothly and by staying positive you can begin to influence everyone around you positively as well. Also keep in mind you can speak into existence the things that you would like to happen around you and perhaps the world around you can help conspire to help you achieve it.

End of Day Reflection

Five Things I am grateful for:

1

2

3

4

5

What did I learn today?

1

2

3

TO DO TOMORROW

1

2

3

4

5

August 17
Leo

"Your current reality or your current life, is a result of the thoughts you have been thinking, and your actions you have or have not been acting upon. All of that will totally change as you begin to change your thoughts and your feelings and start putting the actions into your dreams and goals."

Stay in the positive mindset today and you will not let anything bring you down permanently. Sure you may be struggling but you aren't going to be struggling forever because you are also working towards your dreams and goals and even if you aren't currently doing what is necessary, get back into it, get back into completing these goals and dreams of yours and you will find that purpose and it isn't too late, you may have taken a brief break from accomplishing what you need to but that doesn't mean that you are going to be still stuck in the same position all the time, you eventually will get to where you need to be and I KNOW that you have it in you to do whatever it takes to bring you from where you are to where you need to be, you just need to DO THE ACTION necessary to do it. No one woke up today being told that today or tomorrow is going to be easy, but you can make it easier on yourself by doing today what others aren't willing to accomplish for the week. Look ahead constantly, think about what you can do to help others, what you can do to reach your goals easier. Maybe you need the help of someone that you know to accomplish your dream and goal, find out what their dream and goal is and see if you can help them accomplish their dream and goal so they can help you. Relying on others' help or support is not a failure, it is merely a building block necessary to get to where you want to be in life. Sometimes you just need to reach out to your goals and dreams and open the doors of opportunity and grab it. Only you can control what you do or don't do today. Only you are in control of how you handle certain situations that may arise today. Something is telling me to tell you today that YOU CAN DO THIS! You need to know that you are loved and that you have a great support system of people who care about you around you. Don't be afraid to be yourself and don't be afraid to ask for help. The worst that they can say is, "No." Which is probably already in your head now, so it's time to let the world surprise you! Sometimes even a "No" isn't a complete, "No" it's sometimes a "not right now."

End of Day Reflection

Five Things I am grateful for:

1

2

3

4

5

What did I learn today?

1

2

3

TO DO TOMORROW

1

2

3

4

5

"Surround yourself with dreamers, and the doers, and the believers, and thinkers. Most of all surround yourself with those who see greatness within you, even when you don't see it within yourself. "

By surrounding yourself with those who are supportive of you and your hopes, dreams, goals, and who are there for you during the good and bad times of your life are the truest of all people. By having this type of support system in your life you can overcome anything that is in front of you that you may face. Trust in these people and you will go far. Yes, there are those who are only going to be there for you during your successes and the good times who use and take advantage of you, but there are also those in your life who will be there for you during the bad times, when you are struggling. These people are even going to be there for you when you may not feel like you have the support of anyone else in the world around you there. There are those who are going to be there for you no matter what because they believe in you or what you stand for and what you do for others around you. These are the people who will walk through the darkness holding your hand in guidance and support until you find the light. THESE are the people that you need to also remember during the good times to celebrate your little life's victories with. These are the people who are most deserving of your support during their bad times.

End of Day Reflection

Five Things I am grateful for:

1

2

3

4

5

What did I learn today?

1

2

3

TO DO TOMORROW

1

2

3

4

5

August 19
Leo

"Whenever you find yourself doubting how far you can go, just remember how far you have come. Remember, everything you have been through that you have had to face, all the battles you have won, and all the fears that you have overcome to get to where you are today. You are stronger than you realize, and you have a resilience within you that will outweigh anything that places itself in front of you!"

It is easier to say that "I can't do this." "It's not possible" "I am going to fail" or "I am not good enough" but to do this is not an option, to give in to these thoughts and feelings leads to failure. Sometimes we must remember that to do things the easier route is not always the best route morally or otherwise. I think our aim in life should be 9876543210. 9 glasses of water, 8 hours of sleep, seeing 7 wonders of the world, 6 figure income, 5 days of work per week, 4-wheeled car, 3-bedroom house, 2 furry children, 1 sweetheart, and 0 tensions.

End of Day Reflection

Five Things I am grateful for:

1

2

3

4

5

What did I learn today?

1

2

3

TO DO TOMORROW

1

2

3

4

5

August 20
Leo

"Be true to yourself - It doesn't make sense to try to become someone you are not to please those around you, even you "special person" in your life, the best thing to be is your genuine self. If you are not true to yourself, you will be miserable and drive yourself crazy."

Everyone worries about what others think, in reality nobody really actually cares about how you are. Everyone worries about the thoughts and feelings and opinions of others so much so that they forget that in life, the main goal is to find love, purpose, and your own sense of happiness. If you just focus your choices based on these three life foundations, you will find your own version of yourself within successes and things you are passionate about. Always ask yourself, is this decision I'm about to make going to make me happy? Is this decision that I want to make going to fulfill a life purpose? And lastly, is the decision going to be something that I will find love for or with, or going to be something that I'm truly passionate about?

End of Day Reflection

Five Things I am grateful for:

1

2

3

4

5

What did I learn today?

1

2

3

TO DO TOMORROW

1

2

3

4

5

August 21
Leo

"If they truly love you, it is because they were attracted to your "natural traits.""

Everyone worries about what others think about them because of their appearance first and foremost and yes, it's kind of cliche to say love is based on what's inside that matters more but it's true. Only true unconditional love is based on what someone's heart is and their own inner talents. I have found that the most amazing looking person on the outside can have the most terrible inside personality and heart and you in the end could be treated like shit.

End of Day Reflection

Five Things I am grateful for:

1

2

3

4

5

What did I learn today?

1

2

3

TO DO TOMORROW

1

2

3

4

5

August 22
Leo

"If you aren't happy or if there is something in your life that you don't like, do something about it, change it. It's your life, and you are in complete control of it."

There are times when we feel like we don't have a choice in the things going on around us, whether it's the job we are in or the classes that we are taking or the school or school district we are in. But in reality, you aren't stuck being where you are. You can always change things from where you are to where you want to be and what you want to do.

End of Day Reflection

Five Things I am grateful for:

1

2

3

4

5

What did I learn today?

1

2

3

TO DO TOMORROW

1

2

3

4

5

August 23
Virgo

> "I don't care how scared you are. What you need to do is make bold decisions."

Right now, you've gotta begin training yourself to act. You've got to begin training yourself to act. You've gotta begin training yourself to take chances, to put yourself at risk, to risk embarrassment to know that you are possibly going to fail. That's the only way that you are ever going to get the things that you want out of life. All of us want to do something extraordinary. All of us want to be great. All of us have something inside of ourselves that if we knew we couldn't fail, we would pursue that. And that question - What would you do if you knew you couldn't fail? That question - is one of the most important questions that you can ever ask yourself. The reality is you can do that thing. But you are going to have to be bold, you are going to have to have the courage and be brave. You are going to have to be willing to take the chances. You are going to have to be willing to put everything at risk because it is worth it in the end. The problem is, the reason that people playthings so safely is because it's so comfortable there, it is so easy, and every day passes by without you even noticing. That terrifying passage of time, but once you realize that this is it, that this is the one shot you have, what does it really matter if you fail? What does it matter what other people think? The only thing that really matters is what you think about yourself and let me tell you right now, that self-belief is going to be built on knowing that you are willing to try. It isn't going to be built on whether you succeed, it's built on whether you tried, or whether you showed up. In that moment, that thing that you rehearsed in your head 1000 times where you hope you will be courageous. Be courageous, - know that about yourself. Know that every moment is that moment. Sometimes it's so small it seems imperceptible. It seems like it's not a moment or courage, but every moment is a moment for courage. Every moment right now is your chance to act, to strive to be and to do the thing you were afraid you wouldn't be able to do. But to do the thing that you know could lead you where you want to go to do the thing you know you could do if you knew you couldn't fail. But courage is doing it - even though you might fail.

End of Day Reflection

Five Things I am grateful for:

1

2

3

4

5

What did I learn today?

1

2

3

TO DO TOMORROW

1

2

3

4

5

August 24
Virgo

"Be courageous, Be bold, strike now." - Tom Bilyeu, Fearless motivation.

 Act on your intentions and you never know how far you will go. If you fear the unknown and you lack the ability to act on your beliefs, goals, and dreams, you won't get very far. Have courage no matter what negativity may be running in your head against this idea of going for it. You don't allow negative people around you, so don't be negative to yourself. Know in your mind that you can accomplish whatever you set your goals to no matter who you know, what your background is like or what you think you can or can't do. Don't let you talk yourself out of what you think you can or can't do. Have the will power to withstand any struggle or pain or difficult thing that you are going through. You cannot allow yourself to feel embarrassed about the things of the past, the goal is to move forward no matter the cost and no matter the burden you think you feel you are. You matter, and your success, health and future depend on it.

End of Day Reflection

Five Things I am grateful for:

1

2

3

4

5

What did I learn today?

1

2

3

TO DO TOMORROW

1

2

3

4

5

August 25
Virgo

"Sometimes I feel defeated. But I don't drown in the feeling of failure too long because I look for what life is trying to teach me. In failure, there is always a lesson. You may be one lesson away from changing your life. If you've failed or made a mistake, there is a hidden lesson in it that may bring you success. When I feel disappointed in myself, I tell myself, it's good that I feel this BAD… feeling bad will make me NEVER make this mistake again…. It's just our brains telling us… "don't do this again, ok? When people aren't okay with the education system, you must go to school, but then after school, instead of partying or going to the bars, create opportunities for yourself outside of school. People complain why do I have to go to school? Why do I have to go to college? But they don't do anything after school that will create an opportunity, so they don't have to go to school. People complain and then go out or party after school, that is not right. If you are going to complain, go create an opportunity for yourself. If you go to college and you realize that you don't like it, and think it's a waste of time, then go do something after class that is beneficial for your future. If you are going to drop out, you should at least have something that has potential to be a success. For me, everyone has their own path to success. The most famous Samurai in the world named Musashi said, "There is more than one path to the top of a mountain." I think that everything must be connected. For example, if our goal in life is to help people, our significant other must want to help people, our friends must also want to help people. What we enjoy doing can help people. The moment that everything is connected, you will begin to enjoy yourself at every moment. You will also be getting closer to success at every moment. When you are with your friends you will talk and laugh, go watch a movie, but after the movie you will talk about, "What can we do to help people?" When I am alone and want to learn something new, or when I am taking action, it is fun. I don't separate anything, relationships, friends, or work. Everything is connected to my life's purpose and it's fun, I never feel like I'm working. I feel like I'm always enjoying myself, and I want others to experience this." - Sean Buranahiran

End of Day Reflection

Five Things I am grateful for:

1

2

3

4

5

What did I learn today?

1

2

3

TO DO TOMORROW

1

2

3

4

5

August 26
Virgo

"If you want to be successful, sometimes you have to study and reflect on the lives of others who are on the same path to success that you wish to be on, read and research and reflect on the path that you may choose to take and be willing with an open mind to learn and grow of those that have been great leaders, athletes, and businessmen who have wisdom that may help to also improve your mindset."

We all want to have what I call the "Ah ha" moment in our lives, the moment when we find out our purpose and our reason "why" we want to be successful, and "why" we want to do what we wish to do to be successful and what will make us happy. Two moments happen to us in our lives that are very important, the day we are born, and then the day we learn why. Reflect on your reasons why you want to be successful and what will make you happy in life today. Let that motivate you and push you to the next level every day, let it wake you up every morning before the alarm clock. Be excited for tomorrow!

End of Day Reflection

Five Things I am grateful for:

1

2

3

4

5

What did I learn today?

1

2

3

TO DO TOMORROW

1

2

3

4

5

August 27

"Attitude is everything. The very first level to success in life is seeing it, like it's clear to you, and you know exactly what you want, you know exactly when you want it. You know exactly what success tastes like, you know what it looks like, and you know what success will smell like, before you really blow up, blow up, you literally have it in the palm of your hand without having it. You gotta know what it looks like because if you don't' you are going to compromise, and the problem is you are not intentional and deliberate. You gotta be consistent from Mon to Fri and not just hope it happens to you. Your success has everything to do with how you prepare, how you think, what time you wake up, what time you go to sleep, how you exercise. You must be willing to do and follow through with whatever it takes and whatever sacrifices that you need to make to be successful." - Eric Thomas

The way you think and the way in which the story is running in your head on how things are becomes self-taught if you are not careful with what you are thinking about and assuming how you think people are. A lot of times our self-thought becomes self-taught, so we are self-teaching ourselves negativity and sometimes we assume people think the worst of us when in fact this is not necessarily the case. It's like what Eric Thomas was talking about, "Your success has everything to do with how you prepare, how you think, what time you wake up, what time you go to sleep, how you exercise" Your habits and routine can determine your outcome of success.

End of Day Reflection

Five Things I am grateful for:

1

2

3

4

5

What did I learn today?

1

2

3

TO DO TOMORROW

1

2

3

4

5

August 28
Virgo

"Each bad experience in life should be viewed as an opportunity whether it is a new lesson learned or an opportunity for a new start."

We grow from the experiences we go through and the experiences of those around us. We see what others struggle with around us and sometimes we wish that we could control that we ourselves don't go through the experiences of those around us as well. Take each day at a time and hold on tight to these lessons and change the way in which you think about these situations.

End of Day Reflection

Five Things I am grateful for:

1

2

3

4

5

What did I learn today?

1

2

3

TO DO TOMORROW

1

2

3

4

5

August 29
Virgo

"Passion is the Genesis of genius, most people run out of fuel, and they get tired, burned out, and they are around someone so much and they take things for granted. Hunger is the number one factor that pushes people forward." - Tony Robbins

At the of the day, if you aren't hungry for the success, and you don't want it badly enough and your reasoning as to why you want to become successful isn't strong enough, it isn't going to push you to that next level, it isn't going to make you want the change enough to let it become you. It's cute to say you want to be happy, healthy, successful, and making money doing what you are passionate about but if you don't put forth the action necessary in order to accomplish said dreams, goals, and aspirations, you won't get past that first step and you will allow yourself to wallow in self-pity, and depression, and fulfill other people's dreams and goals. You do what makes you happy, regardless of what other people think and say about you. What they say and think shouldn't matter so long as you are trying your best in doing what you believe that you can accomplish if you follow the steps necessary to accomplish them. Dream and follow through with the actions, and you will see the world change around you before your very eyes. Don't let fear deter you but rather let it fuel you to push further faster! Gas is expensive so don't waste it going the wrong direction or wallowing in self-pity being stationary on that road to success. PUSH YOURSELF! If you aren't happy with where you are and what you are doing in your life, you need to make the changes necessary to find that happiness again and find that sense of purpose.

End of Day Reflection

Five Things I am grateful for:

1

2

3

4

5

What did I learn today?

1

2

3

TO DO TOMORROW

1

2

3

4

5

August 30
Virgo

"Tomorrow is promised to no one - Live each day as if it were your last."

We don't know when our last day will be or when we will take our last breath but living to the best of our abilities trying to be better than we were yesterday is a great way to start.

"I read something this morning that somewhere in your childhood, you and your friends went outside to play for the last time, and nobody knew it. It seems to me that many of life's last times allude to us. We aren't aware of our pages turning, our chapters ending. The phases of life essentially blend into each other. One fading into the next in fact we don't realize to the extent that things have changed until we peer back over our shoulders. See life is happening to us now, while we hope, pray, and plan for better days, 99.9% of life consists of the time that exists between the so-called pivotal life events, the average the ordinary the things we pay no mind to, what's the relevance? Why does this matter? Because the sun coming up every morning is life. Pouring your coffee is life, small talk with your family, the music you are listening to, the art you are painting, the workouts at the gym, they are life, and not in a you better be grateful or else kind of way, but if you don't understand this, contentment will be hard to capture kind of way. I have a lot of favorite quotes but this one tops them all. The Character Andy Bernard from the Office, he says, "I wish there was a way to realize that you are in the good old days before you actually left them." I can't get over how this statement proves itself to be true repeatedly. It's not until we peer over our shoulders before we realize how lucky we were how much fun we had, how much the time meant." – Eddie Pinero

End of Day Reflection

Five Things I am grateful for:

1

2

3

4

5

What did I learn today?

1

2

3

TO DO TOMORROW

1

2

3

4

5

August 31
Virgo

"Never forget to tell someone you love them - you may not get a second chance."

I have never regretted letting my feelings be known to someone that I truly care for. Yes, sometimes it's unrequited love but there are times when the feelings are mutual, and that fire of love burns brightly in the hearts of those that share those same feelings. You won't know how they feel until you reveal and realize your own true feelings and they may feel the same way. There is only one way to find out and only time will tell if it's meant to be by getting to know that person.

Spend time with your significant other today, create memories with those you love around you. Don't forget to take plenty of pictures!

End of Day Reflection

Five Things I am grateful for:

1

2

3

4

5

What did I learn today?

1

2

3

TO DO TOMORROW

1

2

3

4

5

September 1
Virgo

"When you are looking for your "special person" remember, no one is perfect."

Human Perfection isn't possible, even if it were, it's certainly not a reasonable goal to attain to find happiness and there are going to be times when things aren't good and that's okay. The point that should matter more is overcoming the difficult times with our loved ones so that the best of times is even better and worth it. We all have times in our lives when we struggle to be the people we wish to become, and to find that version of ourselves that we wish to be for others and it's okay. Having emotions and being an emotional person is okay no matter the gender of the person. If we weren't emotional beings, we would be less human and more robots in my opinion. Within the realm of a relationship, it is my own personal belief as well that loving someone unconditionally for who they are is a trait that is meaningful and can lead to an even more enduring love with a strong foundation.

Things to work on this month: Work on not being a perfectionist and too obsessive, also work on not being too critical of others. Lastly try not to pay too much attention to insignificant details. Yes, there are times when details matter but if you worry about trying to perfect other people's imperfections you may push them away. Try working on being more positive with people around you and find gratitude in the small things going on around you.

End of Day Reflection

Five Things I am grateful for:

1

2

3

4

5

What did I learn today?

1

2

3

TO DO TOMORROW

1

2

3

4

5

September 2
Virgo

"In life and in relationships - always remember to stop and think about the situation first before taking action."

This is the classic Reacting emotionally versus responding logically scenario. You attract more bees with honey than you do with vinegar. If you live your life always saying "I'm always right, and I know the way in which to do things and things have to be done a certain way (My way or the highway)" you end up being closed minded to seeing what others perspectives and opportunities that are around you and sometimes you may end up stepping on peoples toes without you realizing that you may be making them upset about things. Sometimes it's best to take a step back and pay attention to the reactions of those around you and make decisions based on what is going on and how others feel about the situations. It will ensure that everyone is comfortable with you and to be around you and ensure that you are getting everyone to be themselves around you.

End of Day Reflection

Five Things I am grateful for:

1

2

3

4

5

What did I learn today?

1

2

3

TO DO TOMORROW

1

2

3

4

5

September 3
Virgo

"Today is the day I want you to make a big difference in someone's life in a sometimes-huge way. Help someone to find what their dreams are and help them see clarity as to what they need to get to where they want to be in life."

"Look around and see the beauty in the journey. Understand that nothing is forever, the places you go, the people you see, they all dissipate. The idea is to realize that you are a part of the good times for someone and will be missed by people around you when they look back on "the good old days" of today." – Eddie Pinero

"The time we have here on Earth is limited so don't waste it living someone else's dream" – Steve Jobs

End of Day Reflection

Five Things I am grateful for:

1

2

3

4

5

What did I learn today?

1

2

3

TO DO TOMORROW

1

2

3

4

5

September 4
Virgo

"Words can hurt more (and leave more scars) than any knife, so be careful what you say. You cannot easily take back words once they are said." - Mary Parker

There is no poison stronger than a pen. Sometimes we forget that there is power behind the words and thoughts and ideas that we have. If we look at it, the power of documents in history like the Declaration of Independence broke away our great nation from the clutches of England. People risked their lives in order for the freedom through the power of word. When it comes to conversations that you have on the day-to-day basis, the outcomes sometimes depend on the tone and energy and passion you use in how you say things and the way in which you try to get your point across. Some people are more sensitive than others when conversing with them and staying aware of this thought is crucial so that things are not misinterpreted along the way. When in doubt, conversation in person or over the phone or facetime is always better than any text message. People read messages based on their current mood/emotion that they are feeling at the time.

End of Day Reflection

Five Things I am grateful for:

1

2

3

4

5

What did I learn today?

1

2

3

TO DO TOMORROW

1

2

3

4

5

September 5
Virgo

"If you are having a bad day, maybe this means you were supposed to help someone else to have a better day."

It is easy to get self-consumed by the things and people who are around us. It is true that it is easy to go through life saying, "I am having a bad day!" "I am the victim of today and yesterday!" "Why is everything happening to me?" or "Why isn't today coming any easier for me?"

Never wish life was easier, wish that you were better at handling life, so that it wouldn't try to handle you so much. It is difficult to prepare for the unknowns that happen to us in life, but if you take things moment by moment and see the happiness, joy, and love within the simplest of things then life wouldn't seem so complicated all the time. I can understand this. But one thing I was told was, you may not be able to control what happens to you, but you can control how you react to it and how you handle it and make back up plans for things that don't work out so that you can cope with the change that occurs around you. Instead of looking at today and saying how bad it was for you, I challenge you to find three good positive things that happened to you and to those around you. Look at how everything went right and be thankful you are still alive right now to enjoy it. Look at things from the perspective of another person's life who may be worse off than you. They may not know when their next meal is, or where they will sleep tonight. Be there for those around you, and you will see and understand things in a more loving and appreciative way.

End of Day Reflection

Five Things I am grateful for:

1

2

3

4

5

What did I learn today?

1

2

3

TO DO TOMORROW

1

2

3

4

5

September 6
Virgo

"Always make time for yourself and your significant other. "Date night" is important even in family and relationships." - Mary Parker

Getting caught up in life happens to us all with what is going on around us between family and friends and work and school. Setting aside the time for "Date night" is crucial for bonding and strengthening the foundation of any relationship. Making time for yourself and your significant others is important to maintain an irregular schedule. Planning it month to month on a specific day will have it looking like it's a chore that "needs to be done" so plan something every month randomly with your significant other like a random day in or a random day out. Going to the movies or going bowling or going out to eat or making food to stay in and do game night or movie night in randomly is important. So today do that one thing that you can do with your significant other. Make it a special day today.

End of Day Reflection

Five Things I am grateful for:

1

2

3

4

5

What did I learn today?

1

2

3

TO DO TOMORROW

1

2

3

4

5

September 7
Virgo

"Sometimes it is better to just listen when someone argues with you, even if you disagree so you can hear what their perspective is. By doing this, you might hear what is causing their pain or unhappiness." - Mary Parker

   Not all can empathize with others around them and see things in the perspectives of others and what they are going through. If you are a libra in personality, then maybe this is true, but others may not have the ability to see what is or may or may not be troubling you or making you feel uncomfortable unless you say it aloud. People don't always read into situations around them and sometimes talk and forget to listen as well. When we forget to take the time to listen to the hearts of others around us, we become selfish, and self-absorbed and forget that others may have a contribution to make or something to say in opinion to what is going on. Take the time to be silent and listen to those around you this week. You won't believe the emotions that you can read and social ques if only you take the time. You aren't the only one going through things and struggling. Take the time and be patient with those around you and don't be afraid to reach out a hand to hold others in a hug or to help them.

End of Day Reflection

Five Things I am grateful for:

1

2

3

4

5

What did I learn today?

1

2

3

TO DO TOMORROW

1

2

3

4

5

September 8
Virgo

"Trust, Honest, mutual Respect, constant communication, Loyalty, unconditional love, and living with integrity are the foundation and hallmark of all committed relationships."

If you can't trust your significant other, you can't figure out if they have ulterior motives in the relationship, you can't trust if what they are doing and saying is true or not. If they lie to you, or mislead you, or they disappoint you, it will be hard for them to gain that trust back and then you will have issues with honesty.

If you cannot respect each other's privacy/ or you cannot trust them enough that they will respect, you as a person and your boundaries this starts to become an issue. If they don't respect your feelings, emotions and opinions, then you can't trust their loyalty to you or anyone especially if they aren't honest. Constant communication and living with integrity and unconditional love are also important factors in any and all relationships to those that are around you as well. If you don't have these as your foundation, you don't have anything worth keeping in my mind. It's best to move on clean away at that point.

End of Day Reflection

Five Things I am grateful for:

1

2

3

4

5

What did I learn today?

1

2

3

TO DO TOMORROW

1

2

3

4

5

"Learning to find someone whose faults and inadequacies are something that you can live with and having that same person be able to tolerate yours, and accept you as you are, is the truest meaning of love." - Mary Parker

""Looking back and understanding that you might have done differently is a source of strength. Awareness is a currency of sorts. But being sorry for yesterday and dwelling on the days gone by, that is a waste of time. See those feelings of discontent, the emotions that rise to the surface as our minds go through that catalog of regret. You know, the emotions that try to pull you back down to the very moment in which they occurred. If you let them lead you by the hand back into a manufactured hell, they will, and down you will go, reliving an expired pain that you can neither prevent nor do anything about, after all it is in the past. But alternatively, if we can do one of the hardest things for humans to do which is to depersonalize the occurrence, remove the emotion and find the value, you will stand face to face with an advantage in life that is exponential. Not only are you refusing to be defined or tortured by yesterday's mistakes/regrets you are creating a framework by which you can use that pain to make a better right now. You are acknowledging that your mistakes are not indicative of a current reflection in a mirror. They are not metal bars keeping you closed in, but they are rather opportunities in disguise."

– Eddie Pinero

End of Day Reflection

Five Things I am grateful for:

1

2

3

4

5

What did I learn today?

1

2

3

TO DO TOMORROW

1

2

3

4

5

September 10
Virgo

"Being a parent means accepting your child for who they are, being there for them no matter what, protecting them with your own life, putting their needs ahead of your own, and setting an example for them that you can be proud of."
- Mary Parker

"A Friend of mine once told me, "From our pain, comes our purpose. From our despair comes our hope it's from the times when we got it oh so completely wrong that we can now arm ourselves with the ability to get it right. To be better and faster, and stronger and wiser. The reality of life in the big city, is having to fall in order to rise again. If we don't fall there are no ashes for us to rebuild upon. We change when we lost. We evolve when we are cornered. We become more when life shakes our worldview. There is power in suffering, that is if you choose to find it. That is always a decision that we can choose to make whether we want the memories to bring us down or whether we want to use them to elevate ourselves higher than what we have ever been. There is a saying that says that life is 10% of what happens to you and 90% of what you do about it. You can let life tear you down or you can let it bring you up. Knowledge is only as powerful as our willingness to put that knowledge to work. Yesterday's pain, the lessons learned can be the very reason you transform and evolve to a higher version of yourself but that is only if you can use these lessons right now stop using them as an attack on your self-esteem and start seeing them as the gateway to tomorrow. Otherwise, they will keep your ball and chain around your ankles. Is the mistake that costed you, that inaction that fractured your relationship, or that swing and miss that hurt your pride somewhere along the way, are they going to remain sources of pain in your mind or mental images or reflections of where you fell short or are they going to fuel your comeback, the sequel? When we fall, we are given one of life's greatest gifts, a part two, armed with the knowledge we otherwise we wouldn't have had, with the failure comes the strength." – Eddie Pinero

End of Day Reflection

Five Things I am grateful for:

1

2

3

4

5

What did I learn today?

1

2

3

TO DO TOMORROW

1

2

3

4

5

September 11
Virgo

"The hardest part of being a parent is learning to step back and watch your child struggle so that they can learn for themselves." - Mary Parker

As adults the struggle is real, struggling and learning to be responsible for your bills, living situation, future family is extremely important and watching your children grow up, part of that is watching them make mistakes and learn to fail properly so that they learn how to get back up again. If they don't learn this, then they will become co-dependent on their partners and those around them to get by and grow up. This is a crucial steppingstone that a child needs to learn so that they can learn to stand on their own two feet. The world can be a cruel place sometimes for the naïve but it's best to prepare for the influences and different personality types out there and how cruel people can be to each other and yet realize at that same time how much of an impact you can make on those around you.

End of Day Reflection

Five Things I am grateful for:

1

2

3

4

5

What did I learn today?

1

2

3

TO DO TOMORROW

1

2

3

4

5

"During rough times, especially during times of great trial and depression always remember that this is the moment that you are supposed to hold your family, friends, and significant others even tighter."

"When you are at your lowest point, you are, often without realizing it, positioning yourself to arrive at your highest point. Potential energy preparing you for an atmosphere of new beginnings. Our adversity is life asking that we submerge and dive deep, sometimes very deep just to remind us of how badly we need that oxygen, so that when we come back up for oxygen, and we will, we notice the warmth of the sun on our face and the calming sound of the ocean waves crashing on the beach. Our submergence is our transformation. You don't make the most of what's around you, until you notice that what's around you is the opportunity." – Eddie Pinero

----

Today, don't let yourself wallow in self-pity for too long, raise your head up, and gather yourself together and realize that you are a strong person and that anything that you are up against, any adversity that you can overcome it. Sometimes it may even take you to see things from a different perspective in order to see things easier and in a better understanding to realize that maybe things are meant to be the way that they are. Though that may be a difficult thing to swallow, we cannot control people and things that are around us all the time. Even the best laid plans don't go as planned. Today try to focus on yourself and get into a more positive mindset!

End of Day Reflection

Five Things I am grateful for:

1

2

3

4

5

What did I learn today?

1

2

3

TO DO TOMORROW

1

2

3

4

5

September 13
Virgo

"You need to rely on your loved ones, family, and friends during the rough times and support and love one another even more. Love and support can help you get to the other side easier."

"They say heavy is the head that wears the crown, with the ability to influence comes a burden a worry not felt by the masses, that power like anything has it costs. I can't help but wondering what value lies in the alternative, Today is my empire, each action is my subject, I rule the kingdom with an iron fist because it is mine, I will not let my life be dictated by foreign aggressors. I am king because of the life I lead. When you govern your own beliefs and expectations you bow to no man. My thoughts are loyal, rule or be ruled. Do act or wish or hope, easy to be the subject, but easy will never change your life. To have control is to take on risk, it's dangerous and makes you vulnerable. Courage is what it takes, everyone has a crown at their feet, but the question is will you pick it up? Will you take control of your life? The Universe doesn't control you; it empowers you! No one can make you take the first step. Royalty must decide to rule. Reign over your life, conquer the unconquerable, the possibilities always outweigh the risk." – Eddie Pinero

End of Day Reflection

Five Things I am grateful for:

1

2

3

4

5

What did I learn today?

1

2

3

TO DO TOMORROW

1

2

3

4

5

September 14
Virgo

"No one can make you feel inferior without your consent."- Eleanor Roosevelt.

You may be a shy and reserved person, and you may feel a little surer of yourself so you should try to make people a little more aware of you to take you seriously. It's time people started to respect you more, especially people around you. Today try to think of yourself before you think of others.

No one should have the power to bring you down and affect your emotions to make you feel less of a person. You matter, you are important and there are people whom are around you who have been deeply impacted by the difference that you have made for just being a part of their lives. Don't give up hope and stay strong through any difficult time that you may be having right now.

"From our pain comes our purpose, and from our despair comes our hope. Sometimes you need to fall to rise again, to rebuild on the ashes. We change and evolve and become more when we are lost, or when we are cornered, when life shakes our world view. There is power in suffering if you choose to find it. Memories can pull you down if you let them, but they can also in the same instance be used to elevate yourself." - Eddie Pinero

End of Day Reflection

Five Things I am grateful for:

1

2

3

4

5

What did I learn today?

1

2

3

TO DO TOMORROW

1

2

3

4

5

"Don't ever let the rough times lead you to attacking those same people you love."

I can understand that some have hurt you in the past, I've been hurt too, but that doesn't mean the world is out to get you either. There are bad and good people in the world, and there are some good people in the world who just aim to help others and be there for those who they themselves see great potential in.

****

"Enjoy and realize how beautiful the now is, whether your current situation or season is ideal or a struggle, or in between to feel something at all in its own unique way is a miracle. And if we look, we will find that there is growth here, there are moments that you will look back on and smile knowing that they shaped you and played a role in the person you have become. Save the pictures of the past and engrave them into your memories to look back on when you are older." – Eddie Pinero

]

End of Day Reflection

Five Things I am grateful for:

1

2

3

4

5

What did I learn today?

1

2

3

TO DO TOMORROW

1

2

3

4

5

September 16
Virgo

"Today in this world, it is you, and your loved ones, against the world."

When the water rises, it's sink or swim...

When you pursue your best, you can live your best life. Despair gives you a chance to look at life differently, look at yourself differently and to look in the mirror and understand that the reflection looking back can lead a revolution in your soul. It's hard, we all know that! How detached from reality it might seem but isn't that what tomorrow is a detachment from reality and the rules and the perimeters of Today?

When you're stuck in the chaos of life, you must know that this is where you too and transform into greatness!

End of Day Reflection

Five Things I am grateful for:

1

2

3

4

5

What did I learn today?

1

2

3

TO DO TOMORROW

1

2

3

4

5

"There is no age requirement to learn and keep learning and growing."

Do one thing that scares you every day synonymous with a seed refusing water, you need to grow but only through experiences of trying and failing and understanding things we don't necessarily like will we grow and better ourselves. We are not made to be creatures of comfort but rather creatures of growth and transfiguration into beings who improve and grow and challenge ourselves and who learn and accomplish things that we THINK are unimaginable to bring to life. I dare you to attempt to bring the things and Ideas that are in your mind to life, bring them into attempted fruition and if you make it and accomplish it, it only proves to yourself that it could be done and if not at least you know you tried and attempted it multiple times and you know it won't work instead of being in a state of unsurety of wondering whether or not it would work.

End of Day Reflection

Five Things I am grateful for:

1

2

3

4

5

What did I learn today?

1

2

3

TO DO TOMORROW

1

2

3

4

5

September 18
Virgo

"What's the difference between simple and easy? Simple is straightforward, uncomplicated, Easy means achieved without great effort. The difference between those two words is subtle but essential to understand. One deals with the complexity of an outcome, the other your will and determination to achieve that outcome. Becoming who you most want to be is simple. But becoming who you most want to be is not easy. Just like walking is simple, yet hiking up a mountain isn't easy. The procedure didn't change but the context did. It's not that most people can't grow, it's that most people won't. It's not that most people don't get how, it's that they don't have a strong enough why. The path is laid down before you, you just must be willing to walk down it. Will you? **Step one** - realize there is more out there. It's not that what you are doing right now isn't amazing, it's just that yesterday's act of courage is now today's status quo. What was once spectacular is now mundane. What was once the ceiling you had to jump to touch is now the floor you walk on, so at the very least, it prompts you to ask what's next? Simple, not easy. **Step two** - Acquisition of courage, yesterday's courage was a fight. It took a lot out of you and it's ultimately what got you here. But it dropped you at the curb and went on its merry way and now here you are. You can stay here, a lot of people do, you can reminisce of the glory days of yesterday's triumphs. Or you can do that uncomfortable exercise of vulnerability stepping into tomorrow's unknowns. Yesterday's rewards had a hefty price tag, and that price tag is discomfort. You think you played this game but all you did was learn the rules, now apply it to a new settling. Simple, not easy. **Step three** Mistakes - It's not the mistakes you fear, it's what you think they will mean, ridicule, lack of direction or identity, embarrassment, losing what you have, but here's the catch, when you realize the downside is not greater than the upside you liberate yourself. When you realize there is more to gain than to lose, your potential for greatness is born. How does one act on this? Mistakes, by making them and injecting yourself into the turbulence of progress. Our biology has not yet learned that the uncomfortable thing is the right thing. That's why we get resistance, that's why it hurts. It's why few people accomplish what we want. Mistakes are your curriculum, simple not easy. **Step four** - Trust yourself. Easy… easy when you are getting what you want. But evolution takes time and there is nothing like giving and giving and giving and not getting. So how do you find the strength? Growth is exponential, everything matters, it chisels your future self. Success is sheer will, and discipline. Repetition and adjustment. Simple, not easy. **Step five** - Celebrate and adjust - At some point you will look over your shoulder and you will notice the space between where you started and where you are. It's not sudden, it's gradual. These moments are important to acknowledge a time for celebrating. Victory matters so relish it and transform it. That mountain top is your foundation and your expectations have increased and changed to what's expected now. Fall in love and respect that moment. Your ability to push forward is a huge accomplishment. Simple yes, easy no. But you are not in this for easy, you are in it for growth and the journey and it's not easy. This decision to endure was the best one you ever made!" - Eddie Pinero

End of Day Reflection

Two Things I am grateful for:

1   2

What did I learn today?

1   2

TO DO TOMORROW

1

2

September 19

Four emotions that will change your life by Eddie Pinero (727) TIME TO MOVE ON | Powerful Motivational Speeches | Wake Up Positive - YouTube - https://www.youtube.com/watch?v=gR4Gk6bUVlE To 8:09 Quoted Below:

"Jim Rohn says there are four emotions that will change your life: Disgust, Decision, Desire, and Resolve. I want to start with the first one because there is a story that lines up perfectly with it that goes like this: Disgust - One day there was a Girl scout walking up to the door of this house of a 25-year-old, man comes to his door and he is broke and he doesn't have any money at the time and he tells her what I assumed is a white lie as to why he can't buy the cookies at that particular time right. So he tells her that he can't, she walks away he says after he closes the door and goes back inside, he felt something that completely changed his life. Disgust, an overwhelming feeling that he simply didn't want to live like that anymore. He didn't want to lie, he didn't want to be broke. Jim Rohn once said, "The day you can say I've had it, may not be the day it ends, but the day it begins." And that feeling, which of course on the surface seems like a terrible thing, no one wants to feel disgust with their circumstance, but its ultimately one of the most powerful indicators life can present to us (to show us that something needs to change) There has always been and I assume will continue to.be that point in many different facets of my life where I say enough is enough, I just never thought to categorize it or label it like he did but that's what it is. You know getting to a point where in your life and looking around and realizing that you have conceded too much. You've strayed too far beyond what matters to you. You've left too much on the table. That feeling again, while uncomfortable, is often what becomes the first step towards that which is truly meaningful, a better version of yourself. A realization by the way that is not some denunciation of who you are right. It's not saying, "I'm not good enough." Or "I'm Inadequate." I would describe it as the exact opposite. It's thinking, enough of yourself to acknowledge that you are better than this. It's saying, "Yeah there is a reality where I stay the same, where I don't change, where I allow this to just be my life, but that's not the reality I am going to choose, because I respect myself too much to continue living with that dissonance between my actions and who I know I truly am. I think at a deep level we all understand this. So many times, in life, funny enough, we don't change until we have to. Until our backs are completely against the wall Right. It took me years in my previous professional life to say enough is enough, but ultimately got to that point. I've been there in relationships, been there with my creative work and been there with my finances. What's especially interesting is that as you grow, evolve, and your goals change, what you expect of yourself changes, grows along with you. You will find yourself at that place again, and again, and again. And that's good, listen to it. That's your intuition telling you you are ready for more. That something else awaits that the status quo is no longer sufficient. There lies the opportunity to recognize and associate that feeling of disgust as Rhon calls it with a need to change or an opportunity to change before things blow up or become more difficult than they need to be. Everything in your life has been allowed by you to some extent now that is an important thing to understand. If there's something in your life that's making it hell, you to an extent are responsible for that. No one takes your time without your permission. If you are doing things that don't move, motivate or inspire you, well the reality is, you're choosing those now the circumstances may be specific to you they may be difficult to you and I understand that, but you are asking yourself, how you can begin moving away from it? How can you put walls between yourself and the things that drag you down? The bottom line is it's very easy to become accustomed to things that are a drain on our lives. The old frog in the boiling water right, you throw a frog in a pot of hot water it will jump right out, but you put it in a pot of cool water, and you slowly but incrementally increase the temperature until its boiling, the frog won't realize its burning alive. I think that in the same way we learn to live with that situational disgust. The things that we are unhappy with just become the baseline or normal. It becomes regular. What I love about the girl scout story is that light bulb moment where its like, "No, I don't have to accept this. I can take back control, I dictate how I'm going to live, and I know this isn't it. Now you don't need to have all the answers right away, in fact, you most certainly won't have them but every journey as the saying goes, begins with the first step. That's precisely why the moment is so powerful. You don't start moving to that new place until you realize that you want to start moving away from where you are. Rohn talks about disgust being a powerful motivator, that's why, it's the initial leverage you need to create that momentum, to see the gap between where you want to be and where you are, and this is ultimately a call to that realization. **Do an audit on yourself and your contentment, the places you find lacking. They are calling for your attention. It's normal, it's okay, it's a part of life. But it's also your opportunity to begin making that change. Make two columns to parse through this simpler. On the left everything that brings be some level of anxiety or that is a drain on my peace. And on the column on the right directly across from it simply what you plan to do about each item,** *"You begin to utilize that feeling of disgust or discontent to act. You turn that message into something beautiful, an adventure, some variation of growth, that's where the good stuff is." – Jim Rohn.* By the way it also changes our relationship with those emotions when they emerge. It's no longer "Poor me, I'm stuck, my life is hard." And the list goes on and on. now, its "Oh this doesn't feel good, how can I use it to connect to something that does?"   - Eddie Pinero

End of Day Reflection

September 20
Virgo

"No one is better than you, and you are no better than anyone else. Always be humble. Above all, always love unconditionally those that are around you."

At the end of the day, you don't know what others around you are going through, you don't know what they have just been through, nor do you know what they are about to have to go through.

If you come up as boastful and bragging to others about what you did or are about to do, it can make people feel uncomfortable, jealous, or even cause them to be self-reflective of their own life and compare your accomplishments to that of their own and maybe even effect their own self-esteem and make them feel bad about themselves. Always try to put yourself in people's shoes so you can understand their perspective on things as well. This is something that I have always found useful in my own life along the way. Sure, I am an author but bragging about the books I've written doesn't help others feel good about themselves. I am always and will forever be grateful for my accomplishments and where they have taken me but at the end of the day, being myself with humility and humbleness is more attractive in my opinion from the outside looking in.

End of Day Reflection

Five Things I am grateful for:

1

2

3

4

5

What did I learn today?

1

2

3

TO DO TOMORROW

1

2

3

4

5

September 21
Virgo

"Take pictures of you and your loved ones and friends today. Inside or outside. Make a scrapbook or photo album printed or digital album of you and those you love. Time is too short and precious and it's limited."

"If you live each day as if it were your last, someday you'll be right. Every morning I looked in the mirror and asked myself, "If today were the last day of my life, would I want to do what I do today?" – Steve Jobs

Too many people take their lives for granted and the miracle of living a life that we choose to lead. There are instances when things come about that seem like they are out of our control, but we have the ability to choose how we react and what we do to any and all situations that may or may not arise in our lives. A lot of this has to do with accountability, what we choose to allow or not allow to happen in our lives. We can choose every day to sleep in or choose to take advantage of the day and wake up earlier and get an earlier start in the day. We can choose to follow our dreams and to do the things that we want to do and lead happy and healthy lives and achieve our dreams and goals in life or we can choose not to and decide that you know maybe I can't or its impossible. At the end of the day, whether we think that we can or can't both be usually right.

End of Day Reflection

Five Things I am grateful for:

1

2

3

4

5

What did I learn today?

1

2

3

TO DO TOMORROW

1

2

3

4

5

"Every problem that you come across in life has more than one solution and there is more than one way you can go about resolving it."

"Life is about decisions about what to accept and what to cut away, and it's in our moments of destress we must find calm, when we feel low that we must remember the heights that we can achieve. See beyond that hopeless narrative and look in the mirror and realize that what looks back at you isn't the problem it is the reason you'll succeed. This is the moment that made you and shaped you like a sculptor. Look up and forward because that is where you are going. You weren't made to accept what is, you were made to rise." – Eddie Pinero

End of Day Reflection

Five Things I am grateful for:

1

2

3

4

5

What did I learn today?

1

2

3

TO DO TOMORROW

1

2

3

4

5

September 23
Libra

"Be Spontaneous today. Treat yourself, you deserve it. Also know that you cannot always plan for everything in your life to go your way. It is okay to lose sometimes in life."

At the end of the day, sometimes, even the best laid plans don't' go as planned and that is okay. We all strive to try to accomplish certain things in life by a certain time in life or time in the day and a lot of us get comfortable planning out lives out, sometimes it the days that we don't plan that we can get the most out of. We all stive to find our purpose in life and all wish to be happy, healthy, and successful.

I am personally guilty of not allowing myself to treat myself. Most times I treat others around me and am happy to be the giver in life to those around me. But I forget to buy things that I want or have always wanted when I have wanted to. I feel guilty because I feel like I don't deserve things or don't deserve to have the experiences in life that I wish to experience. But I reflect on this quote and think, what am I truly missing out on in life. What am I not doing that I want to do in my life that I am holding back from doing or having? If we take a deep look internally at the deeper picture sure it's nice to treat ourselves but what is holding you back from it?

Today I challenge you to treat yourself and I will remember to do the same for myself occasionally even if someone has to remind me to do so sometimes…

End of Day Reflection

Five Things I am grateful for:

1

2

3

4

5

What did I learn today?

1

2

3

TO DO TOMORROW

1

2

3

4

5

"Be truthful and honest but not at the expense of being cruel - know the difference. Don't hesitate to love and trust with all your heart. It's never a waste.".

Sure, I may be an author, but I am also human and am not afraid to admit my own mistakes and wrongdoings and still have my own life of my own regrets of things I feel I may have mishandled along the way in life. Making mistakes is also something that is a learning curve for all of us along the way. If we didn't make mistakes along the way in life, how could we grow? Sometimes we want to help those around us along the way from making mistakes and falling. Being honest and truthful with careful awareness of other people's feelings and emotions is also very crucial. Telling someone that they need to do better because they are horrible is cruel but telling someone hey this is how you can improve is different. Loving others around you is very important because you don't know where others are in their lives and sometimes a simple gesture of a smile or a hug of a warm embrace can go along way in the lives of others.

Don't be afraid to help others around you but don't enable them to be, there is a difference. When doing so is just like a caterpillar learning to get out of its own cocoon, helping it to opening its cocoon encased around it doesn't help but it hurts the caterpillar. When trying to help the caterpillar it prevents it from learning how to fly with its own wings. It needs to push itself out of the cocoon to have the strength to hold itself up in the air. Enabling those around us doesn't help them grow or to be better humans, it doesn't teach them how to fly, it teaches them to rely and be codependent on others around them.

End of Day Reflection

Five Things I am grateful for:

1

2

3

4

5

What did I learn today?

1

2

3

TO DO TOMORROW

1

2

3

4

5

September 25
Libra

"Don't blame your "special person" for past mistakes made by exes for the reason why you aren't where you want to be in life., Forgive all."

To add to this, I would also say, "but never forget all."

Yes, it is my belief that it is okay to give people second or third chances in life, but at the same time, never forget and allow what has been wronged to you to be done more than once by the same person. If someone chooses to handle a situation badly sometimes in mistake this is okay as long as it is learned from, but if this is something that now happens out of habit without a care to how it hurts you, then you need to realize that they may not care about you or your feelings and maybe in the end just using you or trying to get a bad reaction out of you which is toxic.

We all should always strive to continue to be better than we were yesterday, the mistakes of those around us should be potholes in the road of life that we ought to avoid. There are always ways to go and handle and maneuver our lives around these potholes. Yes, from time to time these potholes are bigger than others at times and they are unavoidable, but as the passenger to this life, sometimes those around us try their best to avoid and attempts are made with effort to not make these mistakes, but you cannot hold bitterness towards the act forever. Potholes aren't on an unending road to the destination, and they are just a simple part of the journey in the end. Give those around you the chance and acknowledge that yes, potholes happen but as long as the mistakes are attempted to be made in life and are attempted to be avoided by those around you with effort try not to hold it against them when they try their best to impress and please you. I have to admit from time to time, I myself have lost my own temper on people around me with impatience and judgement towards their actions/inactions but I have to remember to take a step back myself and remember that I myself am not perfect and I should allow others to make mistakes around me and be okay with being themselves around me, even when I don't remember to be patient with them and their personalities.

End of Day Reflection

Five Things I am grateful for:

1

2

3

4

5

What did I learn today?

1

2

3

TO DO TOMORROW

1

2

3

4

5

"There are those of us who believe that there is always someone there spiritually listening to what is going on with us. Someone who, when our time comes, will judge us by what we felt, what we said, what we thought, what we chose to act on, and how we chose to live our lives." – Frank Burgesis, Grey Matter Series Volume 1: The story of Mark Trogmyer in the World of the Unknown, Page 38,

"Dream and live big!"

If your dreams don't scare you, they are not big enough.

Our worst enemy is ourselves; we often discount the fact that we ourselves don't believe in us. We don't believe that we are capable of so much and accomplishing what we most want in our lives. We say when we are younger, "I want to be a doctor, or a nurse, or a lawyer when we grow up." But what happened along the way? What changed our direction of the goal that we had in our life? What changed your viewpoint of thinking that it's still not possible.

We say to ourselves, "I am too old now. I have kids now. No one will support me. What if I try it and I fail? What if I try it and I am successful, but I find that I no longer enjoy doing it or I cannot handle the success of it?"

YOU ARE WRONG! No one says that by the age of 20 you need to have your life together or even at the age of 50 for that matter. You cannot allow your own happiness and want to be successful in life be stopped by this negative thinking. You must push yourself forward and not allow yourself to be stopped by waves of good intentions around you. People are going to tell you what you want to do in life and put negativity in your head in order to prevent you from progressing forward but if you figure out what this true path to being successful is and you stick to it, you will find that success and happiness in the end.

End of Day Reflection

Five Things I am grateful for:

1

2

3

4

5

What did I learn today?

1

2

3

TO DO TOMORROW

1

2

3

4

5

"This isn't your birthday, right? Asked Susie Que pointing at us quizzically, "Cuz our birthday parade came and left. We aint got no time to be singing no Happy Birthday or Happy anniversary, or any congratulations to anybody today."

"Oh no, we are trying to cheer up our son with an ice cream sundae since our cat died." Said my father looking at Susie Que's long black hair that was dyed at the end's blond in the braids.

"Oh good, well boy, better get used to death, this happens every day on the streets around here. Just be happy that you are alive and that your cat died instead of you." Said Susie Que rather rudely looking at me. "You gotta tough life as it is out there, it's not all sunshine, daisies, and roses. If you want something in life, you gotta fight for it. You gotta prove not just to others, but to yourself, that you want and deserve success.! Your parents are basically treating you like a pig for slaughter." She continued looking at them as they were open mouthed and shocked at what she was saying to me., "I'm sorry but kids today need to know how bad life is out there, and how fragile it is, and that life needs to be respected. You can't be naïve in life, it's better to be strong and know what you need to do to survive and what you are up against. Your parents need to realize that if something happens to them tomorrow, they can't go and buy you an ice cream to make you feel better. You know that they shouldn't be doing this right? I mean every time someone or something you know in your life leaves or dies, that you shouldn't go out and buy ice cream, otherwise you will turn out to be one fat tub of a kid!" Said Susie Que"

- Grey Matter Series Volume 1: The Story of Mark Trogmyer in the World of the Unknown, Page 18-19.

Life is fragile, today we take it for granted and don't seem to appreciate its value and importance. Around you, the lives of those around us are limited and precious. Today recognize the importance of the lives of the people around you and share with them an act of love and care to show them how important they are to you. By sharing this love of others to others, we not only show them our appreciation of them being in our lives, but you have a unique ability to make a difference on their day.

End of Day Reflection

Five Things I am grateful for:

1

2

3

4

5

What did I learn today?

1

2

3

TO DO TOMORROW

1

2

3

4

5

September 28
Libra

"You may not have had control of your childhood, but as an adult you can control all of your choices."

ONLY A BOWL OF RICE -

One day there lived a sage who was known for his ability to solve difficult problems. One day he had two visitors who needed his advice. Both were polite and each insisted that the other should go first. After some discussion, they discovered that their questions were essentially the same. So, they settled on speaking with the sage at the same time. One of them asked, "Master we are both low level employees being treated badly at work. We get no respect at all, and our employers constantly push us around. Can you please tell us if we should quit our jobs?"

The sage closed his eyes and meditated at length. The two young men waited patiently until the sage opened his eyes. He gave them the answer in five words: "Only a bowl of rice."

The two young men thanked the sage and departed. They contemplated the answer as they walked back to the city. After a while, one of them broke the silence and said, "That was interesting, what do you think the sage meant?"

The other one was thoughtful and said, "Well, it's fairly obvious that the bowl of rice represents our daily meals."

"I agree," said the first young man, "I believe that the sage was telling us that the job is nothing more than a means to make a living. Yes, when you come right down to it, that is all we get out of the job – our daily meals."

They went their separate ways, one of them continued working at the same place, the other submitted a letter of resignation immediately upon his return. He went home to the countryside and took up farming. After several years, this young man had achieved considerable success as a farmer. He used what he had learned in the city to import high quality seeds. The fruits and vegetables he grew became the best in the region. He enjoyed not only great profits but also a great reputation as an expert. The other young man who remained at work also did well. It was as if he became a different person. He took on difficult tasks and demonstrated an ability to handle adversity. He rose up through the ranks and received one promotion after another and became a manager. One day the two of them met again by chance, once they got caught up with one another, they realized that they had taken two very different paths based on the exact same answer from the sage. They were both wealthy and happy. But which path was the correct one? "How strange!" the manager said puzzled, "The master said the same thing to us, and we both heard it the same way. Why did you quit?"

The farmer was also puzzled, "I understood his words immediately, the job was nothing more than the means to get my daily meals, so why force myself to stay in a horrible situation just for a bowl of rice? Quitting was obviously the right thing to do. Why did you stay?"

"I also think it should be obvious," the manager laughed. "The job meant nothing more than a bowl of rice so why was I getting so worked up over it? As soon as I understood this, I realized there was no need for me to get so upset. I didn't need to take the abuse heaped on me personally, so of course I stayed. Isn't that what he meant?"

"Now I am so confused," the farmer said, "Did he mean for us to take my path or your path? Let's go and see him again and get to the bottom of this. Once again, they presented themselves before the stage and explained the reason for their visit. "You see master, we would really like to know the real meaning of your advice, all those years ago, can you give us some insights?"

The Sage closed his eyes and the two men waited patiently like before and he opened his eyes and gave them his answer and again said only five words, "Only a difference of thought. You see in life, your life, we all have our own paths to follow, your Tao/ state of mind, is like a stream flowing downhill. No matter what direction you take, you will get to your point of happiness, each has his own way. So go your own way and reach your happiness. It is only a bowl of rice."

End of Day Reflection

Three Things I am grateful for:

1

2

3

What did I learn today?

1

2

3

TO DO TOMORROW

1

2

3

"Relationships are give and take but they will never flourish if you are the only one taking or giving. Pick and choose your battles with care."

It is my belief that all relationships have the following building blocks as its foundation:

- Unconditional Love - loving someone as they are and where they are in life to be supportive of each other's needs and understand and care about your partner's love language.
- Respect of each other and yourself
- Loyalty
- Communication, talking and listening equally and understanding each other.
- Honesty/ Trust
- Responsibility of each other
- Romanticism/Passion
- Goals/Dreams
- Kindness/Care

If at any time, that any of these are unstable at their core, the relationship is destined to fail in the end. Always be willing to work through things and accept each other and all their faults for there is no perfect person in the world, we are after all, only human. Within a relationship, if you are continuing to improve yourself along the way, and growing and learning from your mistakes, you are striving for success and supporting each other, then the outcome will most definitely be a happy one.

End of Day Reflection

Five Things I am grateful for:

1

2

3

4

5

What did I learn today?

1

2

3

TO DO TOMORROW

1

2

3

4

5

"Making decisions in life is not always easy. Some take more reflection than others. As the saying was once told to me, with great power comes great responsibility and the ability to affect great change with the choices that you make in life. If you aren't careful with the decisions that you make in life, they are in direct correlation with the conditions and consequences in their outcome and to those around you."

There are times when we make decisions that have the ability to affect those around us in positive and negative ways, it is slightly dependent on a matter of perspective. There are positive and negative wings of change that happen around us. The way that I tend to personally look at them are positive winds that help us continue to support ourselves and grow and then the negative winds of change I look at as winds of growth and challenge, these are times that are seemingly unstable but in the end they are there to help us grow and improve ourselves and when looking back they helped us strengthen our resolve and helped us to be successful in our future by helping us understand others as well in empathy.

End of Day Reflection

Five Things I am grateful for:

1

2

3

4

5

What did I learn today?

1

2

3

TO DO TOMORROW

1

2

3

4

5

October 1
Libra

"Never expect or demand more from others than what you expect of yourself."

Sometimes the people around us are people pleasers and their only wish is to ensure the happiness of those around them. Sometimes we tend to ask a lot of those around us and tend to add more to the plate of others and impose on them more than we should or more than they can handle without us recognizing that maybe they too are going through so much in life. Sometimes to understand those around us, we must place ourselves in their shoes and understand the things that they are also dealing with in life and possibly try to help them handle things to the best of our ability. If you don't think that you are in a position to be able to handle a certain situation on your own, don't expect this of others around you to be able to handle it without help. We need to be better supportive of those around us and ensure that they too are okay in their own mental, emotional, and physical health as well… Sure someone may smile all the time, but ALSO realize too that behind that smile is a dark and difficult past or even worse, maybe this is a mask to hide that they themselves are also truly struggling. IF you see someone today smiling a lot in your life or maybe has on a serious face. Do not be afraid to ask them if everything is okay and don't be afraid to get to understand them and talk to them to ensure that they know that they aren't alone and that maybe you can help them in some way to ensure that they are okay.

Things to work on this month: Work on not being so indecisive about your decisions. Know what you want, fight for what you want, and let it be known to others what you want in life. Work on sharing your feelings even when it is not easy too, especially if you think it will cause an argument. Work on being direct with your feelings. Be quicker at making decisions. Don't neglect your partner when making decisions when trying to help everyone else around you.

End of Day Reflection

Five Things I am grateful for:

1

2

3

4

5

What did I learn today?

1

2

3

TO DO TOMORROW

1

2

3

4

5

October 2
Libra

"It is okay to see the doctor when you feel fine."

The worst thing you can do is say to your partner, "I'm Fine" when you know that you are not. I can understand the reason behind not wanting to go to the hospital or see the doctor when you are feeling sick or not well. Not many enjoy the visit to doctors' offices and such places because of the costs and the amount of time spent in these places. But in the end, the result is to ensure that you survive through whatever it is that you are trying to go through or deal with health wise. Seeing a doctor can tell you things about yourself that you may not have known before. Bloodwork and vitals can reveal so much to us. We may think that we know our bodies, but it is at times when the doctors can read whether our bodies can keep up with the activity of our minds or not. Sometimes our minds move faster than our bodies when they try to keep up and things become sorted, messed up. Take time to visit your doctor and make an appointment for a checkup, even if it's just a flu shot or regular blood work and schedule the follow-ups to keep up with the results. Improving yourself also means trying to improve the body, as well as the mind and remembering to take time to be grateful for your health, insurance, and the ability to access a doctor, as many may not have that opportunity.

End of Day Reflection

Five Things I am grateful for:

1

2

3

4

5

What did I learn today?

1

2

3

TO DO TOMORROW

1

2

3

4

5

"When it comes to gift giving, always give from the heart, not last minute after thoughts."

Personally, I have always been a simple person. I am perfectly okay with gifts that are handmade or inexpensive things. I am not a label hoe as Madea says. There are different love languages and gift giving is one of them. Many find happiness in the need of having materialistic things and there is nothing wrong with that as long as we are not using the need of materialistic things in order to get things from others or to help others.

Around the Christmas season, I think a part of the reason why people get so stressed out is due to the need to buy things in order show that they "Love others" and they worry about how much they are or aren't spending on the significant other or they are worried about the fact that they don't have a lot of gifts to open. All these things take away from the true meaning behind the art of gift giving. Yes, I just called it an art, as sometimes and many a times, we don't know what to get those around us and yes, it's nice to be the giver it's also quite stressful as we don't want to disappoint our significant others either. Remember that even if it's not in the holiday season of giving a just because gift, it truly is the thought that matters. Take a deep breath and remember yes, the holiday seasons are coming around the corner but there is no need to stress over them.

End of Day Reflection

Five Things I am grateful for:

1

2

3

4

5

What did I learn today?

1

2

3

TO DO TOMORROW

1

2

3

4

5

"Always be reading."

"Look for an unventured adventure and follow it."

Take a trip to the nearest bookstore today and come out with one book that you can read once a day. Even if it's just for 10 minutes of silence or on a lunch break. We can get through so much in life by taking the time to distract yourself in the world of another book and its pages and learn so much!

Share this delight with your friends and maybe they too can read the book you find too and then you have something else that you can use as a conversation starter as well!

End of Day Reflection

Five Things I am grateful for:

1

2

3

4

5

What did I learn today?

1

2

3

TO DO TOMORROW

1

2

3

4

5

"Play like a child and enjoy life, and its simple pleasures, and always remember to have fun occasionally."

We all get caught up in the days of shift work and grueling homework and school study all the time but remember to take a break and have some fun occasionally even if it's just for an hour a day. We all need a break sometimes and it's okay to relax, loosen up and have fun!

End of Day Reflection

Five Things I am grateful for:

1

2

3

4

5

What did I learn today?

1

2

3

TO DO TOMORROW

1

2

3

4

5

"Every year, take up a new hobby."

   I love watching movies and listening to music and changing it up is interesting. Throughout the years I have switched out writing and reading. If I write, I don't normally read new books yet and if I am reading, I do not write. It makes it easier to keep my thoughts organized. Some can read multiple books at a time. Recently I have taken a liking to collecting chess sets as there are so many unique ones and I love playing chess as well.

   Taking up a new hobby has its advantages, meeting new people and seeing different perspectives from the lives of others around you as you meet them through taking on new hobbies like bowling or cars, or coin collecting, or comic book collecting or getting interested in playing video games or card games is also very interesting.

End of Day Reflection

Five Things I am grateful for:

1

2

3

4

5

What did I learn today?

1

2

3

TO DO TOMORROW

1

2

3

4

5

"Travel and learn new cultures."

  I grew up originally in the Lancaster County area of Pa surrounded by the Amish and their culture and while in school I moved to Texas and Once out of school I had lived in Arizona briefly. Moving into these different areas, you learn about the people, the changes of traditional cultural music and foods and you learn so much more about things that as you do, you begin to be open and accepting of new cultures and people and diversity through understanding them.

  Learn about a new Culture today, you don't have to move there like I did to learn more about a specific area or people.

End of Day Reflection

Five Things I am grateful for:

1

2

3

4

5

What did I learn today?

1

2

3

TO DO TOMORROW

1

2

3

4

5

October 8
Libra

"In life, not everyone is supposed to stay at your side forever."

People move, change schools, change jobs, and at times you lose touch with people along the way. Social media in this aspect does help you stay in touch with people thousands of miles away, but even in distance or even without distance sometimes you outgrow the crowd you surround yourself with and that is okay too. We change our preferences and what we like over time and grow apart from people, it happens. But those that are truly your friends will always remain connected to you that are meant to be.

End of Day Reflection

Five Things I am grateful for:

1

2

3

4

5

What did I learn today?

1

2

3

TO DO TOMORROW

1

2

3

4

5

October 9
Libra

"Life is too short not to take occasional risks only to live with regrets."

"So, you are scared to start. Scared of what could go wrong, scared of what people might say, scared of what you might lose. Perhaps you are scared of hurting your ego, your pride, scared of a world that isn't quite predictable we the world you might live in. This is not a small decision to make, you might think to yourself. How scared are you to not go? How scared are you of things staying the same? How scared are you of looking back at this moment years from now and wishing you had given it a try? How scared are you of watching people around you living the life that you were too scared to try for yourself. Seeing them attempting to live the life you had once thought you wanted to try and didn't? When weighing these two side by side not doing it is even scarier. Being nervous to start something new is human and that's okay. Jumping in the pool and feeling that cold water on your skin is shocking at first but then you get acclimated to it. Being scared to go is diluted, it's the cure. There is no cure for you if you don't go. Fear is the cost of admission; it kicks and screams the hardest. It's not how scared you are not to go, but rather how scared you are not to go. Taking the new journey is scary but considering the alternative not going and what could have been worse. We all fall only few choose to get back up and depersonalize it. Reality is not what happens to you, your reality is how you internalize it, what happens to you, no one gets a pain free life. "To live is to suffer to survive is to find meaning in the suffering." – Nietzsche. Every loss and failure there is an opportunity to gain from it. Look past what is in front of you. When things are hard of challenging you MUST keep going. Your perspective becomes a roadmap to reality. There are no problems, these are steppingstones to overcome. No matter how hard it gets rise above the emotion. Never lose sight of the opportunities." – Eddie Pinero

End of Day Reflection

Five Things I am grateful for:

1

2

3

4

5

What did I learn today?

1

2

3

TO DO TOMORROW

1

2

3

4

5

October 10
Libra

"It is okay to be different, it is what makes you, you."

No one likes to be vulnerable because we open ourselves up for failure or pain but if you are not vulnerable you are not going to grow. Your career is not going to grow because you are not putting yourself in a position for opportunity because you are staying within the limits of your boxed comfort zone. This isn't going to work out well if you remain here, unless you are okay with just being status quo for the rest of your life. In love, someone might walk away because being vulnerable is the first step to say, "Hey I really like and care about you." "You end up trying to show that pers6on the good and the bad and the ugly, so they fall in love with everything about you, which, it also makes you vulnerable. For growth, you just have to suck it up, and be that vulnerable person to people so it will take you to that next level of where you need to be next, so don't be afraid to speak up and put yourself out there. When in fear, realize that FEAR is – False Evidence Appearing Real.

Shift your thinking from what can go wrong to what could go right! When you do this, you create opportunities that could become a reality but when you think about what can go right, things go right and turn out okay in the end. Always think on the bright side and stay positive because then you attract more positivity in most areas of your life. Live in the moment, don't worry about things that are out of your control and things that have yet to pass, keep in the present, don't stress about what is or what could come. At the same time don't think and dwell on the past as you cannot change what was, only what is. No one can predict the future, always stay in the moment, don't overthink.

End of Day Reflection

Five Things I am grateful for:

1

2

3

4

5

What did I learn today?

1

2

3

TO DO TOMORROW

1

2

3

4

5

Keep Life Simple

Try to be understanding of people that are in your life. Everyone has their own unique way of dealing with stress/grief. Be patient. Be kind. Everyone is fighting their own personal demons. Everyone is looking for ways not to shatter, for ways to feel free, for ways to communicate with others. Everyone is just trying to get ahead, just like you. Everyone is trying to move on from some hurtful past, trying to rewrite their story, everyone has some kind of baggage dragging with them. Keep in mind, we all want love, to be told its going to be okay, to have someone to help us make it through the night, to be a part of something special, to make a difference, to be remembered, to be told how much of an impact we have made. We just want to leave behind something that meaningful so that our children's children can look back and say, "they lived, they loved, and in the end, they left all these inspiring moments behind."

"Moving on and finding your own peace is better than getting back at them. Happiness growth, and finding self-love Is the sweetest revenge without being vengeful and to remember to do this for yourself and not them." - @R.M. Drake

End of Day Reflection

Five Things I am grateful for:

1

2

3

4

5

What did I learn today?

1

2

3

TO DO TOMORROW

1

2

3

4

5

October 12
Libra

"You may physically lose a loved one, but they will always remain close to your heart."

Losing a loved one is not easy. There is nothing that we can do to bring back the dead, but we can learn from their lives and hold on to the memories that we have had with them. Death comes like a thief in the night, and we never know when our time will come but the destination remains the same for us all. When considering our own lives, it is important to remember one thing. Are you happy right now? Do you have things that you need to say to people if you were to die tomorrow? What would you change about your life if you knew you were going to die soon? Any regrets? Do you have pictures of those you love?

These are things that we need to think about considering doing and changing now without fear. Take advantage of recognizing now the fragility of life and the necessity of saving time and taking advantage of the time left.

Some memories are good to lose, and some memories are all we have.

End of Day Reflection

Five Things I am grateful for:

1

2

3

4

5

What did I learn today?

1

2

3

TO DO TOMORROW

1

2

3

4

5

October 13
Libra

"Nothing is impossible for you."

You weren't put here to live in the shadows of life. Right now, is just a moment. Just like darkness is temporary. In life we all suffer at one time or another in darkness which cannot be defined without light. Remind yourself today of the sun and infinite beauty that persists throughout the world and that it is around you even in times when it feels like it may not be around.

Remind yourself how much you have been through up to today. You have made it through this year quite remarkably through all your trials and suffering and struggles and yet, by overcoming it all, you have become so much stronger.

There may be people in your life who may be negative constantly towards you, who don't support you, who laugh at you and talk about you behind your back. People who don't want you to be successful and who seem to thrive with your failures and seem to be completely jealous of you. These are Toxic people, perhaps even within your own family. These are people who are in your life not by choice but by default.

"You can remove someone from your life and still truly want what's best for them. Just because there is a distance or detachment, it doesn't mean that hate has to fill that space." – Morgan Richard Olivier.

Never give toxic people too much of your energy as they are like vampires, they tend to suck the life out of you. Vampires love and thrive in the darkness of the night. Just as you would never want negative friends and unsupportive people in your life, do not allow negative thoughts in your head, kick them out, raise the rent.

End of Day Reflection

Five Things I am grateful for:

1

2

3

4

5

What did I learn today?

1

2

3

TO DO TOMORROW

1

2

3

4

5

October 14
Libra

"Be loyal, loving, and supportive."

   Be Loyal: Good friends are hard to come by and being loyal to each other is very important. When going through life having people around you that are dependable, loving, and supportive is important and being that loyal friend to others is just as important.

   Be Loving: Love is the most basic feeling that connects you to others in a special but specific way. Showing others that you love and care about them will help them also care for and look after you. Some people in our lives grow up without love from family and sometimes the support you get from your friends is the next best thing. Showing love and kindness to others is very important in life.

   Be Supportive: When you show others you not only care about them but that you also support them and encourage them to be better and help themselves. It's also a very special connection that you can make with others. Never discount the ability to be supportive, loving, and caring and loyal to others in your life.

End of Day Reflection

Five Things I am grateful for:

1

2

3

4

5

What did I learn today?

1

2

3

TO DO TOMORROW

1

2

3

4

5

October 15
Libra

"There is no growth where there is no pain, struggle, or suffering."

At one point in time, maybe even today, you are going through a struggle or some physical pain. Perhaps you are trying to lose weight or gain muscle. "No pain no gain" as they say. Or perhaps you have recently lost a good friend or coworker or friendship or perhaps someone you know is dying or just died. When going through struggles and pains of grief or loss or if we are suffering through some dark times, you may not realize it, but it only lasts a little while and eventually you pull through. Pain is just temporary, it may last for a minute or an hour or a day, and then this darkness will subside and eventually you will overcome it.

We all have a destination in mind of where we see ourselves and where want to be. We may want to be able to live in a penthouse apartment, but to get to that, we need to work hard and get through struggles in life and work our way up to the top to get to that pinnacle level. It's in these moments of struggle that matter more than the destination in the end. In the end when reaching that destination, we look back and we realize that we have gained so much strength by getting there going through the journey to the top and we end up having that ability to be proud of whom we have become. Be proud as long as along the way you remember where you come from and that you don't lose whom you are along the way, as with great power comes great responsibility and sometimes that power gets to our heads and we lose those whom were closest to us when we should have ensured that they continued by our side through the best and worst of times. Never forget about those who get you to where you are, and those that care about you and who are always there for you. They matter!

End of Day Reflection

Five Things I am grateful for:

1

2

3

4

5

What did I learn today?

1

2

3

TO DO TOMORROW

1

2

3

4

5

"Live in gratitude."

Gratitude is something that I think that people take for granted. We remember what to be grateful for once a year, Thanksgiving. But I think that without this simple act of feeling and being and emotion of being grateful and having gratitude for the things that we have in life, the life that we are leading, and the abilities and talents that we have and our own health and wellness, I think we are in the end lost in some ways without it. Being grateful and learning more about gratitude and trying to find more and more things in which to be grateful for is extremely valuable. It is valuable in that when recognizing everything that we have, and the people who are in our lives, we learn to appreciate life and everything about it. We learn to be content and learn to want more and do more for others than just ourselves. As Zig Ziglar had said in his story about the lady from Birmingham, she was a negative as can be before starting to use the gratitude journal and after her personality changed over time. She realized how much of the world around her changed when its reality it was, she that changed for the better and she found that she was so positive and happy smiling all the time so much so that she could eat a banana sideways. When we are in a state of constant gratitude we learn to appreciate so much and give more of ourselves more. Zig Ziglar had once said" if you care more about others and helping others and showing others you care, the more they and the world around you will care and help to conspire to help you out." Today I challenge you to take some time and think about everything you have written down thus far in the journal as to what you are grateful for. Make sure you didn't repeat anything and if you have, go back, and think of things you haven't used yet to replace them and write new ones down. Also share this journal with as many people as you can think of who could benefit from being more positive and have a better outcome in life. These maybe the negative Nancy's or the complainers in your life. Tell them about this journal! They may see the world around them change as well!

End of Day Reflection

Five Things I am grateful for:

1

2

3

4

5

What did I learn today?

1

2

3

TO DO TOMORROW

1

2

3

4

5

October 17
Libra

"A dream is merely an unreached short term or long-term goal. Don't give up on your dreams, there may be hard times ahead, but they have not come to stay, they have come to pass by you and leave. There are only 10 negative people in the world, they just move around a lot."

At the end of the day, we run into what seems like a roadblock to a lot of negative people but, there are very few in the world, they just move around a lot. When thinking about our dreams, write them down and then write a date that you would like to complete it by next to it, then sign your name next to it. Commit yourself to it. Figure out through research what it is that you need to do to accomplish this dream/goal. Steppingstones along the way may seem like it's impossible, but they aren't problems that aren't easily able to be overcome. Expect problems to happen when trying to reach your goal. Talking about them to people around you might enable you to accomplish them sooner if people know how you can meet your dreams and goals through people or processes that they may be already aware of that you don't know.

End of Day Reflection

Five Things I am grateful for:

1

2

3

4

5

What did I learn today?

1

2

3

TO DO TOMORROW

1

2

3

4

5

October 18
Libra

"Dare to dream. The most amazing feeling in the world is feeling the result of your handiwork/hard work paying off and the difference it has made in the world of those around you!"

May of 2016, I reached by goal by receiving a box in the mail. It was full of my first edition of my first volume books. I was so excited and overjoyed and it was a feeling like no other. Along the way when writing this book, I was told it wasn't possible and that I was wasting time and that it wasn't worth writing because it wasn't going to make a lot of money. That was because I didn't know the right people or have the right background in writing and experience in being an author, it wasn't going to happen. I was determined to get this book out and write this series. Along the way I found passion and through my own determination I finished the book, and I knew that as long as I knew and researched the process, it would be possible to accomplish it. I never believed in those that told me no, or that tried to convince me it wasn't worth it. It never mattered in the end who I knew or didn't know. Only that I had a dream, I envisioned it, I put it into action and made mistakes along the way that I brushed off. When receiving the first book's first edition, I realized how much editing needed to be done. I learned this by hearing my grandfather laughing in the room at a sentence, "Peach through a keyhole" instead of "Peak through a keyhole." My first volume went through 5 editions before realizing it was ready through various changes and editing and cover changes. But I have never been prouder of the journey along the way to reach the destination of accomplishing this dream and I am happy for the steppingstones and barriers I ran into along the way as I would never have learned from them. And now, I can laugh at things like this. No one is perfect and everyone accomplishes their own dreams and goals in their own way, and you can do this too!

End of Day Reflection

Five Things I am grateful for:

1

2

3

4

5

What did I learn today?

1

2

3

TO DO TOMORROW

1

2

3

4

5

October 19
Libra

"Be the change that you want to see in others. There is a satisfaction in helping others to learn and grow and become better than they were yesterday."

They say that if you want something done right or a specific way, its best if you do it yourself, however, if you gain the patience and the time, showing someone else how you accomplish something in your own way of doing things, it may also allow you to see someone else grow and learn and be your protege.

Sometimes, especially within a work retail environment, you come across those who do not want to work or work as hard as you do. It can be overwhelming, and it can.

End of Day Reflection

Five Things I am grateful for:

1

2

3

4

5

What did I learn today?

1

2

3

TO DO TOMORROW

1

2

3

4

5

October 20
Libra

"I challenge you to smile all day today, thinking nothing but positive happy thoughts, no matter what is put in the way."

You will notice after a while of being around people how much they smile and are happy and the positive energy spreads. Trying to have a positive vibe in those around you may attract more positivity to you. It's contagious.

I used to know someone who no matter what kind of day he was having would always be smiling authentically. He smiled so much that he could have eaten a banana sideways. He was a literal ball of positive energy. People were attracted to how he held himself. They would look forward to entering the store he worked at and even the employees around him would fight over the shifts that he would work because they all wanted to be energized by his personality. He cared so much about his job and the people he surrounded himself with. It was during the holiday season that I stopped into his store during his shift and caught a glimpse of him. He had dark circles around his eyes. He hadn't had a day off due to the Christmas holidays, but he was still smiling. I asked him how he was able to do this, and he said he was shown personal development growing up and how his parents raised him. This was something that I wanted myself to be able to emulate to those around me. This is not an easy feat, nor is it for the faint of heart to attempt. Personal development is a huge impact on people's lives, and I've seen difference it can make on those around you and how it can change who and how you are as a person. But it is worth it to study!

End of Day Reflection

Five Things I am grateful for:

1

2

3

4

5

What did I learn today?

1

2

3

TO DO TOMORROW

1

2

3

4

5

October 21
Libra

"Think about what you can plan for today and tomorrow to make it something to look forward to over the coming days."

When we have something to look forward to, you will find out outlook on the days ahead exciting to get through. Your perspective changes and you will find internal happiness through this. If you continue this habit of planning ahead certain activities or meetings with specific people that make you happy or outings for yourself to look forward to, it will also be in the back of your mind and you will be thinking, "I can't wait for the weekend, or I can't wait till Tuesday night or I can't wait for next Saturday!" When you have these thoughts in your mind dopamine will do wonders for you and cure your depression state temporarily!

End of Day Reflection

Five Things I am grateful for:

1

2

3

4

5

What did I learn today?

1

2

3

TO DO TOMORROW

1

2

3

4

5

"Today is your day, so make it something special!"

   Today is happening for you! The strength is in showing up! Show appreciation for the things and people that are around you. Sometimes the results in life may feel like that are not aligning right to your output but in the end it will all make sense. Sometimes life throws us curve ball after curve ball, why? Because if you can get through this and pull through the greatness while under duress just imagine what's around the corner! It's hard to make sense of the dark and the chaos and the hurt but find a way to remember that this life is happening for you and not too you! Hold on to see that seed that you have planted for the spring to begin to grow and rise by the heat of the sun! Look beyond that darkness that is around you and push through it!

   Today may be a great day for you but share that greatness with others around you. Cherish the moments that you have with your family and friends around you today!

End of Day Reflection

Five Things I am grateful for:

1
2
3
4
5

What did I learn today?

1
2
3

TO DO TOMORROW

1
2
3
4
5

October 23
Scorpio

"Go out to eat with your best friend today!"

   We don't know when our last day on earth is, so use your time wisely. Spend time with those that are in your life, and create memories, they don't have to be perfect, just take pictures and do what you have always wanted to do. Maybe you have always wanted to go go-karting or play mini golf or laser tag with your friends and family. So go out and do it, go bowling or go out to eat. Great things are done by doers!

End of Day Reflection

Five Things I am grateful for:

1

2

3

4

5

What did I learn today?

1

2

3

TO DO TOMORROW

1

2

3

4

5

"Trust in what you love, continue to do it, and it will always take you to where you need to go." - Natalie Goldberg

Seek the opinions of others as a guidance, weighing your options and deciding what direction you want to go but it's more important to start than it is to over analyze and over think things. The longer you stand there doing nothing, the louder it gets and the more you dismiss even attempting the thing you most want to do. You don't have to outthink it or out smart things you just must move forward. A sailor cannot predict the wind, but you can trust yourself and find patterns along the way and utilize them going ahead.

End of Day Reflection

Five Things I am grateful for:

1

2

3

4

5

What did I learn today?

1

2

3

TO DO TOMORROW

1

2

3

4

5

October 25
Scorpio

"You have the power in you to overcome anything life throws at you." - Les Brown

When struggling with life, we all have the ability to turn back around if you feel you are going in the wrong direction and your errors are not permanent, take the pain and extract the wisdom around you. Dismantle the delusion of perfection and begin. You may be going through a hard time right now but it's only a temporary thing and you have got this! You have so much potential within yourself to accomplish so much so don't give up! If you have a dream and you feel like it's too much, remember that you have it within you to find the right thing you need to do, to go in the right direction and that you have the power to get through whatever that is place in front of you. Imagine yourself looking back at the darkness of struggles right now, how would you get around this obstacle. Putting things in perspective and keeping yourself from caving in the discomfort. "There is a pain of discipline or a pain of regret, choose your pain." – Jim Rohn

What will this pain do for you? Will it be the type of pain that grows us or the type of pain that reminds you of what could have been? Discomfort, confidence being shaky, are not stop signs. They are the cost of admission to accomplish your goals and dreams. It's a challenge you are capable of overcoming. Life is about stepping into things we don't feel ready for and then learning repeatedly that we can piece together the knowledge along the way. Fear is going to show up regardless of what we do in life, but to grow into the people we are capable of becoming.

End of Day Reflection

Five Things I am grateful for:

1

2

3

4

5

What did I learn today?

1

2

3

TO DO TOMORROW

1

2

3

4

5

October 26
Scorpio

"Be willing to destroy anything in your life that isn't excellent." – Joe Polish, Genius Network Founder

"This is a big statement. Think about your world and run through the things that might not meet your standard in your life. Is excellency the standard for everything? How? Willing. The key word is Willing. Its an acceptance of what is, and a willingness to be rigorously honest with yourself. Take a stand and say, "I want a new standard in my life," I am going to be more caring, more prepared, what we can do is start moving to that best version of yourself. Be more aware that you are not shackled to yesterday. Our paths are not dictated to what was. Every passing minute is another chance to turn it all around. Change doesn't happen without the understanding that more is possible. Maybe you have been building self-induced limiting walls around you. Build a bridge to what is to what can be. You can attain better, you may not be perfect or flawless, but be willing to destroy anything in your life that isn't excellent." – Eddie Pinero, Excellence Video

End of Day Reflection

Five Things I am grateful for:

1

2

3

4

5

What did I learn today?

1

2

3

TO DO TOMORROW

1

2

3

4

5

You need to avoid the victim mentality. You are in control of your own destiny, avoid these 11 Signs of Victim Mentality in your everyday life.

1. They are constantly blaming other people or situations for feeling miserable. 2. They possess a "Life is against me" philosophy. 3. They think others are purposely trying to hurt them. 4. They're cynical or pessimistic. 5. They feel powerless to change their circumstances. 6. They enjoy sharing their tragic stories with other people. 7. They have a habit of blaming, attacking, and accusing those they love for how they feel. 8. They are constantly putting themselves down. 9. They believe they are the only one being targeted for mistreatment. 10. They refuse to analyze their beliefs or improve their life. 11. Even when things go right, they find something to complain about.

Never let yourself be a victim. When you are a kid, you cry and whine, you make your parents feel sorry for you when things don't go the right way that you want. The victim mentality does the following two things: It makes you come across hopeless and weak, it doesn't change the situation or get you what you want. The ball is in your court. What do you want? Become the author of your own story. There is always a way to get from point A to point B.

There are two types of people:

1. People who complain about how they look at things are and who accept reality as truth.

2. People who look at what could be, who make the most of any situation. Look at life like clay to be molded and shaped. If this type of person doesn't like something in their life, they change it, when most people would just complain about it.

End of Day Reflection

Five Things I am grateful for:

1

2

3

4

5

What did I learn today?

1

2

3

TO DO TOMORROW

1

2

3

4

5

"Pride is concerned with who is right. Humility is concerned with what is right." - Ezra T Benson

Courage means to be scared and choosing to do it anyway. Courage is about admitting your most well-kept secrets and dreams — even if you can get mocked, ridiculed, and humiliated for them.— Zita Fontaine

We all get scared and have fears at times, especially when it comes down to going towards the uncharted waters of life that we have never been down. We must remember that it is in these times that courage and humility along with holding on to our own integrity is important. Our bosses and various people in our lives have told us what to do, and sometimes what they want us to do goes against the very nature of the fabric of our being and what we believe. We need to keep our integrity in check and remember to have humility when in making decisions and doing *wha*t is morally right regardless of what others say to us or think. Have the courage to accomplish what you most want in life and what will make you happy even if it means you will get mocked, ridiculed, and humiliated for thinking, doing, or even mentioning your dreams and goals. You must have the I don't care attitude so that you can get through the negative mindsets and the "you can't do it" and "lack of support" of people around you. There are times when you will feel down and out for the count but remember you do have a support system around you, and there are people who think you will accomplish what you most want in life. Do not discount the fact that you have made it thus far and you will get through it.

End of Day Reflection

Five Things I am grateful for:

1

2

3

4

5

What did I learn today?

1

2

3

TO DO TOMORROW

1

2

3

4

5

October 29
Scorpio

"When you talk, you are only repeating what you already know. But if you listen, you may learn something new. "

Do not be quick to talk, take time to listen and to understand what is going on and being said around you. Sometimes we forget to listen and in doing so when we are quick to talk, sometimes there is miscommunication about things. If you take the time to listen to those around, you and understand them and what they are going through by putting yourself first in their shoes you see how you can help them by understanding how they are feeling and perhaps why they are saying what they are saying. Sometimes there is even background story to people around others that they are aware of that they can tell you that you may not know of. Speaking of this, when you are around someone else whom you don't like or trust, and your friends or family don't know them, sometimes its best for those around you to figure out on their own if that person whom you don't like, or trust is someone that they like or trust. Speaking ill of someone is never good karma and isn't classy. Someone else's experience of someone may not be the same as what you experienced with that person. People learn from their past mistakes and aren't always going to ruin friendships the same way twice in a row intentionally.

Today think about giving someone in your life or someone who was in your life a second chance. People change over the years and not everyone is toxic.

End of Day Reflection

Five Things I am grateful for:

1

2

3

4

5

What did I learn today?

1

2

3

TO DO TOMORROW

1

2

3

4

5

October 30
Scorpio

"Chasing your dreams is just as crucial as finding your happiness and ultimately your purpose."

Never give up on your dreams. Keep at it, everything is going to be okay and will work out for the best.

Today find happiness in the simple pleasures in life. A Bowl of ice cream or some chocolate, or some coffee. Treat yourself today and maybe treat someone else special in your life.

End of Day Reflection

Five Things I am grateful for:

1

2

3

4

5

What did I learn today?

1

2

3

TO DO TOMORROW

1

2

3

4

5

October 31
Scorpio

"Do you have a legacy to leave behind? What will people remember about you? Are you satisfied with the life you have led thus far?? Have you always ensured that the last conversation you have had with everyone is a positive one?

If you are overthinking, write it down,
If you are anxious, meditate,
If you are sad, exercise,
If you are stressed, go for a walk,
If you are angry, listen to music,
If you are lazy, reduce your screen time,
If you are burnt out, read a book,
But whatever you do, you need to keep moving forward.

I'd rather be saying, "Oh well," than "What If" and along those things an "Oh well," is really powerful thing to say because if you are saying "Oh well," it that means somethings not going to plan/ You say "Oh well," and move on. Somethings not going to plan means you have learned from it. So, saying, "Oh well," is much better than "What if." Because what "What if has," is the burden of what that could have been. That could have been such an amazing relationship, but it was ruined. That business could have gone so well I had that idea, but I never executed it. That business could have been my whole life's dream and purpose, but I never cared about it because it was too challenging. "What if," "What if," is a dangerous place to be in. But "Oh well," it's like well it happened but I've learned from it and now I'm just not going to do that again. @morechrisgriffin

End of Day Reflection

Five Things I am grateful for:

1

2

3

4

5

What did I learn today?

1

2

3

TO DO TOMORROW

1

2

3

4

5

November 1
Scorpio

"Do today what others are unwilling to do today, so tomorrow you will find yourself one step ahead in success." In life, the most miraculous things grow in silence. Find the silence in yourself to get inner peace.

Things to work on this month: Try not to feel like you have to control everything going on around you, if you do this you could come across as intolerant, jealous, and manipulative. Work on not being too possessive, paranoid, clingy, and vindictive. Try not to think too much in situations going on around you because then you will start to dream up things that aren't actually going on around you. If you start assuming the worst in everyone and everything it can be self-destructive in behavior. Work on not being a vengeful person. People make mistakes and yes sometimes we get feelings of "wanting to get even" but the way I see it, there are already enough bad and mean people in the world, why would you want to be another one? People often get what's coming to them in other ways when they mess up in life and they end up learning from their mistakes, even sometimes when it is too late. Life is too short to hold grudges against others, it will hurt you more than it hurts them in the end. Sometimes its just better to forgive others and move forward.

End of Day Reflection

Five Things I am grateful for:

1

2

3

4

5

What did I learn today?

1

2

3

TO DO TOMORROW

1

2

3

4

5

November 2
Scorpio

"Go where you can grow. If you have reached the maximum growth that you can reach in and around where you are at in your life, change and do something about it so you can further yourself. It's your education and your life. This way you can face new challenges and grow head on constantly.

@morechrisgriffin introduces Jim Forton – Transform your life from the inside out Podcast, "Be Do Have" mindset versus a "Have Do Be" mindset

"He talks about living in a "Be Do Have mindset versus a "Have Do Be" mindset. Most people live in the "Have Do Be" mindset and that's when its like "When I Have these things, I am doing to be able to Do these things, and then I am going to be able to Be this person. The problem is where that all stems from is, "When I have these things, I can do this." You don't have those things now; you can't stop being that person until you have them, so you are constantly waiting. Or when I move here, I am going to have a better life, or when I meet the man of my dreams, I am going to have a better life. It's always when I do this, and I need to have this before I can do this. <u>No switch that</u>, **Be** the person you want to become and **Do** the things that that person does in her or his day-to-day life and then in return you will **Have** the life you want to live. Be Do Have, it was a complete switch in mindset from what people normally think and act, to a new framework. It comes down to belief in yourself. Problem is when your inner dialogue is something negative or something that is not getting you closer, like saying "when I have this, I will be able to have these things," as soon as your inner dialogue says this that's you battling you, battling your own brain and your own subconscious mind. Telling yourself about this day in and day out, that you can't do that until you have this. You're reframing the conversations you are having with yourself, so that then you can get closer and closer to your goals, because in your mind you have already done it, time is just catching up."

End of Day Reflection

Five Things I am grateful for:

1

2

3

4

5

What did I learn today?

1

2

3

TO DO TOMORROW

1

2

3

4

5

November 3
Scorpio

> "Lead others around you by example, and help out those that are struggling."

At the bare minimum, upon my reflection about life in general, that if one goes through life struggling to get by, it is at these moments when we hope to have that support system that we have chosen to surround ourselves to be there for us. That they would without thought, reach out a hand to help us out in our times of great need with empathy, care, and love. I know that there are those whom people tend to enable and ensure their needs are always met without consequence or ability to grow up, but at times it is always too good to bear in mind that we all need help at some point in our lives. That no one is meant to be put through the trials of life without a helping hand occasionally, especially if there is proof that there is a need for help. I find reaching out to help others is easier for me than to ask for help. I don't know if this is able to connect to you today, but this is the time of giving and being thankful for what we have. Not to take it all for granted is an understatement. There are those who have less than us and who are still willing to give more of themselves to others without expectation of help from anyone else in return. Be aware of those who have helped you in times of need and don't hesitate to check on them to see if you could give them a helping hand as well today. There is nothing wrong with helping others and nor is there anything wrong with asking for the help of others. Sometimes people take joy in the ability to be able to help others. Give someone that chance to be there for you too this week.

End of Day Reflection

Five Things I am grateful for:

1

2

3

4

5

What did I learn today?

1

2

3

TO DO TOMORROW

1

2

3

4

5

November 4
Scorpio

"People think you always have to be happy, but that couldn't be further from the truth. Behind every strong person is a past that gave them no choice. Behind every warrior are scars and bruises that made them stronger. Sometimes the unplanned things lead you to the most amazing, beautiful destinations. You didn't plan to be the strong person you are today, but, here you are!"
@cross.novia

"Maybe not today, but one day. Maybe soon, or maybe not. Healing is not always a straight line. You are going to have your ups and your downs. You are going to feel like you are on top of the mountain and then the next day there is another mountain to climb. But trust me, you have to keep going because someday is just around the corner."
@cross.novia

Everyone heals and deals with things differently and that is okay.

End of Day Reflection

Five Things I am grateful for:

1

2

3

4

5

What did I learn today?

1

2

3

TO DO TOMORROW

1

2

3

4

5

November 5
Scorpio

"Find your purpose to find contentment in your life."

What are you passionate about? What makes you happy. Yesterday is in the past. You cannot change it. You may plant an orange tree, and yet you may wish for an apple or peach tree, but it will always be an orange tree. However, knowing that yesterday was the past, and today is the present, you can make today an even better day. There are things that are out of your control like the weather but focus on what you can control and how you can make today a great day! We all strive to try to be perfect or at least the best we can be but there is no greater reward than seeing the happiness in someone else around us who may be having a bad day. We easily forget that everyone else who we meet on the day to day, has their own struggles that they are dealing with. The server at the restaurant, the teacher in the classroom, the janitor in the hallway of an office building, the construction worker, the concierge at the hotel, the bus driver on our route to work or school. These are everyday people with shift jobs like us that we run across and not everyone has it easy. Reach out to someone today and show them that it's okay, and that today is going to be a good day. Be that positive light in their darkness. Sometimes it's a simple smile or a tip to the server that can make someone's day.

End of Day Reflection

Five Things I am grateful for:

1

2

3

4

5

What did I learn today?

1

2

3

TO DO TOMORROW

1

2

3

4

5

November 6
Scorpio

"Don't be afraid of what is and what you think that you cannot change."

Any power that surpasses reason, still comes from reason, right? Believing in yourself to be able to accomplish your own dreams and goals isn't some kind of miraculous power. It is a talent that only works when the flow of positive energy inside of us and the flow of energy in the natural world are in perfect synchronization. Meaning if you know what you want and you speak it into existence the world around you will help conspire to try to make it happen. To put your dreams and goals into action, one must have a strong mind and the ability to focus with consistency. Your reason why should take over your being and come pouring out of your soul from within. If all we do is worry about following the rules of what you think can and can't be possible, then your self-esteem, self-belief, and by extension your own hopes dreams and goals will never progress. Don't let those blowhards that are around you scare you! Follow the path you believe in. We cannot choose another's path. It's best to let them be if you see someone who is determined to go their own way in life but be a support system for others too when you can.

End of Day Reflection

Five Things I am grateful for:

1

2

3

4

5

What did I learn today?

1

2

3

TO DO TOMORROW

1

2

3

4

5

November 7
Scorpio

"You can die tomorrow, so with this realization, what do you want to do today so you don't go through tomorrow in regret?

Life is too short and fragile to waste it living a fake life. Say things to people as they are and as you mean it to an extent, mind professionalism and the right way to truthfully say things. Some people are sensitive and cannot handle bluntness but realize today that if you don't speak about things as you feel them, not saying what you mean, and feel can lead things astray. For example, someone is presenting you with an idea for a project to work on. Yes, you enjoy working with that person but the idea that they have has some Swiss cheese holes in them that you can foresee. If you don't speak up and tell them that you see the holes and you don't share with them that things will not work according to plan and to prepare for certain situations, you are not helping that person out. Yes, it may seem hurtful to tell that person it won't work but better than when they are more than fully invested in the project only to be told later that something has gone awry. It is in these moments you can say, "I love the idea but there is a slight flaw in the plan, *so let's do it this way*." And offer a new solution. Better to lift someone up and suggest that you are all going to tackle the project by saying "So let's do it this way" and offering a new solution than just turning it down completely without rhyme or reason. It comes down to how you handle the conversation and how you emotionally sensitively break it down to someone that matters more as they will respect you as a person more instead of shutting them down in front of everyone during the presentation.

End of Day Reflection

Five Things I am grateful for:

1

2

3

4

5

What did I learn today?

1

2

3

TO DO TOMORROW

1

2

3

4

5

"Nothing and no one lasts forever, so don't waste today and don't waste your tomorrow, live it to the fullest."

Today go out and enjoy the day. If it's a rough day weatherwise instead of going on the walk, go to the mall or the movie theatre. Take some time to yourself. Enjoy a meal at a food court. Change your scenery up a bit.

End of Day Reflection

Five Things I am grateful for:

1

2

3

4

5

What did I learn today?

1

2

3

TO DO TOMORROW

1

2

3

4

5

November 9
Scorpio

"YOU GOT THIS TODAY! So, push yourself to a new unreached level!"

Get back into gear and get yourself to that next level. Do what you can to get ahead of things for the week and impress people around you. Today is your day, show the world what you got and motivate everyone around you to make their mark in the day, to give it all they got and to make two steps towards the right direction! Don't let anyone bring you down and realize that people are very grateful for what you do for them! You are loved and appreciated and even though no one has told you this, just think how much of a difference you are making in the lives of those around you by doing what you do!

End of Day Reflection

Five Things I am grateful for:

1

2

3

4

5

What did I learn today?

1

2

3

TO DO TOMORROW

1

2

3

4

5

November 10
Scorpio

"Don't be afraid to work more than another person."

Being afraid of hard work is like a salesman being afraid of people. You need to work to survive, you need the sales to pay for a roof over your head and food on the table. Sometimes you have to do things that you don't like in life in order to get to that next level. If you work harder than the person next to you, then you are that much harder to replace in the job. Show others in leadership above you that you have what it takes to handle more. Eventually as you are noticed and the numbers and production improve you might be offered new doors of opportunity for you to seize and as you open them, they will change your life. Have the foresight to see that you could move up where you are, leadership wise, or pay wise! Never give up! Keep pushing forward! Stay positive! Find the things that you have to be grateful for in life!

End of Day Reflection

Five Things I am grateful for:

1

2

3

4

5

What did I learn today?

1

2

3

TO DO TOMORROW

1

2

3

4

5

November 11
Scorpio

"The quality of your life is a direct reflection of the quality of your beliefs, thoughts, habits, and perspective."

Increasing the healthy habits in your life and seeing things in a better more positive perspective and being open minded are just a few things that you could do to increase the quality of your life in small simple steps. Even the simple idea of making your bed every morning increases the feelings of accomplishment that you need to start off your day right. First positive thought of the day, I made my bed. It is a healthy habit and a good positive thought, and it will increase your positive perspective of the day. Find more things that will increase that dopamine in your everyday life.

End of Day Reflection

Five Things I am grateful for:

1

2

3

4

5

What did I learn today?

1

2

3

TO DO TOMORROW

1

2

3

4

5

November 12
Scorpio

"Your words become your thoughts. Your thoughts become your beliefs; your beliefs become your life. Be careful what you speak about in your life."

Stay positive today! No matter what is placed in front of you, you need to know that you are going to be okay, everything happens for a reason, even if you don't see the silver lining right away. Have faith that it will all work out for the best in the end.

End of Day Reflection

Five Things I am grateful for:

1

2

3

4

5

What did I learn today?

1

2

3

TO DO TOMORROW

1

2

3

4

5

November 13
Scorpio

"When it feels scary to jump, that is exactly when you jump, otherwise you end up staying in the same place your whole life and it's never too late to make the jump chance to change the rest of your life!"

"I left a 15-year career in human resources to become a baker."
—Liz Berman, 43, Natick, MA

"I started off making cakes for my kids and quickly realized that baking provided me with a creative outlet that had been missing from my work in human resources. I started posting pictures of my work on Facebook and soon developed a large following. Friends and friends of friends started asking me to make cakes for them, so I figured I should give this a shot as a business! After several years baking at night while working in my office during the day, I decided to take the leap and go full-time with it. That was five years ago, and I never looked back! Since then, the business has grown dramatically! It was clearly the best decision for me because it taps into a creative and entrepreneurial side of me that had previously been unfulfilled. The added bonus is I'm able to be home for my kids every day when they come home from school!"
https://www.rd.com/list/never-too-late-change-your-life/

Today think about the ways in which you make money into your home. Most millionaire's have at least 6 sources of income coming in for profits and some of its residual income. How prepared are you for your next car breakdown or emergency? Think of ways in which you can increase your ROI (return on investments) or ways in which you can earn more income coming in using your passion, or doing things that you are passionate or most knowledgeable about. Or think about doing things that you always wanted to learn more about that you can do on the side to increase your income.

End of Day Reflection

Five Things I am grateful for:

1

2

3

4

5

What did I learn today?

1

2

3

TO DO TOMORROW

1

2

3

4

5

November 14
Scorpio

"You had a purpose before anyone had an opinion. Keep going." - Danny Castilho

Meeting people is never an accident. Someone cannot walk in and out of your life without reason. Lessons and the growth that you experience are never spontaneous. It is always meant to be. There is a higher purpose, and end beyond you and I, which we will never know until we reach it. So, I want you to stop treating your experiences as casual experiences that just happened and start looking for deeper meaning, and end or a goal. Something that helps you flourish, that teaches you the important lessons that only people and their existence can give you. There is a plan for you – Think about it. In a world consisting of 7 billion people, each capable of teaching you something. Why did your path cross with this person? Because you needed a particular lesson at this point of your life. Think about it deeply, only then will you stop treating your growth as an accident and start appreciating it as a beautiful journey meant for you! There is so much in life to be grateful for even within the lessons of life that we learn along the way. Take it all in!

End of Day Reflection

Five Things I am grateful for:

1

2

3

4

5

What did I learn today?

1

2

3

TO DO TOMORROW

1

2

3

4

5

November 15
Scorpio

"Sometimes you must hurt in order to know, fall in order to grow, lose in order to gain, because most of life's greatest lessons are learned through pain."

Looking back at your life, how many times have you been hurt? How many times have you fallen? When these things happened to you what did you learn from them? How did you grow? What did you gain? What lessons have you learned since then? These are lessons that you might have gained and learned from people who were or are no longer in your life. Sometimes the cruelest teacher is experience and through the swords of truth of people around you. When going through life's battles hold that shield of positivity up, never let it bring you down, learn and grow, and continue pushing forward.

End of Day Reflection

Five Things I am grateful for:

1

2

3

4

5

What did I learn today?

1

2

3

TO DO TOMORROW

1

2

3

4

5

November 16
Scorpio

"We are all in the same game, just different levels. Dealing with the same hell, just different devils."

When looking at Facebook, Instagram, twitter, or even if you are hearing about your high school or college friends getting married or already having kids or adoptions or having baby showers, sometimes we just get jealous and compare ourselves to them. Not everyone's chapter 12 is your chapter 4. For some, sometimes life happens faster or slower for others and sometimes life doesn't always go the way we planned and that's okay, as long as you are happy, and you are successful or on your way to success of accomplishing your dreams.

End of Day Reflection

Five Things I am grateful for:

1

2

3

4

5

What did I learn today?

1

2

3

TO DO TOMORROW

1

2

3

4

5

November 17
Scorpio

"Know your worth, you must find the courage to leave the table if respect is no longer served." - Tene Edwards

A strong relationship with anyone has Loyalty, honesty, trust, communication, Unconditional love, and most of all Respect. If these values are not there at this table with the other person, you must leave it. You must value yourself and love yourself enough to surround yourself with people who value you, your time, and your opinion, and who love and care about you in all aspects of life. Surround yourself with doers, and thinkers, and go getters, people who are always willing to learn and grow and be better than they were yesterday. Being in an environment with these values and types of people will only encourage and enable your successes in life even further. If you find that your circle of people around you are no supporting you and you are missing these core values, maybe you have outgrown your circle and need to find a new one. Surround yourself with "Only Quality People, OQP" as Les Brown says, "birds of a feather, flock together."

End of Day Reflection

Five Things I am grateful for:

1

2

3

4

5

What did I learn today?

1

2

3

TO DO TOMORROW

1

2

3

4

5

"If you want to change, if you really want to change, you need to make a statement. A statement says, "No more." A statement says, "Never again." A Statement says, "today everything is different." If you are serious about change, you will make that statement. Not just a statement of words, but also you will follow through with a direct intentional statement of action."

"You have chaos in your soul, and lightning in your veins. You my dear, we are made for wild, magical things." – Erin Matlock

End of Day Reflection

Five Things I am grateful for:

1

2

3

4

5

What did I learn today?

1

2

3

TO DO TOMORROW

1

2

3

4

5

November 19
Scorpio

"Surround yourself with people who remind you that you matter and support you in ways that matter most to you. No person, situation, or circumstance can define who you are. Don't give up, don't cave in, or stop believing that it's possible. It's not over until you win." - Les Brown.

You love so hard because you have been hurt so much. You never want anyone to feel as lonely as you have felt so you give and give until you have nothing left. You need to trust that you are still loveable without giving all of yourself away. This is the hardest thing you will ever have to do. Tell yourself that you are worthy of love and fully believe in it. You are worthy of the same devotion that you give to others, and this is the truth.

End of Day Reflection

Five Things I am grateful for:

1

2

3

4

5

What did I learn today?

1

2

3

TO DO TOMORROW

1

2

3

4

5

November 20
Scorpio

"If you have got the time to worry about what other people think of you, you are not living big enough. Focus on your own path, your own passion, and your own purpose."

Can you remember who you were before the world told you who you should be? – Charles Bukowski

7 Signs that you are a healer.

- People naturally feel drawn to confide in you.
- You have compassion for all living beings.
- Cities, crowds, and shopping centers can drain your batteries very fast.
- You feel other people's emotions.
- You get the urge to go and be in nature.
- You have a deep sense of calling to be of service and help others.
- Your pain and suffering become your strength and motivation.

End of Day Reflection

Five Things I am grateful for:

1

2

3

4

5

What did I learn today?

1

2

3

TO DO TOMORROW

1

2

3

4

5

November 21
Scorpio

"Shoutout to the people who haven't felt okay recently but are getting up every day and refusing to quit. Stay strong."
- Unknown

10 Deep feelings that you may have experienced without realizing it:

o Nostalgia for a moment that has yet to happen.
o The bittersweet joy of watching loved ones grow older.
o The ache of missing someone you've never met.
o The profound connection felt with a stranger in a fleeting moment.
o The yearning for a place you've never been to
o The quiet satisfaction of finding beauty in the simplest of things.
o The inexplicable sadness that accompanies profound happiness.
o The comfort found in solitude and embracing your own company.
o The heartache of witnessing the passage of time and the fleeting nature of life.
o The overwhelming gratitude for the small moments of everyday life.

End of Day Reflection

Five Things I am grateful for:

1

2

3

4

5

What did I learn today?

1

2

3

TO DO TOMORROW

1

2

3

4

5

"Self-control is strength. Calmness is mastery. You have to get to a point where your mood does not shift based on the insignificant actions of someone else. Don't allow others to control the direction of your life. Don't allow your emotions to overpower your intelligence."

Things that happened today that you didn't notice:

- Someone heard a song and was transported to a memory with you.
- Someone thought of you today and smiled.
- You appeared in someone's list of things to be grateful for.
- Someone saw something that reminded them of you and thought, "they'd like this."
- A stranger admired something about you but was too nervous to say anything.

End of Day Reflection

Five Things I am grateful for:

1

2

3

4

5

What did I learn today?

1

2

3

TO DO TOMORROW

1

2

3

4

5

"Learn how to be happy with what you have while you pursue all that you want." - Jim Rohn

"I think the saddest people always try their hardest to make people happy because they know what it's like to feel absolutely worthless and they don't want anyone else to feel like that." – Robin Williams

Some people are like books, they don't reveal much on the cover, but they have a whole world inside of them. They don't talk much but they have a lot to say. They just need someone who can read them, understand them, and remember them.

End of Day Reflection

Five Things I am grateful for:

1

2

3

4

5

What did I learn today?

1

2

3

TO DO TOMORROW

1

2

3

4

5

November 24
Sagittarius

"Doubt kills more dreams than failure ever will."

If someone is falling behind in life, you don't have to remind them. Believe me, they already know. If someone is unhealthy, they know. If someone is struggling in their relationships, with money, with self-image, they know. It's what consumes their thoughts each day. What you need to do for those who are struggling is not to reprimand them but encourage them. Tell them what's good about their lives, show them the potential that you see. Love them where they are. When we can't see clearly for ourselves, we need others to speak greatness over us. People don't need you to tell them what's wrong with their lives, they already know. They need you to reassure them that they can still make it right and try to better themselves.

End of Day Reflection

Five Things I am grateful for:

1

2

3

4

5

What did I learn today?

1

2

3

TO DO TOMORROW

1

2

3

4

5

November 25
Sagittarius

"Life is like riding a bicycle. To keep your balance, you must keep moving." - Albert Einstein

When riding a bicycle, the gentle wind serves as a reminder that we can feel things even if we can't see them, which brings us a sense of calm. Sometimes, we form stronger connections with others when we talk less and listen more.

Today take some time to yourself and feel yourself in peace and calm.

End of Day Reflection

Five Things I am grateful for:

1
2
3
4
5

What did I learn today?

1
2
3

TO DO TOMORROW

1
2
3

"Problems are like washing machines, they twist us, spin us, knock us around, but in the end, we will always come out cleaner, brighter, and better."

I've been told, "You are too kind." And sometimes I feel frustrated with myself for being so compassionate. But then I remember that having a good heart is an essential part of who I am. If I were to lose that, then I would lose my true self.

The most beautiful people we have known are those who have known defeat, known suffering, known struggle, known loss, and have found their way out of the depths. These people have an appreciation, a sensitivity, and an understanding of life that fills them with compassion, gentleness, and a deep loving concern. Beautiful people do not just happen.

End of Day Reflection

Five Things I am grateful for:

1

2

3

4

5

What did I learn today?

1

2

3

TO DO TOMORROW

1

2

3

4

5

"There is a difference between being liked and being valued. A lot of people like you. Not many value you. Be valued."

Plato was asked what are the behaviors of people that surprise you the most?

o When they get bored in childhood and hurry to grow up but then they miss their childhood they lose their health to earn money but then they pay their money to regain their health. Worried tomorrow, they forget about today, in the end, they live neither in today nor tomorrow, they live as if they will never die but they die as if they have never lived.
  o So, what do you suggest?
    ▪ - Don't try to make everyone like you, the only thing to do is to leave yourself to be loved, and the most important thing in life is not to have the most but to need the least.

End of Day Reflection

Five Things I am grateful for:

1

2

3

4

5

What did I learn today?

1

2

3

TO DO TOMORROW

1

2

3

4

5

"Sometimes you have to distance yourself from people and that is okay. "

"You must do the work to heal yourself, even when it hurts – especially when it hurts, so that you don't continue to approach life within the boundary of just surviving. Be unapologetic in the way you exist. Take up space. Because our existence is finite. And as hard as that is to understand, from time to time remind yourself that in the most human way we are all living on borrowed time. And that is liberating, because it is pressing there is urgency to let go and live.

End of Day Reflection

Five Things I am grateful for:

1

2

3

4

5

What did I learn today?

1

2

3

TO DO TOMORROW

1

2

3

4

5

"Sometimes it takes ten years to get to that 1 year that will change your life. Keep going. "

Five wise quotes to embrace before your journey ends:

o A good partner is an investment, and an immature partner is a liability, their mindset will shape your children and not just their body and looks. Choose wisely.
o Act as if you can't afford the bread until they find out you own the bakery.
o Be shameless about learning new skills, nobody will support you if you become broke.
o Being broke is a part of the game but staying broke is a personal choice.

End of Day Reflection

Five Things I am grateful for:

1

2

3

4

5

What did I learn today?

1

2

3

TO DO TOMORROW

1

2

3

4

5

"Give. But don't allow yourself to be used. Love. But don't allow your heart to be abused. Trust. But don't be naive. Listen. But don't lose your own voice."

Hard Hitting Quotes Ep 9 – You came into their life, to show them the meaning of true love, they came into your life to show you the meaning of self-love. - @morechrisgriffin

A soulmate isn't someone who completes you. No, a soulmate is someone who inspires you to complete yourself. A Soulmate is someone who loves you with so much conviction, and so much heart, that it is nearly impossible to doubt just how capable you are of becoming exactly who you have always wanted to be. - @thespiritualmagic

End of Day Reflection

Five Things I am grateful for:

1

2

3

4

5

What did I learn today?

1

2

3

TO DO TOMORROW

1

2

3

4

5

December 1
Sagittarius

"If you think success is only about the money…. You have already lost."

Maybe you are like me, you like taking care of people because it heals the part of you that needed someone to take care of you. You know how it feels to be alone, to be hurt, to be ignored. You don't want anyone else to go through that. You want to be the person you wish you had when you were struggling. You want to give what you didn't receive. You want to make a difference in someone's life. You like taking care of people because it makes you feel whole. It makes you feel like you matter. It makes you feel like you are not alone.

Things to work on this month: While it's good to have an open mind, one thing to understand is that not everyone is open-minded and sometimes are not able to see things fully in a clear picture as you. Work on following through with your ambitions in life and not being lazy and feeling easily bored. Another thing to work on this month is being more responsible, making sure you are on top of bills, and other responsibilities that you may have. While it is good to be optimistic in life about things sometimes, we also must see that there may come times when things don't go as planned or things take a turn for the worst, but you can't let that bring you down or prevent you from trying. Lastly, take a chill pill, quite literally I mean this. Sometimes, we get bored with things as they are, and you might feel restless about things in life. I have learned that by looking at things generally and more simply and by having gratitude for the small things, you will find yourself more at ease about things. Keep pushing yourself by being optimistic and open minded and enthusiastic about the future, there are more good times to come!

End of Day Reflection

Five Things I am grateful for:

1

2

3

4

5

What did I learn today?

1

2

3

TO DO TOMORROW

1

2

3

4

5

"In any given moment, we have two options; to step forward into growth or step back into safety. Growth must be chosen again and again. Fear must be overcome again and again."

- Abraham Maslow.

Things to deeply think about:

• What's something you want to ask me but are too afraid to say?
• If you walked into a room with everyone you've ever met, who would you go looking for?
• What's the thing you regret the most?
• How would you describe the most beautiful thing in the world?
• What's the most admirable aspect of human nature and the worst?
• What does 'live in the moment' mean to you?

End of Day Reflection

Five Things I am grateful for:

1

2

3

4

5

What did I learn today?

1

2

3

TO DO TOMORROW

1

2

3

4

5

December 3
Sagittarius

"If you expect the world to be fair with you because you are fair, you are fooling yourself. That's like expecting the lion not to eat you because you didn't eat him."

3 things to give up in life - If you are willing to give up all three it is highly likely that your overall life quality will be significantly enhanced:

- Give up excuses.
  o Excuses hold you back from reaching your goals, take responsibility for your actions and focus on finding solutions instead of making excuses. Embrace determination and perseverance to overcome challenges.
- Give up Toxic Habits
  o Negative Habits drain your energy and hinder personal growth and identify and let go of habits that no longer serve you. Replace them with positive actions that align with your goals and values. Surround yourself with supportive people who inspire you.
- Give up Fear of Failure
  o Fear of failure prevents us from pursuing our dreams, embrace failure as a steppingstone to success. View setbacks as opportunities for growth, take risks and believe in yourself and learn from each experience. Finish what you start.

End of Day Reflection

Five Things I am grateful for:

1

2

3

4

5

What did I learn today?

1

2

3

TO DO TOMORROW

1

2

3

4

5

December 4
Sagittarius

"You are responsible for your own reality. Decide what you want of the world and go make it happen. No clarity, no change, no goals, no growth." - Brendan Burchard

Self-control is strength. Calmness is mastery. You must get to a point where your mood doesn't shift based on the insignificant actions of someone else. Don't allow your emotions to overpower your intelligence.

I made peace with me. I stopped finding fault with me and I stopped trying to find fault in you. I stopped looking for reasons to feel bad. I started to look for reasons to feel good. I stopped making the worst of things and I started making the best of things. I stopped asking other people to be the reason for me feeling better, and I decided that I can be the reason for me feeling better. And for that decision I found ultimate freedom.

End of Day Reflection

Five Things I am grateful for:

1

2

3

4

5

What did I learn today?

1

2

3

TO DO TOMORROW

1

2

3

4

5

December 5
Sagittarius

"It's not important that you become a good fighter in this world. It is not important that you become a good spiritual guide in this world. It is important that you find a way to live a pleasant life, and in the best-case support other people so that they also find the same. This is what it is about, no matter what form or culture background you put it. The main idea is If you don't find a way to reduce the suffering of your surroundings, your suffering won't stop." – Master Shi Heng Yi

"You've probably heard the saying "Pain is inevitable; suffering is optional. For many years, I didn't understand how pain and suffering were different from each other. They seemed inextricably wrapped up together, and I took it for granted that one was the inevitable consequence of the other. However, as I have grown to understand my own capacity to create happiness, I noticed something interesting about the nature of my suffering. As I reflect on painful episodes in my life, I can recall losing people who were dear to me. I remember abrupt changes in jobs, housing, and other opportunities that I believed were the basis of my happiness. In each of those experiences the immediate visceral pain was searing, like a hot knife cutting through my heart. Then afterwards came grief, an emotional response to loss that arose quite naturally. But closely on the heels of physical pain and emotional grief comes something else, something that I create in my own mind even though it feels quite real. That something else is "suffering." …Suffering is the "extra" that our mind adds to an already painful situation. It is at this very point, when your mind starts to fiddle with the pain and grief, that you have the possibility of doing things differently. If you're amid great pain right now, it might help to know that the old saying really is true: While the pain can't be avoided—it's the price of being a human with a heart—there are ways we can reduce this kind of self-generated suffering.
….

1. Don't "spin" your story "Spin doctors" are media maestros who take an event and distort it to serve their political goals. We often do something similar when it comes to our emotional life, although we don't realize that it doesn't serve us. We tell ourselves all kinds of stories about what it

could mean based on our past experiences or future fears. When we tell ourselves that the end of a relationship will ruin the rest of our lives, or that no one else could ever understand what we are going through, or that there is no way out of our suffering, we are adding layers of meaning that don't exist within the original feeling. We have no way of knowing any of these things with any certainty. This is a sure source of suffering. Mindfulness meditation can be a very effective way to work with our mind's habitual tendency to spin a story. By practicing noticing our thoughts and feelings just as they are and gently stopping ourselves when we catch ourselves creating a story on top of them, we can begin to liberate ourselves from this tendency.

2. <u>Embrace change.</u> During difficult situations, I've sometimes said to myself in a very gloomy way, "My life will never be the same again." Then I realized how silly that statement is—or at least how deceptive it is to think of change only in the negative sense. The statement that our life will never be the same again is not false. In fact, it's true every moment! Change is always happening. Sometimes the change is for the "good," sometimes it's painful. But we can never know the ultimate outcome of a change. What might seem horrible today may in the long run turn out to be just what we need to take us to the next step of our life. If we can learn to lean into change rather than resist it, we'll find the possibility inherent in a situation.

3. <u>Smile, even if you don't feel it inside.</u> Thich Nhat Hanh once said, "Sometimes your joy is the source of your smile, but sometimes your smile can be the source of your joy." This is a wonderful reminder that we have more power to change our mood than we realize. Something as simple as finding the smile that is inside of us, even when life hurts, can help us access that deep well of joy. It may feel forced at first but watch what happens to your state of mind when you practice smiling. And notice how people react differently to you when you smile at them. These kinds of positive feedback loops can make a big difference in overcoming our own suffering rather than being entrenched in it.

4. <u>Jolt yourself out of your usual routine.</u> Sometimes suffering comes about because we've ground ourselves down into a rut. We obsess over our loss and can't seem to think of anything else. At times like these, it helps to give our psyche and soul a jumpstart by doing something we wouldn't normally do. Maybe it's time to take that trip to Europe that you've dreamed of. Maybe it's time to register for that yoga class that you've been considering. Maybe it's time to say a kind word to a stranger you pass on the sidewalk. Whatever

it is that may pull you out of your rut, give it a try and see how it changes the nature of your suffering.

5. Soften someone else's suffering. When we experience pain, it's easy to isolate ourselves and believe that no one has it worse than we do. While whatever pain you are experiencing is unique to you, it helps to remember that all human beings share the capacity for joy and suffering. Having contact with someone else who is also having a difficult time and offering them simple kindness can be a great antidote to our own suffering. Bring flowers to an elderly aunt at a nursing home and take time to listen to her stories. Look into the eyes of a homeless person as you walk down the street and give him a kind word. Volunteer on the children's floor of your local hospital and play a game of checkers with the kids there. You may not be ready to do this right away. But once you've made it through the acute phase of a painful experience, see if you can push yourself a bit beyond your comfort zone to spend time with someone else who is going through a hard time. Offer some simple kindness to that person. And watch what happens inside of you.

6. Remember your basic goodness. "Basic goodness" is a wonderful concept that comes from the Shambhala Buddhist tradition. It reminds us that no matter how chaotic or negative the circumstances of our life, there is a ground of basic goodness in ourselves and in the universe that we can count on. Tibetan Buddhist teacher Chogyam Trungpa Rinpoche put it like this: "If we are willing to take an unbiased look, we will find that, in spite of all our problems and confusion, all our emotional and psychological ups and downs, there is something basically good about our existence as human beings." When you are amid deep pain, allow yourself to touch back into this truth—or at least the possibility of this truth. You can do this in very simple ways. Take a walk outside and appreciate the warmth of the sun on your face. Drink a sip of cool, fresh water. Each of these actions can help to remind you that in a multitude of ways, the universe is supporting you. This basic truth is deeply healing and deeply reassuring. Finally, it's good to remember that while there is self-generated suffering, there is also self-generated happiness. May you make some for yourself today!

6 Ways to Decrease Your Suffering (tinybuddha.com)
https://tinybuddha.com/blog/6-ways-to-decrease-your-suffering/

End of Day Reflection

Five Things I am grateful for:

1

2

3

4

5

What did I learn today?

1

2

3

TO DO TOMORROW

1

2

3

4

5

December 6
Sagittarius

"Accept that you are not perfect but that you are enough. and then start working on everything that destroys you. Your insecurities, your ego, your dark thoughts. You will see in the end that you are going to make peace with yourself. And that's the greatest thing in the world." - Finja Brandenburg

They say when two people are angry at each other, do you know why they shout when they are so close together? Ancient Sufi Saint – The reason why they shout is although they are next to each other physically their hearts have become so far apart, they need to shout because they feel that they need to make up the difference that has been created. It works the other way as well. When you have a very loving relationship and your heart is close to someone, sometimes you can be with them in the room and you don't have to say a word and you make even just a movement of your face, and then they can read you and what you are trying say without even you saying anything at all to them and you understand each other

End of Day Reflection

Five Things I am grateful for:

1

2

3

4

5

What did I learn today?

1

2

3

TO DO TOMORROW

1

2

3

4

5

"The world is but a canvas to our imaginations."- Henry David Thoreau

Canvas fabric has very strong rugged material that is difficult to tear. But even the smallest snip of cloth from scissors can damage the integrity of the cloth which ruins the cloth and makes it easier to rip apart. Even the strongest fabric of friendship can unravel when there is a loss of integrity.

What is a best friend? It isn't the one that makes your problems disappear, it's one that doesn't disappear when you are facing your problems.

End of Day Reflection

Five Things I am grateful for:

1

2

3

4

5

What did I learn today?

1

2

3

TO DO TOMORROW

1

2

3

4

5

December 8
Sagittarius

"Because in the end, we are all just dreamers in the endless universe."

There are only two ways to live your life:

One is as though nothing is a miracle.

The other is as though everything is…

If you let people's perception of you dictate your behavior, you will never grow as a person. But if you leave yourself open to experience despite what others think, then you will learn and grow.

Stop and look at your life… You are exactly where you are meant to be today. Stop looking at everyone else's life and thinking you are behind, stop thinking that you would be happier if… x happens. It's important to appreciate where you are right now because this is your life. And it is what you make it. You are doing amazing things, and you don't give yourself enough credit. Yes, it's great to have something to work towards, but don't forget that where you are right now: Someone is probably wishing for at the moment. Be Present and love hard because you are not going to get this moment again. Social media makes you think you are being, you are not rich enough, you are not popular enough, you are not skinny enough, but listen to this, you are perfect just the way you are and remember that you are loved and cared for.

End of Day Reflection

Five Things I am grateful for:

1

2

3

4

5

What did I learn today?

1

2

3

TO DO TOMORROW

1

2

3

4

5

"For in our dreams we enter a world that is entirely our own." - Albus Dumbledore

   This is for you: I want to remind you of something important: I am so proud of you. Yes, you read that right. Despite the struggles and hardships that you have faced, you have shown incredible strength and perseverance. I see your journey and all the obstacles you have overcome. You have endured so much, and I want you to know that I am here with you, every step of the way. I have witnessed your determination, your unwavering spirit, and your refusal to give up. It fills my heart with joy and admiration. You may not always realize it, but you are a shining example of resilience and courage. When the weight of the world feels heavy on your shoulders, you continue to press on. You choose to keep going, even when it feels easier to quit. That takes incredible strength, and I am in awe of you. I want you to know that you are worthy beyond measure.

   There comes a time in your life when you walk away from all the drama and the people who create it. You surround yourself with people who make you laugh. Learn from the bad and focus on the good. Love the people who treat you right and pray for the ones who don't. Life is too short to be anything but happy. Falling is a part of life, getting back up is living.

End of Day Reflection

Five Things I am grateful for:

1

2

3

4

5

What did I learn today?

1

2

3

TO DO TOMORROW

1

2

3

4

5

"In the end, we only regret the chances we didn't take."

But what if I fail, what if it doesn't work, what if everyone around me judges me? Ask yourself this: What if it works, what if you become a huge success in everything you've ever dreamed of? You won't know unless you try. - @janzin.chillz

I was walking past a cemetery and on the headstones they all have in common that There is a birth date and a death date. If our lives are between that B and the D and that means that in that Hyphen is the C – that C is the choice. Change your environment, escape your comfort zone. Yeah its hard and sometimes you have to cut friends out of your life and it will be sad and you need to hang out with friends who have a common future not just a common past and don't worry about your past and mistakes second chances do exist the universe allows for U Turns but you must make a new choice, decide on a new path, and I pray that when your time comes in the middle of your B and D is a squiggle not just a dash.

There are 2 days in the year that nothing can be done. The first day is called tomorrow and the second day is called yesterday. YOU NEED TO FOCUS ON TODAY. I think sometimes that we get so caught up on what's next, or what's new or what am I going to do tomorrow or the next day. Or we get so caught on what happened yesterday and something that happened that we can't change or racking your brain on rethinking about what happened and overthink. I think that living in the present moment is so difficult but if you just sit with yourself and breathe then that's living, that's letting it be.

Forget about the past, it doesn't matter who you used to be. How are we going to build and learn as a person if we are not faced with diversity and trauma? our past is what molds us into the character that we are today. Mistakes are mistakes and the past is the place to learn from, not to live in.

End of Day Reflection

Five Things I am grateful for:

1

2

3

4

5

What did I learn today?

1

2

3

TO DO TOMORROW

1

2

3

4

5

"Accept what is, let go of what was, and have faith in what will be."

If you are willing to do only what's easy, life will be hard. But if you are willing to do what's hard life will be easy.

"The difference between depression and sadness is sadness is just from happenstance, whatever happened or didn't happen or you. Depression is your body saying "F-U I don't want to be this character or avatar that you made me to be anymore. I don't want to hold up this person that you've created to be anymore." – Jim Carey

Signs of personal growth: You stop blaming. You stop trying to impress. You stop asking for validation. You stop making excuses.

Hard Hitting quotes: Ep 19: At some point you need to realize that some people can stay in your heart but not in your life. - @morechrisgriffin

End of Day Reflection

Five Things I am grateful for:

1

2

3

4

5

What did I learn today?

1

2

3

TO DO TOMORROW

1

2

3

4

5

"It does not do to dwell on dreams and forget to live."

- Albus Dumbledore.

- Reasons to be alive by @n1ckwilkins
  - Imagine all the things you have yet to experience, there are great people waiting to meet you and waiting to love you. These people will change your life, they could be your soulmate or an animal.
  - There are places that stand still until you set foot in them.
  - There are movies you haven't seen that will change your perception.
  - A song that will make you want to dance or will make you cry or make you feel alive again.
  - If you aren't here who is going to eat your favorite meal or play with your friends. You have yet to find another moment that makes you feel truly alive again.
  - You have the power to make someone else feel truly alive again and feel loved and who knows maybe tomorrow morning something great can happen because life is unpredictable.

You will always have good and bad days, but the good ones do come.

"Your new life is going to cost you your old one, your comfort zone and your sense of direction. It's going to cost you relationships and friends, and it's going to cost you being liked and understood, but it doesn't matter because the people who are meant for you will meet you on the other side. And you are going to build a new comfort zone around the new things that will move you forward. Instead of being liked you are going to be loved, instead of understood, you are going to be seen. All you are going to lose is built for a person you no longer are. So let it go." – Brianna Wiest

End of Day Reflection

Five Things I am grateful for:

1

2

3

4

5

What did I learn today?

1

2

3

TO DO TOMORROW

1

2

3

4

5

"The distance between you and your dreams and reality is called action."

You are suffering from self-doubt when others are intimidated by your full potential.

Let no person or circumstances diminish or derail your quest for excellence, your spirit of adventure, or your compassion for your fellow human beings, it is of these that great leaders are made. – President of Caribbean Island, @leomagnusolsson

7 Rules of life:

- Let it go – Never ruin a good day by thinking about a bad yesterday.
- Ignore them - Don't listen to other people. Live a life that's empowering to you.
- Give it time – Time heals everything.
- Don't compare – the only person you should strive to be is better than you were yesterday.
- Stay calm – it's okay not to have everything figured out and know that over time you will get there.
- It's on you – only you are in charge of your own happiness.
- Smile – Life is short, enjoy it while you can.

End of Day Reflection

Five Things I am grateful for:

1

2

3

4

5

What did I learn today?

1

2

3

TO DO TOMORROW

1

2

3

4

5

"A dream without a plan is just a wish." - Antonie de Expuery

"Be the person who still tries. After failure, after frustration, after disappointment, after exhaustion, after heartache, be the person who musters up the courage to believe that a new attempt can manifest a new outcome. Be the person who still tries. – Michell C Clark.

Life is not linear. It's a mix of ever-changing scenarios, situations, relationships, and people. Because nothing lasts forever, and because you are supposed to go through everything, in order to grow and acquire the wisdom that you need to live peacefully. And so, with everything that changes in life, you also change with it. You become wiser, stronger, kinder, and more compassionate. You choose what you take out of every situation by the way you respond to it. Know this – Everything that you go through, you have two choices: you either grow with it or let it take you further away from your authentic self. Chose wise, and don't turn away from opportunities to evolve.

End of Day Reflection

Five Things I am grateful for:

1

2

3

4

5

What did I learn today?

1

2

3

TO DO TOMORROW

1

2

3

4

5

December 15
Sagittarius

"There are far, far better things ahead than any we leave behind." - C.S. Lewis

It's easy to look back and get angry at yourself for certain decisions that you have made in the past, but it's unfair to punish yourself for them. You can't blame yourself for not knowing then what you know now, and you made each decision for a reason based on the person you were in that time. As we grow up, we learn, and we evolve. Maybe the person you are now would have done things differently back then, or maybe you are the person you are now because of the decisions you made back then. Trust your journey; it's all going to make sense soon.

Happiness is amazing, it's so amazing it doesn't matter if it's yours or not. It's that lovely thing, a society that grows great when old men plant trees, the shade of which they know that they will never sit in in their lifetime. Good people do good things for other people. That's it, the end.

I wanted to take a moment and remind you of the incredible strength and potential you possess. Life may present challenges and setbacks. But remember that within you lies the power to overcome anything.

End of Day Reflection

Five Things I am grateful for:

1

2

3

4

5

What did I learn today?

1

2

3

TO DO TOMORROW

1

2

3

4

5

"There is a pain of discipline or a pain of regret, choose your pain." – Jim Rohn

"One of the things that makes life challenging is that we must be open to some level of discomfort in our lives, it is just what it is to be human. Now our power is that we get to choose where we let that pain in and what it means and what it will do for us. The type of pain that grows us or that type of pain that reminds us of what could have been…" – Eddie Pinero

So, when people ask, "What are you doing?
Respond with – Things that please me.
Towards what end?
– Pleasure.
What are you working on?
– Having a good time.
What do you hope to accomplish?
– To live happily ever after
What is it that you want to leave as your legacy?
– I was a happy one.
But what is the mark you want to leave?
– Life is joyous.
What is the value of what you are contributing to this time space reality?
I'm Joyful.
What do you hope to accomplish?
– Being happy.

It's hard for people to wrap their head around this concept but this is the goal of all of existence and what it's about.

You really should reflect on the following today:

Things that it's not too late for:
- Healing
- Being kind
- Starting over
- Working on yourself
- Forgiving yourself
- Finding your voice
- Putting yourself first
- Meeting new people
- Believing in yourself
- Creating new dreams
- Showing up for yourself
- Learning something new
- Being who you want to be.
- Speaking kindly to yourself

Remind yourself it's not too late, someone else's Chapter 4 can be your chapter 10 or 20, its okay to do things on your own time when you are ready.

End of Day Reflection

Three Things I am grateful for:

1
2
3

What did I learn today?

1
2
3
4
5

TO DO TOMORROW

1
2
3
4
5

"The moon is always full, it's just our view that is partial."
- Jackie Deakin

You don't always need a plan, sometimes you just need to breathe, trust, and let go.

If you stay in your comfort zone, that is where you will fail. You will fail in your comfort zone; success is not a comfortable procedure. It is a very uncomfortable thing to attempt so you gotta get comfortable being uncomfortable if you ever want to be successful.

I Asked for strength and God gave me difficulties to make me strong. I asked for wisdom and God gave me problems to solve. I asked for Courage, and God gave me Dangers to overcome. I asked for love and God gave me troubled people to help. My Prayers were answered.

End of Day Reflection

Five Things I am grateful for:

1

2

3

4

5

What did I learn today?

1

2

3

TO DO TOMORROW

1

2

3

4

5

Things to think about today:

Always go with the choice that scares you the most because it is the choice that is going to help you grow.

You have got three choices in life, give up, give in, or give it all you have got.

The hardest walk you can make is the walk that you walk alone. But that is the walk that makes you the strongest, that is the walk that builds your character the most.

8 things that can change your life in one year.

o Stop complaining and appreciate how lucky you are every single day.
o Embrace loneliness and reinvent yourself in that process.
o Say goodbye to people who don't bring positive energy into your life.
o Take control of your thoughts remember "whatever you grow in your garden will grow whether it's good or bad."
o Pick one skill you want to cultivate and put all your effort into developing that.
o Commit to every single goal you set and never look back.
o Sweat a little bit every day to boost your mood.
o Fail forward and learn from every mistake that you make in life.

End of Day Reflection

Five Things I am grateful for:

1

2

3

4

5

What did I learn today?

1

2

3

TO DO TOMORROW

1

2

3

4

5

"All our dreams can come true if we have the courage to pursue them." - Walt Disney

  In the beginning of all uncharted courses in life, there are supposed to be these feelings of doubt and unsureness. These are fears that occur that make us question whether we should pursue these dreams and goals. Don't let them stop you, continue with courage in knowing that even if you fall a few times, you only need to remember to get back up again, dust yourself off, and keep going and everything you will get there. Have the bravery and the courage to be persistent with healthy habits and the want and the need to grow to that next level of success. We all fall sometimes but when falling do not look around and see who is laughing. Stand strong and keep walking and gradually get into that run again, and within this consistency and pace, you will accomplish so much come rain or shine, or hell or high water. Once you envision yourself accomplishing your goal, you will get there once you set certain actions in place towards the right direction, even if you get lost along the way or have a few setbacks, these are merely steppingstones to get back right on the right path again. Keep your chin up, and always stay positive and don't let anyone bring you down or make you think that you can't or that you are wasting your time trying to accomplish your hopes, dreams, and goals. You've got this, and everything is going to be okay today!

End of Day Reflection

Five Things I am grateful for:

1

22

3

4

5

What did I learn today?

1

2

3

TO DO TOMORROW

1

2

3

4

5

December 20
Sagittarius

"No man, no matter how great, can know his destiny. He cannot glimpse his part in the great story that is about to unfold. Like everyone, he must live and learn." Merlin, Season 1 Intro

There is a stage in our lives that we go through that I like to call the "I know, I know" phase. It's when we easily for some reason get annoyed and we tell people "I know I know" because we no longer want to listen, sometimes it our pride and our ego talking. Or because we think we know but when shit hits the fan we get embarrassed and sometimes those same people come back and tell us, "You know, if only you listened to what I was trying to tell you, to how I was suggesting you try doing things. Maybe then you could have learned something."

When you forget to listen and you don't take others' advice, or guidance we are still apt to make mistakes and are still liable to have to go back and correct things.

Remember you don't know what you don't know. Remember to listen and remember to understand other people around you. Sometimes people want to help us without anything in return. Communication is very important and sometimes miscommunication can darken things around us. Respect your elders and other wisdom offered to you from adults as you never know what you will learn and experience from them.

End of Day Reflection

Five Things I am grateful for:

1

2

3

4

5

What did I learn today?

1

2

3

TO DO TOMORROW

1

2

3

4

5

"Lessons in life will be repeated until they are learned." - Frank Sonnenberg

- 4 Sentences that will make you rethink your life:
  o Happiness is not the absence of problems, it's the ability to deal with them.
  o Feeling sad after deciding, doesn't mean it was the wrong decision.
  o You are not stressed because you are doing too much, you are stressed because you are doing too little of what makes you feel most alive.
  o The lesson you struggle with will repeat itself until you learn from it.

You know sometimes your mind plays tricks on you, it can tell you that you are no good and that it is all hopeless, but I have discovered this, "You are loved, and you are important, and you bring to this world what no one else can, so hold on, and things will get better. Stay positive."

End of Day Reflection

Five Things I am grateful for:

1

2

3

4

5

What did I learn today?

1

2

3

TO DO TOMORROW

1

2

3

4

5

December 22
Capricorn

"Just four days away, begins a new year; we will be forced once again to reflect on another year gone and striving forward to discover our new path to finding peace and happiness and ultimately our true purpose in life. Along the way good and bad things may have and will occur, but if you set small, short-term goals daily you will eventually get to where you want to be in life. It's best to set short term attainable goals and you will most likely reach them. Yes, for example, we may want to lose weight but remember even losing a few pounds is still achieving greatness. Never sell yourself short or think that enough is never enough otherwise you may never find your happiness, and nothing will ever be good enough. Take gratitude in the small things and you will see the world around you change in seeing things in a new perspective.

"There is nothing outside of yourself that can ever enable you to get better, stronger, richer, quicker, or smarter. Everything is within, everything exists. Seek nothing outside of yourself. - Miyamoto Musashi

Your impact on people is much bigger than you think. Someone still laughs when they think of that funny thing you said to them. Someone still smiles when they think of the compliment that you gave them. Someone still silently admires you, the advice you gave made a difference to someone's life.

End of Day Reflection

Five Things I am grateful for:

1

2

3

4

5

What did I learn today?

1

2

3

TO DO TOMORROW

1

2

3

4

5

December 23
Capricorn

"Start by doing what's necessary, then do what's possible, and suddenly you are doing the impossible." -St. Francis of Assisi

The moment you realize that the next step isn't going to kill you, and that next step is the next step to evolving; changing growing and learning and becoming literally the best version of yourself, that is the most beautiful thing. It is not going to kill you, and putting yourself in the game you are giving yourself the opportunity to achieve something that everyone else would say is impossible.

Staying positive doesn't mean that you must be happy all the time, it just means that even on hard days, you know that there are better days coming. It's not how we make mistakes, but how we correct them that defines us.

What you focus on expands, if you focus on the goodness in your life, you create more of it. If you live with an open palm rather than a closed fist you leave yourself open for more immeasurable blessings to flow through your hands.

Sometimes you feel like you have healed from something and out of nowhere it will hit you again, and sometimes it will feel like you haven't even healed at all. The reality of it is, is that it is a part of healing, even though you feel like you haven't healed, the chances are that if you look back to a few weeks or months ago you realize how much you have grown. Realize that you are always growing, and that healing isn't linear.

End of Day Reflection

Five Things I am grateful for:

1

2

3

4

5

What did I learn today?

1

2

3

TO DO TOMORROW

1

2

3

4

5

December 24
Capricorn

"We don't receive wisdom; we must discover it for ourselves after a journey that no one can take for us to spare us." - Marcel Proust

Things to start doing for yourself:
o Spend time with the right people who appreciate you.
o Be gentle with yourself and talk to yourself like you would to your best friend.
o Forgive yourself for your mistakes.
o Accept things even if they're not perfect.
o Stop waiting and start doing it. Start believing in yourself.
o Get out of your comfort zone 0 this is the only way you can grow.
o Respect your own boundaries.
o End toxic relationships.
o Take care of your body and be gentle with it
o Celebrate your wins, even the smallest ones.
o Be yourself. Don't try to be someone else. You are one of a kind and that makes you unique!
o Enjoy the things you already have and appreciate where you are.

You may not always see the results of your kindness but every bit of positive energy you contribute to the world makes it a better place for all of us.

Everything is going to be okay! Don't worry about things that happen out of your control over the next few days!

'Life is not just the passing of time, life is a collection of experiences, their frequency, and their intensity. Life is not just watching the clock just tick away. Whatever the span of your life turns out to be, here is what you fill it up with, experiences and the intensity of those experiences. "– Jim Rohn

End of Day Reflection

Five Things I am grateful for:

1

2

3

4

5

What did I learn today?

1

2

3

TO DO TOMORROW

1

2

3

4

5

December 25
Capricorn

"At the end of the day, we can endure much more than we think we can." - Frida Kahlo

Today is a special day, Christmas, a day that we all spent the last few days stressing over. Financially, Socially, and Emotionally it's probably been a rollercoaster up to today. Today, take a step back and realize the purpose of these stresses that we put ourselves in as a whole. Is this true happiness or is it the feelings that we want behind the act of giving that pushes us to want to please and give to others that we love and care about?

Walk away from anything that gives you bad vibes. There is no need to explain or make sense of it.

"When you work, work. When you play, play. Don't mix the two. When at the beach, be at the beach physically and mentally, DO NOT be at the office. When at the office never think about needing to get the family to the beach." – Jim Rohn

"You can't change people. You can change your expectations. You can set boundaries and make decisions about how much time and effort you give. You can refocus your attention. You can practice acceptance and letting go. But you can't mold someone into who you want or need them to be. You can't force them to make a shift before they are ready. You can't ask them to become someone different than who they authentically are. You shouldn't have to and that can be a painful truth to sit with. That no matter how much you beg and explain things. No matter how many times you say what you need and communicate what hurts, that person you care about can't show up for you in the way you need. That sometimes, there's no one to blame and nothing to fix." – Daniell Koepke.

End of Day Reflection

Five Things I am grateful for:

1

2

3

4

5

What did I learn today?

1

2

3

TO DO TOMORROW

1

2

3

4

5

December 26
Capricorn

"The struggle you are facing is a test to see if you are truly committed to the life, that you say, that you want."

Grow with it or change what you can to make it run smoother and do it without skipping a beat. We all have great ideas that come to us and it's up to us whether or not that we do it or share it with others. Fear and of others opinions tend to hold us back and we forget that ideas can be built upon and when shared with others around us, can grow into things that we could never have imagined possible before!

Where you are in life, it doesn't mean that you are "stuck" it only means that you just must either reach out to those around you to ask for help, share the struggle with someone else around you, or grow to figure out a way to overcome. If you want to follow through with a dream or goal, sometimes we see that there are challenges to get to where we want to be. If you look at that and say it's not possible and give up its different then saying, "Look here is the challenge, what am I going to do about it to overcome it and get through it?"

The abilities that we have within ourselves are great potential to overcome great adversities in times when we don't think that it's possible because we don't give ourselves enough credit for being able to accomplish them and get to that next level needed for our own growth as we need to. You are an amazing person, who has lived and grown so much this year. You may or may not need to know this, but you are loved so greatly just as you are by those around you! You are special and unique and full of great and many talents. You are loved even by those who don't realize it because of your influence on their lives and others of those that are around you. You have so much great courage and bravery for accomplishing what you have dared to do thus far, even by taking advantage of utilizing a tool like this book. Never be afraid to share this process that you have gone through with this book with others in your life to show them how you have grown to be the amazing and wonderful person that you are! Always, always remember it's okay to dream, it's okay to have a wild and spectacular imagination, and you can overcome anything that is set before you, so don't give up!

End of Day Reflection

Five Things I am grateful for:

1

2

3

4

5

What did I learn today?

1

2

3

TO DO TOMORROW

1

2

3

4

5

"Success is liking yourself, liking what you do, and liking how you do it." - Maya Angelou

This is extremely true to its core. If you aren't happy, healthy, relatively able to support yourself and you are able to have a work/personal life balance, how can you feel positively successful? Adulting is rough for us all and as I have said before, "the struggle is real" but these are moments for growth and warning signs for the need for growth, and to realize that something must change or be updated in your life to possibly allow for it to run smoother. No one should have to deal with being stressed if you have others around you willing and able to help you be able to get back on track.

"I found that nothing in life is worthwhile unless you take risks. Nothing. Nelson Mandela said, "There is no passion to be found playing small and settling for a life that is less than what you are capable of living." – Denzel Washington

Don't give up on your dream, I don't care if you don't have the money, you don't have the help, you don't have the background for it, and you don't have a friend for it. Don't give up on your dream! Don't you do it! It will take you twice as long, you must take courses or classes. You may not read as fast. You might not move as quickly; you may not have as much. DO NOT QUIT!

You are not where you want to be, you feel like you are supposed to be somewhere else. Say You can snap your fingers and you could be where you want to be, I bet you would still feel this way, that you are not in the right place. The point is you can't get so hung up on where you would rather be that you forget to make the most of where you are. The point is to take a break from worrying about what you can't control, live a little.

End of Day Reflection

Five Things I am grateful for:

1

2

3

4

5

What did I learn today?

1

2

3

TO DO TOMORROW

1

2

3

4

5

December 28
Capricorn

"In the end, everything will be ok, and if it's not, it's not the end," - John Paul Dejoria

Understand one thing: You can't change what has already happened. You must learn to stop victimizing yourself and let go. You must free your mind from the weight of the past. Good or bad, your past experiences occurred to mature you, not to keep you stuck. Forgive yourself for them, accept what happened, and gracefully let go. You have better things to be creating with your mind right now. - @sarcasticjeevan

Your next chapter in life begins whether you are ready for it or not. Sometimes they feel like they are the end of the world, but tomorrow if not tomorrow, maybe perhaps next week, things will bring you to that next level of understanding and perspective.

End of Day Reflection

Five Things I am grateful for:

1

2

3

4

5

What did I learn today?

1

2

3

TO DO TOMORROW

1

2

3

4

5

December 29
Capricorn

"Be happy with what you have while working for what you want."

- Hellen Keller.

"There is a blessing in everything. Behind every moment of adversity there is a blessing and a lesson. Every moment of adversity has those two things. Pain always leaves a gift." – Steve Harvey.

Sometimes you are unsatisfied with your life, while many people in this world are dreaming of living your life. A child on a farm sees a plane fly overhead and dreams of flying. But a pilot sees that farmhouse and dreams of returning home. That's life. Enjoy yours. If wealth is the secret of happiness, then the rich should be dancing on the streets. But only the poor kids do that. If power ensures security, then officials should walk unguarded. But those are people who live simply, and soundly. If beauty and fame bring ideal relationships, then celebrities should have the best marriages. Live simply. Walk humbly. And love genuinely. And all good will come back to you.

There are many who aren't as fortunate as I am. In fact, many don't have a bed or a heater to sleep with at night tonight. Many don't even know what it is to sleep in peace, silence, and comfort. Take enjoyment and gratitude in the simplicities in life, and they will bring you greater appreciation.

End of Day Reflection

Five Things I am grateful for:

1

2

3

4

5

What did I learn today?

1

2

3

TO DO TOMORROW

1

2

3

4

5

December 30
Capricorn

"The number one reason people fail is because they listen to their friends, family, and neighbors." - Napoleon Hill

One of the most important quotes that I have ever heard was – If it makes you happy, it doesn't have to make sense to anyone else. You have grown so much this year! Encourage others to get this book especially if you have noticed a difference this year than last year in your day-to-day life after using this book!

An experience that happens to you in life doesn't define who you are, it is a momentary moment of growth, and a lesson to be learned. Enjoy your day today and step forward fearlessly into the spotlight!

I hope to see you again next year!

End of Day Reflection

Five Things I am grateful for:

1

2

3

4

5

What did I learn today?

1

2

3

TO DO TOMORROW

1

2

3

4

5

December 31
Capricorn

"Dream as if you will live forever, live as if you will die today." - Jimmy Dean

If you have not at least given yourself a chance to consider your dreams and goals this year, NEXT year is YOUR year! Continue, press on and push forward, and even if you aren't where you hoped you'd be by right now, at least you know you are heading in the right direction. You haven't yet given up because you keep reading this journal and studying it and its quotes daily, and as soon as you get your next new copy of this book, you will be better prepared daily going forward into next year. You have got this, and this next year is going to be a year full of loving, enjoyable, growth experiencing memories! If you have not given up yet, you have not failed at following your hopes, dreams, and goals!

End of Day Reflection

Five Things I am grateful for:

1

2

3

4

5

What did I learn today?

1

2

3

TO DO TOMORROW

1

2

3

4

5

Another year has gone… Today I would like you to go back and look back into this book and look at all that you have learned this year. Look how much you have grown. Look at how much you are grateful for now. Look at what you have done as a person. Step by step, day by day you woke up and started your day afresh and made it to be something meaningful for someone else in your life. You made many people smile this year. You may have made some mistakes; you may have lost some friends or people you thought were your friends. You may have started some healthy habits. Take a step back and be proud of yourself as I am proud of you and what you have done this year. You may not have had a chance to write in this book every day and that is okay. You got back into the habit.

I hope that this book helped you relax at night to get a fuller night's sleep without thinking about what you had to worry about the next day. I hope that this book encourages you daily to wake up and be excited for another day. I hope this book can be shared with someone else in your life to make a difference in their life. I am sure you noticed that as you became more grateful for the people and things in your life, you noticed how much everyone changed around you. If you can believe it, the only reason things seem better is because you changed positively this year because you completed this journal. Get another one of these books for next year if you would like and if you thought that this book was helpful get one for someone else who struggles with stress, anxiety, depression, negativity, or someone who just seems lost in life.

Thank you for being you and remember that people love you for who you are no matter what! You are loved, you are important, and you make so much of a difference in the lives of those around you whether you realize it or not. Enjoy the life that you have right now and realize that you are special and that without you in people's lives the world wouldn't be complete. You are such an important person and the person who may have given you this book feels the same way I do about you. No matter who you are on the outside, it's inside and the journey that you have made so far that matters so much more! Don't let anyone bring you down or tell you otherwise. Raise the standards of those around you if you haven't already and realize that you deserve to be happy and to have so much more in your life! I wish you the best and that you have many more great years to come full of happiness, love, joy, health, and success.

Source Pics:

Capricorn Pic

https://media.istockphoto.com/vectors/capricorn-zodiac-sign-flat-astrology-vector-illustration-on-white-vector-id856162916?k=6&m=856162916&s=170667a&w=0&h=DIdFc-TwmlcacdF-RvTPHWrNjiaQm052ZDpjSs8rvZI=

Aquarius Pic

https://thumbs.dreamstime.com/z/aquarius-zodiac-sign-isolated-white-background-star-astrology-horoscope-line-stylized-symbol-astrological-calendar-130468117.jpg

Book Summary:

This is a unique one-of-a-kind gratitude journal full of daily messages, wisdom, and motivation to help you on your day to day. Also, in the back of each day of the week to help you go to sleep at night there is a place where you can write what you need to remember to do the next day, things you learned today, and things that you are grateful for. This is a daily guidebook to help you out and it's fit for every day of the year.